# Heroic Personal Finances for Christians

## Accelerating Past Average With Your Money Plan

LARRY JONES

HEROIC PERSONAL FINANCES FOR CHRISTIANS. Copyright © 2016 by LJones Enterprises, LLC. Manufactured in the United States of America. All Rights Reserved. No other part of this book may be reproduced in any form or by any electronic or mechanical means including information storage and retrieval systems without permission in writing from the author, except by a reviewer, who may quote brief passages in a review.

First Edition: February 2017

ISBN-10: 0-9979286-2-X
ISBN-13: 978-0-9979286-2-4

For additional information on the book *Heroic Personal Finances for Christians*, and to receive a FREE Healthy Personal Finances Checklist, visit heroicpersonalfinances.com.

Edited by: Karen Engle
Cover Design by: pixelrocket on Fiverr®

Copyright © 2016 LJones Enterprises, LLC
All rights reserved.

# CONTENTS

|  | | |
|---|---|---|
| | Acknowledgments | 1 |
| | Disclaimer | 2 |
| | Introduction | 4 |
| | Part One: Laying the Foundation | 8 |
| | Part One Introduction | 9 |
| 1 | God Is The Source | 11 |
| 2 | Living The Generous Life | 22 |
| 3 | Morning Routines and Habit Formation | 37 |
| 4 | Energy Management | 56 |
| 5 | Take On The Wealthy Mindset | 67 |
| | Part Two: Next Level Financial Strategies | 81 |
| | Part Two Introduction (An Explanation and Framework) | 82 |
| 6 | Invest In Yourself | 86 |
| 7 | Emergency Preparedness | 109 |
| 8 | Interlude: Tax Strategies | 122 |
| 9 | Stock Market Investing: Part 1 | 130 |
| 10 | Put Your Money To Work Like Banks, Insurance Companies and the Wealthy | 137 |
| 11 | Property Ownership | 158 |
| 12 | Stock Market Investing: Part 2 | 174 |
| 13 | Wrap-up: Putting It All Together | 195 |
| | Outro: Crank the Flywheel of Success! | 201 |

Time to Take Action . . . . . . . . . . . . . . . . . . . . . . . . . . . . 205

About the Author . . . . . . . . . . . . . . . . . . . . . . . . . . . . . 207

Endnotes . . . . . . . . . . . . . . . . . . . . . . . . . . . . . . . . . . . . 209

# ACKNOWLEDGMENTS

This book has been a labor of love for over eighteen months, but the idea behind it has been living inside my head for much longer than that. A few years ago, the initial idea for a book was planted into my mind by my brother Evan when having discussions about our experience with a certain Christian financial expert's views on precious metals. The book idea blossomed during a lunch meeting with my financial advisor friend Stephen Stricklin (wisewealthkc.com). During that lunch, I remember having a similar conversation with him. A few months later, I found myself putting together a rough outline for this book, and the rest is history. You didn't even know it at the time, but thank you Evan and Stephen for sharing your wisdom and ideas that helped me formulate this book.

This book would not have been written if it were not for the loving support of my wife Jennifer. The majority of the book was written between 4:30-5:30 a.m. each day. She has allowed me to be "crazy Larry" and get up way too early, just so I had time to write before she had to go to work and I had to get our children ready for school. Thanks, Jen, for allowing me to fulfill a life goal that has been burning in my heart for many years.

Finally, I acknowledge my Lord and Savior Jesus Christ for the wisdom He has given me to write the book. Each day during my prayer time, I asked Him for wisdom as I wrote. I also asked Him to bless the book so that it might be a blessing to others in their own financial journey. I pray that you the reader are blessed beyond measure for taking the time to read the words written here.

The Baroque composer Johann Sebastian Bach (1685-1750) wrote the initials "S.D.G." at the end of his church compositions. "S.D.G." stands for the Latin phrase "Soli Deo gloria" which is usually translated "glory to God alone." This is how I would like to begin and eventually end. Ultimately, this book is a result of His wisdom and power in my life. I give Him all the honor, praise, and glory for everything He has accomplished through me. Thank you, Lord.

S.D.G.

## DISCLAIMER

The intention of this book is for informational and motivational purposes only. It was sold with the understanding that the author is not bound to give any type of financial, legal, psychological, or any other type of professional advice. The advice and actions proposed in this book are not intended as a substitute for counseling. The author will not be liable for any physical, psychological, emotional, financial, or commercial damages. The reader must test everything for his or herself according to their own unique situation, talents, finances, and aspirations. Each person is responsible for his or her own decisions, choices, actions, and results.

This book is a synthesis of ideas taken from hundreds of personal finance, self-help, and spiritual growth sources. Any third party sources mentioned in this book may include products and opinions expressed by their owners. As such, the author does not assume responsibility or liability for any third party sources of products or opinions. The fact that certain individuals, organizations, or websites are mentioned does not mean the author endorses the information or recommendations these individuals, organizations, or websites may make. Also, readers should be aware that any website listed in this book may have changed or disappeared between the time the book was written and when it is actually read.

The author did his due diligence and made every effort to ensure the information presented in this book was correct at press time. Therefore, the author does not assume any liability to any party for any loss, damage, or disruption caused by errors or omissions, whether such errors or omissions result from negligence, accident, or any other cause. No warranty may be created or extended by sales representatives or written sales materials. The advice and strategies contained in this book may not be suitable for every person's unique situation; consult with a professional when appropriate.

The rights to any trademarks, quotes, and/or excerpts from books, movies, TV shows, brands, or other media mentioned in this publication belong to their respective owners. As such, they are presented in this book according to fair use doctrine.

No part of this publication may be reproduced, transmitted, or sold in whole or in part in any form, without the prior written consent of the author. All trademarks and registered trademarks appearing in this book are the property of their respective owners.

# INTRODUCTION

When you hear the word "hero," who comes to mind? A popular comic book character? Superhumans who fight courageously on the big screen in the movie theater? Or, maybe a family member or friend who has battled through some difficult times and emerged victorious on the other side?

Heroes are around us each and every day, and we probably don't even realize it. Heroes who are fighting difficult battles in their relationships, emotions, health, careers, and yes, even their personal finances.

Heroes don't always have the answers. But, they remain confident that they will be victorious if they keep fighting hard until the end of their journey, whatever that may be for them. They help guide the way for the rest of us to be victorious when we have similar life challenges as well.

The first time I climbed out of debt in July 2007, I paid off somewhere around $30,000 in nineteen months. Because of this accomplishment, I became a Financial Peace University™ (FPU) coordinator as well as the stewardship pastor of my church.

The second time I dug myself out of debt (it's a long story) on October 27, 2014, my wife and I paid off almost $100,000 in thirty-five months. The good news for us is that we had more income coming in, giving us a "bigger shovel" to dig ourselves out faster . . . time to cue up the Dave Ramsey radio show *Braveheart* recording, "We're Debt Freeeeeeee!"

For three years, my wife and I focused on shoveling our way out of a big financial mess. Since I had been debt free in the recent past, I knew what an incredible feeling it is to not worry about the bills. I knew the joy of financial peace.

This second journey through freedom from debt was different for me, though. This was not only a journey out of debt but also a journey into abundance.

My wife and I both have great jobs with good pay, excellent benefits, and a lot of flexibility. God has blessed us, and I comprehend His goodness to us as a family. Because of God's blessing on our multiple income streams, we were able to climb out of a lot of debt, fast.

Don't misunderstand me, though. I'm not some "health and wealth" preacher as seen on TV. I'm not saying if a person does all the things presented in this book they will automatically be healthy, wealthy, and wise. The truth is God will do what He's going to do in each person's life. He may give one person a little to manage for the kingdom, or He may give them a lot. He has eternal purposes for everything He does.

I do believe, though, that there are financial principles that work when applied to what God teaches in His Word. There are also universal laws such as the Law of Sowing and Reaping[i] (also known as the Law of the Harvest[ii]) that work for everyone. Generously planting "money seeds" will reap a bountiful harvest over time.

A few months before my wife and I completed our debt-free journey in late 2014, my mind began a shift into what was next. First, we needed to build up our "3–6 months of expenses" emergency fund. Second, we needed to save for a down payment on a house. As a side note, during our two trips to financial freedom over the last decade, we had been renting a house. We were completely over paying off someone else's house note!

As we prepared ourselves for these next money steps, we anticipated even greater things to come. We could see a wonderful bright light at the end of a long, challenging tunnel of massive debt. We were walking from a place of lack into a position of great abundance.

But, the next big step in the whole Christian personal finance experience I have found somewhat lacking—stock market investing advice. By this part of the journey, consumer debt should be paid off using the debt snowball. Cash reserves equal to three to six months of expenses are built up, and the next step involves putting fifteen percent of one's income into good growth stock mutual funds. Then according to certain experts—with fingers crossed—hope for the best! Don't invest anywhere else. Don't diversify investments beyond stocks.

In my mind, I'm not sure this is the wisest move to make with investment money. Why would I think this?

Stop and consider these financial experts' own wealth. Are they wealthy because they have invested 15% of their income into good growth stock mutual funds, funded their kids' college accounts, and paid off their home? I don't think so.

These experts have been engaged in next level, wealthy-people activities. They invest in themselves through reading, writing, and public speaking. They have developed strong relationships. They invest tremendous amounts of time and energy creating products to help people. They have built great businesses. They have been busy building tremendous brands for many years.

Knowing this is the path these experts have taken, I wanted to determine how to maximize my family's financial potential. I wanted to understand how wealthy people think and act. I wanted to know how to make money with money. I started reading every book I could find on the topics of personal finance, a wealthy mindset, making money, and investing money. *Heroic Personal Finances for Christians* is the result of my own financial journey over the last several years.

Let me pause here and explain that this journey hasn't been about me making more money so I can buy more stuff, either. I am a minimalist. I don't like a lot of stuff, and I'm always trying to purge as much stuff out of my life as possible. For me, this has been more of a game or a personal financial experiment. Money is like a game in many respects. Understanding the basic and advanced rules of the money game will result in above average game play. That's why I pursue this game. I believe God has called me to be a manager of His stuff—to excel in money management. I want to be the five-bags-of-gold guy that He expects to double His investments for the kingdom (see Matt. 25:14–30).

I have several assumptions of each reader of this book. I assume each knows and understands the most popular Christian personal finance principles that are being taught today in many churches and faith-based organizations. Some may be in the middle of a seven-step financial program, wondering if there is more to consider for their financial journey. Each of us is in good company! My family is in this exact same position in our financial plan. This is the reason I wrote this book.

*Quick Tip:* If not familiar with the seven Baby Steps in Financial Peace University™, here they are:
1. $1,000 in the bank. This is the "baby" emergency fund to help people avoid using credit cards.
2. Debt snowball. Pay off all consumer debt (everything except a first mortgage) from smallest debt down to the largest. This is more of a psychological approach to pay everything off faster.
3. 3-6 months of expense money in savings. This is a fully funded emergency fund. For example, if a person's expenses are $5,000/month, they will need $15,000-$30,000 in the bank.
4. Invest 15 percent for retirement in pre-tax retirement plans or Roth IRAs.
5. College savings (if the person/couple has children).
6. Pay off mortgages early.
7. Build wealth and give![iii]

My prayer for each reader of this book is that they will become the hero of their own money story. That they will learn to be excellent managers of what God has entrusted them to manage. I pray they will maximize their financial potential in a greater way than ever before.

But first, a strong foundation must be laid. Begin by searching deep within, to establish a firm financial support structure through a mindset of right thinking and a pattern of excellent habits. True wealth begins here.

*Quick Tip:* To better determine where you stand in your own financial journey, I have created a Healthy Personal Finances Checklist on my website. You can download your FREE copy at http://www.heroicpersonalfinances.com/free-financial-checklist-download/.

HEROIC PERSONAL FINANCES FOR CHRISTIANS
PART ONE: LAYING THE FOUNDATION

# PART ONE
# INTRODUCTION

The One World Trade Center building replaced the twin towers in the New York City World Trade Complex. This was a result of the devastation caused by terrorist attacks on September 11, 2001.

Actual construction on this building began in 2004 and wasn't completed until 2014. One World Trade Center is now the tallest building in the United States. It is also the fourth-largest skyscraper in the world by pinnacle height. Get this, though: the foundation of this huge building took several years alone to complete.

The foundation for One World Trade Center is some seventy feet below street level and required dynamite blasting down into solid bedrock. Officials laid down the symbolic cornerstone in a ceremony on July 4, 2004. Further construction of the tower stalled until 2006. Then, on November 18, 2006, the construction crew poured 400 cubic yards of concrete, carried by 40 trucks, onto the foundation. The first steel beam was welded on to the building's base on December 19, 2006.

On January 9, 2007, a second set of beams was welded to the top of the first set. Later in that year, the construction company completed a row of steel columns at the perimeter of the construction site. By the end of 2007, the tower's footings and foundations were almost complete.[iv]

The builders had to create a solid foundation before the beautiful steel and glass structure could rise high in the New York City skyline. A lot of time, energy, resources, and money were required to build it. This was a carefully executed piece of the building plan. In no way did it happen on accident.

The foundation is the most critical component for building anything of importance. This includes the financial plan for you and your family. Get this part right, and you can create a magnificent financial legacy for your family for generations to come.

A class such as Financial Peace University™ provides a great start to establishing a strong financial foundation. These foundational steps include the following: a baby emergency fund, becoming debt free, building up 3–6 months worth of expense money in the bank, and investing a percentage of income for retirement. The first four FPU Baby Steps lay a solid foundation for personal finances. I know this personally. At the time I wrote these words, my family was at Baby Step 4.

T. Harv Eker[v] often says, "Thoughts lead to feelings. Feelings lead to actions. Actions lead to results." An important part of building a solid foundation in personal finances includes the internal struggle of a person's mind. So in Part One of this book, we're going to deal with exactly that: thoughts, feelings, and habits. The reader may wonder if some chapters have anything to do with money at all. I would argue that they do.

I was recently reminded of an important truth: "Little things ARE the big things." Little things, or habits, are the small ways in which a person lives their life—habits established in managing time, relationships, and finances. Every day people develop little habits they don't think much about. These small, daily habits will either make a person's life wealthy, mediocre, or destitute over the course of time.

Wealth isn't about completing a sequence of Baby Steps. Sure, there's a tremendous amount of peace that comes with being completely debt free. It's amazing to have a stash of cash in the bank. There is a sense of accomplishment when properly funding retirement and college accounts. True wealth, though, is more about what a person is becoming on the journey. A wealthy experience comes from the favor of God poured out in someone's life. God blesses His people when they follow His financial wisdom found in His Word.

When people establish this money foundation correctly, their financial house will rise majestically just like the One World Trade Center.

Join me, now, on the financial journey of a lifetime.

# CHAPTER 1
# GOD IS THE SOURCE

"But remember the LORD your God, for it is he who gives you the ability to produce wealth, and so confirms his covenant, which he swore to your ancestors, as it is today."
– Deuteronomy 8:18, NIV[vi]

"God meets daily needs daily. Not weekly or annually. He will give you what you need when it is needed."
– Max Lucado

George Müller was a Christian who understood his source of wealth and resources. Müller was an evangelist in England during the 1800s. He believed God had called him to help the orphans in the city of Bristol. He also led other ministries such as pastoring a church as well as founding the Scripture Knowledge Institution for Home and Abroad. He made a vow to the Lord that he would not receive a salary from his church. He refused to receive government funding or to fundraise. George also made the decision to never sink into debt. He trusted in God alone to meet all the financial needs of his family, as well as the various ministries he led.

Several stories have survived over the years about Müller's prayer life and God's provision for his orphanage. In one of these stories, there were three hundred children living in the orphanage. One morning, they were dressed and ready for school, but there was no food for breakfast. He had the children assemble in the dining room. Müller prayed, thanking God for the food they were about to receive, and then they waited.

A few minutes later, a baker knocked at the door. He explained to Mr. Müller that he couldn't sleep because he knew that the orphanage needed bread. He arose from his bed in the middle of the night and baked three batches for the orphanage.

Not long after the baker left, there was another knock on the door.

This time, it was the milkman. His cart broke down right in front of the orphanage. The milk would spoil by the time he could repair the cart. He asked Mr. Müller if he could use some free milk. The milkman brought in enough to provide for three hundred thirsty children.

Even though times were difficult in England, God's hand was on George Müller. God supernaturally provided for him his entire life! During Müller's lifetime, his organization received and disbursed approximately £1.5 million ($2,718,844 USD). This money was used for supporting the orphanages as well as for distributing almost two million Bibles. Some of the money also supported missionaries around the world, such as Hudson Taylor.

Not only was Mr. Müller an excellent steward but also an excellent leader. More than a century after his passing, his work continues on through the George Müller Foundation.

George Müller's story can be a convicting one. How many Christians, especially those of us who live in the richest nation on earth, have that kind of faith? How many are that kind of manager of God's resources? I would say that all who claim the name of Christ can learn a lot from the life of George Müller!

A person's financial foundation begins with God. In making this statement I'm assuming my readers are Christians—followers of Jesus Christ. Perhaps I shouldn't make that assumption, though.

In 1976, around the age of six years old, I was sitting in junior church at the First Baptist Church of Washington, Michigan. I was listening to a Bible story about Jesus taught by Mr. and Mrs. Peters, the directors for that ministry. At the end of the story, Mr. Peters asked if anyone would like to ask Jesus into their life to be their Lord and Savior. In that moment, I fell under the conviction of the Holy Spirit and raised my hand. Minutes later, I was talking with Mr. Peters about my decision. I prayed with him to receive Christ into my life. My life has never been the same since.

God created human beings to be in a relationship with Him. Unfortunately, Adam and Eve's sin in the Garden of Eden (Genesis 3) caused a spiritual separation between God and man. But God provided a way to restore that relationship with Him through the death, burial, and resurrection of His Son Jesus Christ. The only thing a person needs to do is accept the free gift of salvation through faith in Christ.

I don't know where you are in your spiritual journey, today. Perhaps you have already accepted the Lord as your Savior—fantastic! I look forward to meeting you one day in the kingdom of God in the life to come. But maybe, all this Jesus talk is completely new to you. If so, can I encourage you to do a few things to learn more about Him?

First, find a copy of the Bible or go online at Biblegateway.com (they also have a free app available). Read through the gospel of John in the New Testament. This book of the Bible provides an excellent foundation to the good news of Jesus Christ.

Second, find a solid, Bible-believing church to visit (www.churchfinder.com). In church, you will learn more about the Bible and gain a deeper understanding of what the Christian life is about.

Third, as you become more familiar with Jesus and the gospel story, and you're ready to make the decision to follow Him, pray this prayer:

*Dear Lord Jesus,*

*I know I am a sinner, and I ask for your forgiveness. I believe you died for my sins and rose from the dead. I trust and follow you as my Lord and Savior. Guide my life and help me to do your will. In your name, amen.*[vii]

One final word of caution: Christianity isn't about praying a prayer and checking something off a to-do list to secure fire insurance from hell. It's about a relationship with Jesus Christ that begins here on earth and lasts for all eternity. I wouldn't even pray the prayer unless you're serious about developing a relationship with Him. Developing this relationship is key to the rest of this book.

We cannot begin to "dig a hole, blast dynamite, set the steel rebar, and pour concrete" for our financial foundation until we acknowledge that God is The Source for everything we have.

God is creator God. He created everything in the universe. He spoke it into existence. As a result, everything is His. He owns it all.

Amazing spiritual and financial forces will be released into a person's life once they acknowledge that God owns it all. In turn, He can do a great work through His people when they wisely manage His resources for the kingdom of God.

Acknowledging God as the source of everything is the first layer to a solid, financial foundation.

## Story of the Bags of Gold

In Matthew 25:14–30 (NIV), Jesus taught the following parable, or story, to His disciples:

*"Again, it will be like a man going on a journey, who called his servants and entrusted his wealth to them. To one he gave five bags of gold, to another two bags, and to another one bag, each according to his ability. Then he went on his journey. The man who had received five bags of gold went at once and put his money to work and gained five bags more. So also, the one with two bags of gold gained two more. But the man who had received one bag went off, dug a hole in the ground and hid his master's money.*

*"After a long time the master of those servants returned and settled accounts with them. The man who had received five bags of gold brought the other five. 'Master,' he said, 'you entrusted me with five bags of gold. See, I have gained five more.'*

*"His master replied, 'Well done, good and faithful servant! You have been faithful with a few things; I will put you in charge of many things. Come and share your master's happiness!'*

*"The man with two bags of gold also came. 'Master,' he said, 'you entrusted me with two bags of gold; see, I have gained two more.'*

*"His master replied, 'Well done, good and faithful servant! You have been faithful with a few things; I will put you in charge of many things. Come and share your master's happiness!'*

*"Then the man who had received one bag of gold came. 'Master,' he said, 'I knew that you are a hard man, harvesting where you have not sown and gathering where you have not scattered seed. So I was afraid and went out and hid your gold in the ground. See, here is what belongs to you.'*

*"His master replied, 'You wicked, lazy servant! So you knew that I harvest where I have not sown and gather where I have not scattered seed? Well then, you should have put*

*my money on deposit with the bankers, so that when I returned I would have received it back with interest.*

*"'So take the bag of gold from him and give it to the one who has ten bags. For whoever has will be given more, and they will have an abundance. Whoever does not have, even what they have will be taken from them. And throw that worthless servant outside, into the darkness, where there will be weeping and gnashing of teeth.'"*[viii]

In this story, a wealthy master hands over five bags of gold to one of his servants. Another servant receives two bags of gold. Finally, the last servant receives one bag of gold.

Scholars believe the reference to one bag of gold in this passage equaled almost a year's wages. If this is true, let's put these bags of gold into numbers relatable to today. In 2015, the year I'm writing this book, an average year's wages for an American family is close to $50,000. Knowing this, let's go back to the story.

One servant received approximately 5 x $50,000, which equals $250,000. Another servant received 2 x $50,000, which equals $100,000. The last servant received $50,000. The story continues.

The servant with $250,000 invested the money entrusted him, doubled it, and as a result possessed $500,000. The servant with $100,000 doubled it and had $200,000. But the servant with $50,000 buried the money entrusted to him because he was afraid of both losing it and what the master would do if he lost the money.

Jesus said the master was gone for a long time—potentially the equivalent of a lifetime. When he returned, he asked his three servants for a financial report on what they did with the bags of gold he entrusted to them. Both the five and two-bags-of-gold servants happily reported that they had doubled their master's money. The master was very pleased with their investments. His response, "Well done, thou good and faithful servant!"

The one-bag-of-gold servant, though, admitted his financial fear and his failure to invest. The master was furious with him for his failure to invest what he entrusted to him. He took the one bag of gold and gave it to the servant who now had ten bags of gold, or $500,000.

The master had expected his servants to invest *all* the bags of gold to receive a return on that investment. The servants understood their master's expectations. Two of the servants put the master's money to work and doubled it. But the third servant was fearful and hid his bag of gold. No investment meant opportunity cost and loss for the master.

**Servant Managers**

The parable of the bags of gold as told by Jesus is an excellent reminder of whom the source of everything is. In this story, God the Father is the Master, and those who follow Jesus are the servants.

God the Father gives His children exactly what He knows they can handle. In turn, He expects them to invest whatever He gives in order to reach their maximum potential. When the master handed off the five bags of gold to the first servant, he knew that servant was capable of doubling that amount of money. When he gave the two bags of gold to the second servant, the master knew that he was capable of doubling that amount of money. And, finally he only gave the third servant one bag; he knew at the end of the day this servant wouldn't invest the money for greater growth.

God the Father owns it all. Period. Psalm 24:1 says, "The earth is the Lord's, and everything in it, the world, and all who live in it" (NIV)[ix] He owns all the money, possessions, resources, relationships, talents, abilities, and time that every person currently has in their temporary control. He has given all these things for a purpose: to be multiplied and utilized to expand His kingdom—not our own. When people get this part of the stewardship equation right—as they yield everything back over to God—He is able to work in amazing ways.

Why is it so important to recognize this fact? Does it really matter if I view everything as God's and not my own? Yes, I believe it does matter, because only then will God's people view all these things in a completely different light. They will understand the importance of generous giving on a consistent basis. They will desire to have healthy relationships with those God has entrusted to them. They will understand the importance of a monthly cash flow plan for family finances. They will desire to dig into Scripture and learn even more about what God has to say about money. They will avoid debt. They will have cash reserves. They will give to those in need as God prompts their hearts. They will understand that the

American dream isn't always God's dream for our lives.

The financial journey begins with acknowledging that God is the source of everything, and Christians are simply managers of all that He has entrusted them to manage for Him.

## Story of the Wealthy Father

In Luke 15:11–32 (NIV), Jesus tells another parable—a parable about a wealthy father and his prodigal son:

*Jesus continued: "There was a man who had two sons. The younger one said to his father, 'Father, give me my share of the estate.' So he divided his property between them.*

*"Not long after that, the younger son got together all he had, set off for a distant country and there squandered his wealth in wild living. After he had spent everything, there was a severe famine in that whole country, and he began to be in need. So he went and hired himself out to a citizen of that country, who sent him to his fields to feed pigs. He longed to fill his stomach with the pods that the pigs were eating, but no one gave him anything.*

*"When he came to his senses, he said, 'How many of my father's hired servants have food to spare, and here I am starving to death! I will set out and go back to my father and say to him: Father, I have sinned against heaven and against you. I am no longer worthy to be called your son; make me like one of your hired servants.' So he got up and went to his father.*

*"But while he was still a long way off, his father saw him and was filled with compassion for him; he ran to his son, threw his arms around him and kissed him.*

*"The son said to him, 'Father, I have sinned against heaven and against you. I am no longer worthy to be called your son.'*

*"But the father said to his servants, 'Quick! Bring the best robe and put it on him. Put a ring on his finger and sandals on his feet. Bring the fattened calf and kill it. Let's have a feast and celebrate. For this son of mine was dead and is alive again; he was lost and is found.' So they began to celebrate.*

*"Meanwhile, the older son was in the field. When he came near the house, he heard music and dancing. So he called one of the servants and asked him what was going on. 'Your brother has come,' he replied, 'and your father has killed the fattened calf because he has him back safe and sound.'*

*"The older brother became angry and refused to go in. So his father went out and pleaded with him. But he answered his father, 'Look! All these years I've been slaving for you and never disobeyed your orders. Yet you never gave me even a young goat so I could celebrate with my friends. But when this son of yours who has squandered your property with prostitutes comes home, you kill the fattened calf for him!'*

*"'My son,' the father said, 'you are always with me, and everything I have is yours. But we had to celebrate and be glad, because this brother of yours was dead and is alive again; he was lost and is found.'"*[x]

Through this parable, Jesus taught His disciples another principle about money. From a theological perspective, this parable's focus isn't about money. Money, though, is an important element within the story itself. Here Jesus teaches about money within the context of family relationships—a father and his two sons.

In this familiar story, the youngest son approaches his father about receiving his part of his father's estate. His father grants him his request and the son moves away. The son then proceeds to blast through his financial inheritance and finds himself completely broke. All his friends desert him. To survive, the son ends up becoming a slave on a pig farm. This was not the greatest place to work for a young, Jewish man!

The son finally comes to a realization. He would be better off going back to his father's house and work as a servant than in his current location. He packs up and heads home to apologize to his father, and asks him to take him back as a household servant.

The father pours out affection for his son and takes him back into his home with loving arms. Instead of enslaving him, though, the father throws a party!

From a financial perspective, this is a great reminder for Christians. Christians are not only servant managers in the kingdom of God, but God has also adopted them as sons and daughters. God loves His children and will help them in spite of financial failures with His money. All that is required is humility before Him and submission to His authority in this important area of life. Being a part of the family of God has its own unique privileges that the world will never know or understand.

**Be Rich Versus Get Rich**

In today's American culture, it's really easy to chase riches—to pursue getting rich by whatever means necessary. People play the lottery with the hope of "getting rich." People gamble their life savings away in casinos with the hope of "getting rich." People speculate in stock market day trading with the hope of "getting rich."

And what happens to those who play, gamble, and speculate with their money? A majority of people who do this end up flat broke. Even when they win, though, they still end up blowing through their winnings in a pursuit of stuff. They rapidly consume all that comes into their lives.

Robert and Lara Griffith were a married couple that hardly ever argued . . . that is until they won a $2.76 million lottery jackpot. They ended up buying a million-dollar house and a Porsche. But six years after they won the lottery, Lara confronted her husband over emails suggesting he was interested in another woman. Their fourteen-year-marriage ended. A freak fire gutted their house. Robert drove away with the Porsche. Every penny of their winnings was gone.[xi]

"Winning the lottery isn't always what it's cracked up to be," said Evelyn Adams, and she would know! Evelyn won the New Jersey lottery not just once, but twice (in 1985 and 1986 - WOW!) for total winnings of $5.4 million. The money is now completely gone and Adams lives in a trailer.[xii]

Instead of attempting to "get rich" though, God wants His people to "be rich." Believers in Jesus Christ are already rich! Now, God wants believers to *act* like it. So how is it possible to act rich or "be rich?"

The Bible, God's Holy Word, teaches His people *how* to be rich. Believers are rich in Christ when they acknowledge that God owns all wealth. He has given His children a part of His wealth to manage—a rich inheritance! In return, God expects them to manage and invest His resources and multiply them for His purposes.

Another way to "be rich" versus "get rich" as a Christian is to be transformed in one's thinking and to avoid being conformed to this world. In Romans 12:2 Paul says, "Do not conform to the pattern of this world, but be transformed by the renewing of your mind. Then you will be able to test and approve what God's will is—his good, pleasing and perfect will" (NIV).[xiii]

The world's pattern of finance includes many practices that go against biblical best practices. For example, debt is highly encouraged in the modern world. People finance everything from cars, boats, snowmobiles, home improvement projects, computers, and pets! "Ninety days same as cash" has been the mantra from retailers and creditors for many years now. They make it easy to buy on the front end and difficult to repay on the back end. But the Bible teaches to avoid debt.

In Proverbs 17:18 Solomon—known for his wisdom—writes, "It's stupid to try to get something for nothing or run up huge bills you can never pay" (MSG).[xiv] Wow, that verse seems pretty blunt and straightforward to me! And over in Psalm 37:21 the psalmist writes, "The wicked borrow and do not repay, but the righteous give generously" (NIV).[xv] The New Testament also speaks of God's view on debt. Writing to the Roman church Paul says, "Don't run up debts, except for the huge debt of love you owe each other" (MSG).[xvi] Christians should be the most debt-averse people on the planet. Unfortunately, though, they are often as bad (or worse) than their worldly friends. Christians and non-Christians alike have allowed the world's financial culture to infiltrate their thinking. The vast majority of Christians are financed up to their eyeballs with little hope of ever getting out from under their debt.

Let's move on to another example. Worldly thinking says, "Get rich quick." Conversely, biblical teaching says, "Get wealthy slowly." Proverbs 13:11 tells God's people that "Wealth gained hastily will dwindle, but whoever gathers little by little will increase it" (ESV).[xvii]

I could go on with even more examples of worldly financial thinking. In a nutshell though, if the world's system says to do one thing with money, then the wiser choice would probably be to do a 180 and go the exact opposite direction!

Before I wrap up this section, let me offer one final thought when it comes to money, God, the Bible, and an attitude of *"be rich versus get rich."* Focus time and energy on a pursuit of wisdom, rather than money. Listen again to Solomon's wisdom:

> *My son, if you accept my words*
> *and store up my commands within you,*
> **turning your ear to wisdom**
> **and applying your heart to understanding—**
> *indeed, if you call out for insight*
> *and cry aloud for understanding,*
> *and if you look for it as for silver*
> *and search for it as for hidden treasure,*
> **then you will understand the fear of the Lord**
> **and find the knowledge of God.**
> **For the Lord gives wisdom;**
> *from his mouth come knowledge and understanding.*
> **He holds success in store for the upright,**
> *he is a shield to those whose walk is blameless,*
> *for he guards the course of the just*
> *and protects the way of his faithful ones.*
> – Proverbs 2:1–8 NIV[xviii], emphasis added

According to these verses from Proverbs, success is the product of living a life in pursuit of wisdom and knowledge, not money. Put more time into reading books, watching informative videos, and listening to podcasts. While learning about wise financial habits, create a database of notes in a program such as Evernote[xix], storing that knowledge for further review and insights.

The ultimate test, though, in *being* rich versus *getting* rich is living a generous life. Pastor Andy Stanley[xx] says that being rich is not about what a person has, it's about what a person does. This will be covered in the next chapter on living a life of generosity.

*Quick Tip: For a FREE list of the Action Steps and Resources for each chapter of the book, simply go to:* http://www.heroicpersonalfinances.com/for-christians-book-action-steps/

# CHAPTER 2
# LIVING THE GENEROUS LIFE

"Give freely and become more wealthy; be stingy and lose everything."
— Proverbs 11:24 NLT[xxi]

"No one has ever become poor by giving."
— Anne Frank

In his book *Money: Master The Game*, the famous "self-help guru" Tony Robbins tells a wonderful personal story. This story takes place several years ago when he was living out in California and going through a financially tough time. As Tony was experiencing this rough patch, he suffered a series of setbacks. He found himself angry and frustrated with himself and the world around him.

One night around midnight, Tony was driving on the 57 Freeway near Pomona, California, wondering what was wrong. He was working hard, but nothing was coming together in his life. He felt like a complete failure. Suddenly, tears welled up in his eyes, and he pulled over to the side of the highway. He dug out his personal journal that he always had with him. Using the light coming from the dashboard, Tony wrote in giant letters a message to himself, "THE SECRET TO LIVING IS GIVING." He had forgotten what life was about. Joy is found in being focused on "we" not just "me." Tony drove his car back on the highway with a refocused and renewed personal mission.

He did better for a while, but then slowly slipped back into old patterns. His revelation on the side of the highway was more of a concept that he hadn't fully internalized. Tony encountered more difficulties and six months later, he lost everything financially. He found himself at the lowest point of his life. He was living in a 400-square-foot bachelor apartment in Venice, California. He was resentful, and he blamed everyone else for all the challenges he was currently experiencing. He threw himself a pity party. He became even angrier and more frustrated. Tony started eating large amounts of bad fast food as an escape mechanism. He ended up gaining more than thirty-eight pounds in just a few months! He also started watching shows on TV that he used to make fun of others watching, such as daytime television. He got sucked into the show General Hospital. He now says that it's both humorous and humiliating to see how far he dropped during this time in his life.

Tony was down to his last $19, and he didn't have any prospects for more cash flow. He was also upset with a friend of his who had borrowed $1,200 from him but never paid it back. He reached out to his friend by phone with the hope of getting his money back, but his friend wouldn't return any of his phone calls. Tony was furious! He had to figure out a way he was going to be able to survive on such little money. Tony then remembered a time in his life when he was younger and trying to survive. He would go to those inexpensive all-you-can-eat buffets and gorge himself. This gave him an idea.

His apartment wasn't far from the beautiful Marina del Rey, where the wealthy of Los Angeles dock their yachts. There was a restaurant called El Torito that had a wonderful buffet for $6. To save on gas money, Tony walked the three miles to the restaurant, which was positioned right on the marina. He took a seat by the window and gorged himself on plate after plate of food. While he ate, he watched the boats going by and dreamed of what his life could be like. Over the next few minutes, the anger left him and he started feeling better.

As he was finishing up his meal, he glanced over and noticed a young boy who was maybe eight years old. The boy was all dressed up in a little suit, and he was escorting his mom over to a table.

Tony walked over to the table and complimented the young man on what a gentleman he was and for taking his mom out to lunch. The boy then acknowledged that he didn't have any money to be able to pay for their lunch.

In that moment, Tony reached into his pocket and took out whatever remaining money he had left to his name and placed it on the table. It was a grand total of $13 and change. The boy looked up at Tony and said, "I can't take that." "Of course you can because I'm bigger than you!" Tony told him. And with that, Tony turned and walked out the door.

Tony didn't just walk out the door, though. He flew home! Tony recalls that he should have been freaking out because he was now completely broke, but instead, he felt free. He claims that was the day his life changed forever. On that day he became a wealthy man—it was the day he moved past the feeling of scarcity and fear when it came to money. Tony realized he had been so busy trying to *get* that he had forgotten to *give*. He felt joyful and free!

That evening, Tony committed himself to a plan of massive action. He decided what he was going to do and how he was going to find employment. He knew he could make it happen but still didn't know where his next paycheck or next meal would come from.

Then, a miracle happened. The next day, Tony went to his mailbox and found a handwritten letter from his friend who owed him money. In the letter, his friend apologized for avoiding Tony's phone calls. He knew Tony was in trouble, so he decided to pay Tony back plus a little more. He looked inside the envelope, and there was a check for $1,300. It was enough to last Tony a little more than a month. He cried in relief.

He didn't know if this was a coincidence, but he chose to believe that these two incidents were connected. Tony believed that he had been rewarded because he not only gave to the young boy but also wanted to give. He didn't give out of obligation or fear, but he gave as an offering from one soul to another.

Tony says, "The secret to living is giving. Our giving should be free, open, easy, and enjoyable! Give even when you think you have nothing to give. You'll discover there is an ocean of abundance inside of you and around you."[xxii]

In Acts 20:35b in the New International Version the apostle Paul recalls the words of Jesus when he wrote, "It is more blessed to give than to receive."[xxiii]

Living a generous life *is* the secret to living a wealthy life.

It seems counterintuitive, so oxymoronic. Human logic says to keep a tight, closed fist on every penny and doing so will build wealth.

It doesn't work that way, though.

To be wealthy, one must live in a wealthy manner. I'm not just talking about having piles of money in the bank, either.

True wealth is much more than money. Life is more than money.

True wealth includes health, relationships, career, calling, time flexibility, abilities, and talents. These things have the capacity to create a rich life here on earth. Investing in these areas here on earth will reap eternal benefits in the life to come.

This chapter will explore ways in which to live out a generous life on earth. The result of living a life of generosity will be an investment in the kingdom of God in this life as well as the next.

**Gratitude**

Isn't it funny that people who moan and complain the most often tend to struggle financially? They have difficulty keeping a job. They can't seem to achieve lasting success in their business. Their marriage is on the brink of separation and divorce. They hate their current home. Their car is always breaking down. They struggle with debt. Everything in their life is substandard and inadequate.

Based on my observations, I would say that people who have an upbeat, thankful attitude are wealthier and happier than their complaining counterparts. The research on the subject seems to bear this out as well.

There was an article written by two psychologists, Michael McCollough of Southern Methodist University and Robert Emmons of the University of California. This was a report of their findings of an experiment they performed on gratitude and its influence on well-being.[xxiv] In the study, McCollough and Emmons split several hundred people into three groups. They asked the first group to keep a daily journal of anything they wanted to write about. They asked the second group to only write about their daily unpleasant experiences. They directed the third group to write down a daily list of the things they were grateful for. The results of the study revealed that the third group of people who wrote down positive, grateful information were more alert, enthusiastic, determined, optimistic, and energetic. This group of individuals also experienced less depression and stress. They were more likely to help others, exercise regularly, and make greater progress toward achieving their personal goals.

I don't know about you, but I have a tendency to drift into a complaining, whiny attitude if I'm not careful. That's the flesh, the sin nature taking control. I never gave it much thought until a few years ago when someone pointed it out in my life. Problems crop up at work, and I complain. My kids give me issues at home. I complain. I have to get the air conditioner fixed on my car, for the fifth time in three years (Ugh! Yes, that has happened to me). I complain.

Complaining is a bad habit. It's easy to slide into and it's difficult to get out of. I have learned a few techniques to break out of this bad habit over time.

First, remember the Scripture that states, "Give thanks in all circumstances; for this is God's will for you in Christ Jesus" (1 Thess. 5:18 NIV).[xxv] In this verse, the Apostle Paul didn't say give thanks for the best circumstances and not for problems. No, he's very clear—in *all* circumstances give thanks. And the reason Paul says to give thanks in everything is because it is God's will for the believer's life.

Second, be sure to always include thanksgiving when praying. I usually pray in my car as I drive from home to work. I take time to worship God for who He is (Adoration). I ask Him to forgive me where I have failed Him (Confession). Next, I spend time in a spirit of gratitude, thanking Him for all the amazing things in my life. I thank Him for my salvation, my wife, my four daughters and one son, a roof over my head, clothes on my back, freedom from consumer debt, money in the bank, and cars to drive. My list could go on and on!

A third act of thanksgiving I have practiced in the past is keeping a gratitude journal. This can be done few different ways. Create a simple list of ten things to be thankful for each day (this is a great practice, by the way). Or, write out in paragraph form (journal style) something to be thankful for on a given day. There are no right or wrong answers here.

Fourth, write more thank-you notes. A strange thing happens when writing thank-you notes—people become more thankful in the process! They begin to realize that because of the generosity of others with their time, abilities, or finances, their life is enriched as well. I know from personal experience that if it were not for the help of others at key, desperate times in my life, I would not be the man I am today. I wrote these generous people thank-you notes, and I continue to be grateful for their gifts to me and my family.

When I take the time to step back and assess all the amazing things in my life (even if some are bad), I can't help but feel wealthy with all the good things God has blessed me with. And when I feel wealthy, I think wealthy. I act wealthy. I become wealthy. There lays the key to true wealth!

## Abundance Versus Lack

Also related to an attitude of gratitude is a mindset of abundance versus lack, especially during periods of struggle. When I feel I don't have the necessary resources to "do life" at the level I would like to, when I don't have the money to buy the house or car that I "think" I need to buy, when I don't think I have the necessary resources to run my business or do my job at the level I believe it needs to do done, I often fall into an attitude of lack.

An attitude of scarcity in today's society is completely understandable. Politicians have put their own spin on the American capitalistic economic system. They have conditioned people about the "haves" and the "have-nots." The world labels the wealthy as "cheaters" who don't deserve what they have. Some politicians have gone so far as stating that the wealth of the top 20 percent should be redistributed to the poorer 80 percent of people. They want the government to operate as a modern day Robin Hood on a massive societal scale.

An abundance mindset looks at the world from a different viewpoint, though. It's like putting on a different set of glasses when viewing the economic world. Tremendous wealth is evident and amazing possibilities abound. Instead of being jealous of the wealthy for tapping into abundance, celebrate their genius and hard work. You want to know how they achieved what they have accomplished.

Have you ever noticed how the less financially resourced in the world behave about money? They're "tight" with whatever they have. They have a closed-fist mentality with their money. Dave Ramsey uses this example in Financial Peace University™. He demonstrates that when tight-fisting money, holding on desperately, money can't escape. What's also true, though, is money can't flow *into* that closed hand either.

In an open-handed approach with money Dave demonstrates some money can escape—but even more, flows back in. Work to remain open to a world of financial possibilities. The abundance mentality looks at the world as a world of infinite possibilities, not a world of lack and limited choices.

This abundance approach doesn't mean being wild and free with money, throwing it around and hoping for the best. No, a monthly budget that assigns every dollar a place is paramount. The abundance approach plugs financial leaks—such as taxes and other expenses—in a family's finances. We definitely don't want to be wasteful with what God has entrusted us to manage.

The main idea I want readers to come away with from this section is that we live in a world of abundance, even in a struggling economy. Wealth surrounds us, flowing all around us every day. Our job as managers of God's wealth is to tap into the financial flow of abundance around us, to multiply the financial resources He gives us.

The poor dwell on thoughts of lack and need, while the wealthy focus on abundance and endless possibilities. Right thinking, and making the mental shift from thinking about abundance instead of lack will open up a whole new world of financial possibilities!

## Tithing

As a pastor of generosity and stewardship, I believe the word "tithing" upsets many Christians more than any other biblical word. I've heard every complaint and problem associated with tithing. "It's an Old Testament principle under the Mosaic Law," some say while others insist, "It doesn't apply to the church." Still, others question, "Why does the church always have to talk about tithing and giving?"

My question for these people is "Then, why did Jesus talk about money so much with His disciples and those He ministered to?" I believe that Jesus talked so much about money while He was here on earth because He knows that human beings are by nature sinful. Because of this, they inevitably have *big* problems when it comes to money.

People are selfish with money. They hoard money. They waste money. They buy stupid stuff that doesn't last. They don't manage the money they do have well. They lust after more money. They covet other people's stuff. In the flesh, people are simply not good with handling money.

But as believers in Jesus Christ, God has called us to a higher standard. Recall the first chapter—God has called His children to acknowledge Him as their ultimate source of wealth. They are to be servant managers of what He has given to them. He wants His children to invest and multiply what He has given them to manage. Those who trust Jesus are God's adopted children whom He loves and has given a rich inheritance to be used for His glory. And because of this, believers are to "*be* rich," and not attempt to "*get* rich."

What is "tithing" anyway? From a biblical perspective, the definition of tithing means giving 10 percent of what is earned back to God. God required by law that the nation of Israel give at least 10 percent of everything they had to Him through the tabernacle or temple system. In modern times, church leadership communicates tithing as giving to God 10 percent of all income sources through the local church. If a person makes $1,000 a week, for example, he or she should give God $100 through their church. If they make $10,000 in a month, then they should give $1,000 each month. It's not that complicated. The reality, though, is that the modern day American church Christian gives between 2 and 2.5 percent of their income on a regular basis. This level of giving is far below what I believe God teaches in His Word—and Christians wonder why they struggle so much with finances. The majority of American Christians look exactly like their unbelieving neighbors around them. They are heavily in debt. They have no cash reserves in the bank. And they are unable to give much away.

Here's something interesting in the area of giving. Many non-Christians, secularists, and atheists are beginning to support the concept of tithing through giving 10 percent to worthy causes. They now understand the benefits of generosity. They recognize the help organizations receive from their financial gifts as well as the intrinsic value they receive through giving. Living a generous life benefits everyone!

In my opinion, the whole tithing issue boils down to the universal Law of Sowing and Reaping, also known as the Law of the Harvest.[xxvi] Plant a corn kernel in the ground and what is the expected result? In most cases, the result is a mature corn plant, which will produce many more corn kernels on the ears of corn. When people live healthy lifestyles, eat the right foods, drink plenty of water, exercise, and get an appropriate amount of rest, what is the expected outcome? A healthy, energetic life. The interesting and powerful result of sowing and reaping is there will always be more to reap than what is sown. If that's the case, why are so many people afraid to sow?

The same thing is true about money. When a person gives part of their income away, many more seeds are planted. Don't misunderstand what I'm saying here. I'm not advocating we *give* only to *get*. That's not an appropriate attitude for a Christian. What I am saying, though, is Christians should give at least 10 percent of what God gives to them to manage, in order to live a healthy, balanced financial life. I know that God blesses those who are healthy in this area. I've seen it over and over, again. I've heard testimony after testimony of God blessing those who give at least at the level of 10 percent. I've never heard a negative testimony from someone who tithes. Why? Because God promises in His Word He will bless those who give generously as a result. And He can't violate His promises, ever! That would completely go against His nature and character.

The lead pastor at our church conducted a tithing challenge with the congregation a few years ago. One of our church members who took on the challenge shared the following giving testimony:

*Prior to my walk with God, tithing was not a part of my life. I was raised in church, but it wasn't until I made the decision to accept Jesus Christ as my Savior, that I began to tithe. Even then, I still wasn't giving what I could have. Worrying about not having money for a rainy day or worse, wanting to shop. I didn't have enough faith in God.*

*It wasn't until Pastor mentioned something about a 90-day guarantee. He said if we tithed 10 percent for ninety days, and didn't see God return it, plus some, we'd receive our money back. I figured, what could I lose? So each week, I tithed 10 percent of my income. The great feeling of being able to give that amount to the Lord and my church home was blessing enough for me.*

*But God wasn't finished yet. I received my year-end invoice from tithing in the mail. When I saw how much I had given, I was overjoyed. I'd never given that much in my life! It felt good! The very next day, I was offered a position at my job and was given a 22 percent raise. This was a position that I originally didn't want to apply for, and a raise for the position was never mentioned by management when posted. I knew that this was the work of God!*

*After receiving the raise, I now give more than 10 percent of my income and plan to continue to do so. The Lord works in mysterious ways. Who would've thought that a 90-day guarantee would change my life? – J.S.*

After all the positive testimonies about tithing from both Christians and non-Christians alike, why don't more Christians give at least at the level of

10 percent?

Proverbs 11:25 (MSG) tells us, "The one who blesses others is abundantly blessed; those who help others are helped."[xxvii] If you want to be financially healthy and wealthy, be generous.

## Blessing Israel

The blessing of tithing can be incredible, but nothing compares to what happens when giving at the next level by blessing the nation of Israel.

Over a year ago, a fellow stewardship director at another church recommended a book to me to read called *The Blessed Life* by Robert Morris. I had heard of the book before, but when my friend recommended I read it, I finally knew it was time to check it out.

In my opinion, this is a must-read book for all Christians. Every church staff member should read this. Every church member sitting out in the pew needs to consider purchasing this book. Many people are struggling because they just don't understand the blessings of the Lord, especially when it comes to finances. We are ignorant on so many levels.

In the book, Morris defines the "blessed life" as one in which God's supernatural power works for the believer. Everything they touch does well. Blessings work their way through every area of life—marriage, family, relationships, health, career, calling, and finances. A "cursed" life is one in which His supernatural power works against the person.

One of the claims by Morris deals with a next level of giving and blessing related to the nation of Israel. Scripture supports this claim as well. In Genesis 12:3 God makes the following promise in Scripture: "I will bless those who bless you, and whoever curses you I will curse; and all peoples on earth will be blessed through you" (NIV).[xxviii] Then in Numbers 24:9b, at the end of Balaam's Spirit-led blessing on the Israelites, Scripture says (in relation to the nation of Israel), "May those who bless you be blessed and those who curse you be cursed!"[xxix] The prophet Zechariah also writes, "For whoever touches you touches the apple of his eye"(Zech. 2:8b).[xxx] Finally, in the Apostle Paul's directive about the gospel message he writes, "For I am not ashamed of the gospel, because it is the power of God that brings salvation to everyone who believes: first to the Jew, then to the Gentile" (Rom. 1:16).[xxxi]

From a modern-day perspective, when nations decide to bless or harm the State of Israel, a pattern of blessings or curses is evident. Looking back in history for the last several decades, both Great Britain and the United States have benefitted from God's promise in this area. When Great Britain and the U.S. were strong allies of Israel, God blessed them. However, when the leaders of these countries backtracked on promises and pressured Israel to give back land to their Arab neighbors, disasters have occurred. In fact, a researcher recently discovered twenty instances in which a disaster in the United States coincided with pressure on Israel to give back land. Those who bless Israel are blessed. Those who curse Israel are cursed.

Not long after I read *The Blessed Life* book, I contacted some friends who support Israel in many different ways. I asked them the question: "If the Jones family was to give to bless the Jewish people over in the nation of Israel, what would be the best organization to give to accomplish that goal?" We went back and forth a few times on some possibilities, and then we landed on the organization [OneForIsrael.org](OneForIsrael.org). I like this non-profit for two primary reasons. One, they share the gospel of Jesus Christ with the Israelis living in Israel. Two, they give humanitarian aid to Jewish Holocaust survivors in Israel. I'm not advocating that everyone give to this specific charitable organization. In fact, I would encourage personal research. Find some friends who are pro-Israel and ask them about other reputable Jewish charities. Ask a bunch of questions. Discover what charity fits best and blesses the people of Israel—and begin giving.

We started with giving a small financial gift of $25 a month, and we plan to expand that gift up to 1 percent of our family's income. We can bless the nation of Israel through giving our top 1 percent, and then give our tithe or 10 percent to God through our local church.

Have you ever heard one of those disclaimers on a TV or radio commercial that says something like, "Individual results may vary?" Yeah, that one. The same is true in people's personal lives. Individual results will vary. The blessing of God will look one way in one person's life and a different way in another person's life—and that's okay. Since our family has started blessing Israel, we can testify that God has blessed us even more than He has blessed us in the past.

We are seeing the blessings of God in many different ways. He has helped us achieve some financial goals in a shorter time frame than we thought possible. He has blessed my wife and me this year with a son. He has blessed us by carrying us through various trials and tribulations.

God cannot violate the promises in His Word. He has been faithful to us as we have been a financial blessing to His chosen people Israel as well as tithing to our church. Malachi 3:10 says, "'Bring the whole tithe into the storehouse, that there may be food in my house. Test me in this,' says the LORD Almighty, 'and see if I will not throw open the floodgates of heaven and pour out so much blessing that there will not be enough room to store it.'"[xxxii] Try God at His word and see what happens!

## Giving to the Poor

God loves the poor and needy. From Old Testament to New Testament, Scripture is clear that God cares for those who are less fortunate.

In the Mosaic Law, God gave specific instructions to the Jewish people. He instructed Israel to do certain things in a certain way to take care of the poor and less fortunate. For example, Leviticus 19:9–10 says, "When you reap the harvest of your land, do not reap to the very edges of your field or gather the gleanings of your harvest. Do not go over your vineyard a second time or pick up the grapes that have fallen. Leave them for the poor and the foreigner. I am the Lord your God" (NIV).[xxxiii]

Over in Deuteronomy 15:11 God says, "For there will never cease to be poor in the land. Therefore I command you, 'You shall open wide your hand to your brother, to the needy and to the poor, in your land'" (ESV).[xxxiv]

Proverbs 19:17 says, "Whoever is kind to the poor lends to the Lord, and he will reward them for what they have done" (NIV).[xxxv]

I love the promise God gives in this next verse. Isaiah 58:10 in the English Standard Version states, "If you pour yourself out for the hungry and satisfy the desire of the afflicted, then shall your light rise in the darkness and your gloom be as the noonday."[xxxvi] The favor of the Lord will be mighty on believers who sacrifice for the poor and needy.

Jesus tells His followers in Matthew 5:42 "Give to the one who begs from you, and do not refuse the one who would borrow from you."[xxxvii]

In Galatians 2:10 the apostle Paul told the church at Galatia about his meeting with the other apostles in Jerusalem, "Only, they asked us to remember the poor, the very thing I was eager to do."[xxxviii]

Today is no different. Christians serve the same God of both the Old and New Testaments. He loves the poor and needy in the 21st century as much as He did back in the book of Genesis. If God loves the poor, then what does He want believers to do? How does He want the Body of Christ to help them?

Helping the poor and needy isn't only about handing a couple of bucks to the homeless guy hanging out on the street corner. There are a variety of ways people can help those who are less fortunate. Here are a few thoughts to get the creative ideas flowing.

- Support a food pantry with food, money, and volunteer time
- Buy a meal for a homeless person
- Help a military family who has a spouse deployed overseas
- Raise foster children
- Adopt orphaned children or a poor widow at church
- Support a teen pregnancy center

People have passionate concerns in different areas and should focus time, energy, and money into those areas in which they feel a burden to help.

My dad became a believer in Christ later in life when he was in his early 30s. Around the year 1976, when I was a young boy around six years old, I remember being with my dad on a Sunday morning. He was driving my brother and me to church in his burnt orange Chevy Nova—man, I wish he had kept that car! As we were driving down the main road to get to church, we saw a rough-looking young man carrying a green duffle bag attempting to "hitch a ride." My dad thought he might be a Vietnam War vet but found out later that he had just been released from jail! My dad invited him to get in the passenger side of his Nova and drove him down the street to our local McDonald's to buy him breakfast. As the man ate his breakfast, my dad shared the gospel with him.

I have to think that God the Father smiled that Sunday morning way back in the 1970s. My dad reached out to someone less fortunate and attempted to meet both a physical and a spiritual need. As believers in Jesus Christ, this is what He has called His body to do.

Do you want the blessings of God poured out all over your life? If you answered "yes," then check out what King David wrote in Psalm 41:1–3: "Blessed is the one who considers the poor! In the day of trouble the Lord delivers him; the Lord protects him and keeps him alive; he is called blessed in the land; you do not give him up to the will of his enemies. The Lord sustains him on his sickbed; in his illness you restore him to full health."[xxxix]

How are you helping those around you who are less fortunate?

## Happy Money

In this chapter, we have discussed living the generous life. I have mentioned three levels of giving. The first level involves giving a tithe (10 percent) to the local church. The second level involves blessing the nation of Israel with a gift of 1 percent of income. And the third involves helping the poor and needy. This amount of generosity may seem overwhelming and out of reach to many reading this book—it may be a challenge depending on income, budget, and obligations.

I feel your pain. I do understand. For many, giving 10 percent and beyond can seem like a lot to give, especially if you've never given before on a regular basis. No worries! Our God is a loving, gracious God. Tithing is not a salvation issue. My encouragement to you would be to just start small and then grow into giving at least 10 percent of your income back to the Lord through your local church.

I recently read a simple eBook I discovered on Amazon.com called *Happy Money* by Lania Buenostar.[xl] I can't recall that much from the book, except the idea of giving a small amount of money once a week or once a month, in a discreet and anonymous manner. I think many of Lania's ideas about giving could be used by the Christian community, and help move people onto the generosity path. Here's what the author says about her method:

*For the Happy Money method, we do something similar to tithing and money seeding. The difference is that we do it anonymously and the recipient is also unknown. What's good about our method is that it doesn't require a generous amount of money or 10 percent of our income to do it. We only need $5 to start, five one-dollar bills to be exact (or the smallest bill in your country). This is what I do: I write a blessing on a piece* *of post-it paper, and then I stick the note to the money. I roll up the bill with the sticky note inside, then I go out of the house and leave this* Happy Money *in a public place where a lucky stranger is sure to find it. Most of the time, I just leave the rolled up money in one of the elevators in my apartment building. I push it under the mirror that covers the upper half of one of the elevator's wall. I leave the money sticking out a little so that it would be hard to miss. But I do this only when I'm alone in the elevator. If there's already someone inside or someone gets in before I have time to do my good deed, I go to the corner grocery instead and leave the Happy Money there ...*

*... What kind of blessing do I write on the sticky note? I usually just write, "May all your days be filled with happiness, love and wealth." Sometimes, I add the words "This is your lucky money." ... "Share your blessing so more blessings will come to you" as encouragement to the money finder to give money as anonymous gifts. I do this regularly, four to five times a month. Okay, that's the first part of our method. Sound easy, right? Even children can do it ...*[xli]

If giving 1 percent of your income seems like a stretch, let alone 10 percent, then I would recommend Lania's *Happy Money* approach. In my opinion, something is better than nothing. Start out small. Give without recognition. Grow into a higher level of generosity as I have mentioned in this chapter. I know God will bless those who live out the generous life.

*Quick Tip: For a FREE list of the Action Steps and Resources for each chapter of the book, simply go to:* [http://www.heroicpersonalfinances.com/for-christians-book-action-steps/](http://www.heroicpersonalfinances.com/for-christians-book-action-steps/)

# CHAPTER 3
# MORNING ROUTINES AND HABIT FORMATION

"In the morning, Lord, you hear my voice; in the morning I lay my requests before you and wait expectantly."
— Psalm 5:3 NIV[xlii]

"If it's your job to eat a frog, it's best to do it first thing in the morning. And if it's your job to eat two frogs, it's best to eat the biggest one first."
— Mark Twain

Scott Adams is the creative cartoonist who came up with the "Dilbert" comic strip. He has done many interviews with online magazines and podcasts about his own unique morning routines.

Several years ago, Mr. Adams created a morning routine in which he could manifest his best, most creative work in the early morning hours. Now, he is the first to admit that he isn't always creative during this time. He structures his morning schedule in such a way, though, to allow himself to get into a creative state if at all possible. Adams says, "Creativity is not something you can summon on command. The best you can do is set an attractive trap and wait. My mornings are the trap. I wait for the ideas to arrive at their leisure, like a hunter in a duck blind. And in order for the trap to work, I exercise tight control over my physical environment."

Scott wakes up early each day, anywhere between 3:30 and 5:00 a.m. His first twenty minutes of the day are always the same. He makes it to his home office desk within ten minutes of waking up. He then sits down, eats a protein bar, and drinks a cup of coffee to be energized for the morning.

After eating, he then "primes the creative pump" with positive news. His favorite news source is *Business Insider* (businessinsider.com). He claims they have a good mix of business and technology, which is the perfect fit for the "Dilbert" comic strip.

He says that four hours of creative time each morning flies by. He hardly notices the clock, and by 10:00 a.m. he states that he has written "two 'Dilbert' comics, a blog post, a few experimental comics posted on Twitter, four clever tweets, a 'Dilbert' movie scene, and an email about a new idea for my startup team at CalendarTree.com."

By late morning, Adams finds he has spent his creative energies. As he approaches lunchtime, he prepares to go workout at the gym. He will repeat the exact same routine the next day.[xliii]

In Stephen Covey's classic book *The 7 Habits of Highly Effective People*, Covey gives us the well-known illustration of the glass jar. In this example, you take a large clear container and attempt to fit water, sand, pebbles, rocks, and then several large rocks. In this visual illustration, Covey demonstrates that in order for everything to fit in the jar, it must be put in the jar in descending order: large rocks first, followed by smaller rocks, then pebbles, sand, and water. This illustration is a visual representation of our daily schedules. In order to accomplish the "big rocks" in life (in Covey terminology, the important but not urgent), important items must be scheduled first before all the smaller stuff crowds them out.

In the life of Scott Adams, we see the "big rocks" principle at work. Adams knows exactly what he needs to do in his creative work life to be successful and generate the income he needs to accomplish his goals. He has engineered his entire morning routine to complete all those important tasks before anything else gets done in his day.

A few years ago, I went through a process of establishing a regular morning routine. My routine came about as a result of going through one of the absolute worst experiences in my entire life.

Professional counselors have ranked divorce as the second most stressful life event. According to the Holmes-Rahe Stress Inventory,[xliv] it carries a stress level of 73 out of 100. I can testify from personal experience that this statistic is true.

During this challenging time in my life, I dove deep into an early morning routine just to keep my sanity! I would usually wake up around 5:00 am and spend some time reading through my Bible. Then, I would spend time on my knees in prayer, asking God to bring healing to an impossible situation. After that, I would spend time writing a couple of pages in a journal about my problems and personal journey. I would wrap up my morning routine with writing blog posts on my first Christian personal finance blog.[xlv]

My own experience with establishing a solid morning routine for the last seven years has been nothing but positive. I am more productive and focused in every area of my life, including the spiritual, emotional, physical, relational, and financial. By setting aside time in the early morning hours, I am also working on my major life goals with intentionality and consistency.

This chapter will explore various aspects of potential morning routines. Some of these activities will most likely be familiar. Some may seem a little "out there." Just hang in there with me through this section of the book. I believe practicing these activities on a consistent, daily basis over time will produce amazing results in all areas of life. I can testify that these morning routines are just as critical to financial success as a well-diversified retirement portfolio.

Having a solid, purposeful morning routine will propel a person on a path to successful living that translates to every area of life.

## Meditation

Based on the title of this section, I know what my readers are already thinking. Larry's lost it. He's into some kind of crazy New Age mysticism, "woo-woo" nonsense.

This is not the kind of meditation I'm referring to. This is not an Indian, "ohm," or spiritual kind of meditation. This meditation is more of a deep breathing exercise focusing on present state awareness for ten to twenty minutes.

And now readers are probably exclaiming, "But Larry, there's no way I can carve out ten to twenty minutes just to close my eyes and do deep breathing exercises. You don't know my schedule!"

I hear and understand this concern. I'm busy too. I spin many plates and have too much on all these plates!

Over the last year, I have listened to several podcast episodes that have referenced the power of this style of meditation. On one of these podcasts, I heard an interview with WWE wrestler Paul Michael Levesque, better known as Triple H, who gave a great explanation for meditation. He said, "It's like hitting the reset button for the mind."[xlvi] That statement is an excellent analogy for the purpose and power of meditation.

On an episode of his podcast titled "5 Morning Rituals That Help Me Win The Day," best-selling author Tim Ferriss has described meditation in this way: "You are developing your powers of concentration. The muscle you are working is bringing your attention back to something. Concentration is like a muscle that needs continual conditioning and reinforcement. If you will do your meditative practice first thing in the morning, it's like a warm-up to avoid distraction during your day. And if you do get distracted or interrupted, you can return to your primary task more effectively."[xlvii]

The personal testimonies I was hearing about meditation began to grow to the point that I decided it was worth further investigation and personal trial. I started small—maybe five minutes at first—and now I'm up to fifteen to twenty minutes each morning. I also find myself practicing my meditation exercises at other times. If I've had a hectic, busy beginning of the day with my two youngest daughters, I'll hide in the office, lock the door, turn off the lights, and practice ten minutes of breathing exercises. This helps to bring back a sense of calm and peace into my life so that I can be more productive at work.

I'm no meditation expert. I'm more of a newbie. I can tell you, though, that practicing deep breathing meditation has been a game-changer for me. It has brought a new level of calm, peace, confidence, and focus into my life. I'm addicted to doing it. I've made meditation one of my Stephen Covey "big rock" habits that I must do in my personal schedule before anything else. I'm even finding myself doing these deep-breathing exercises when I get myself into stressful situations. This style of present state awareness meditation does work!

Here's a quick thumbnail sketch of my own approach to meditation each day. First, I attempt to practice this not long after I wake up around 4:00 or 4:30 a.m. each morning. I get dressed and go downstairs to my home office. I sit in my office chair, eyes closed, back straight, and feet flat on the floor with my hands resting palms up on my thighs. I then start breathing in through my nose for five counts—I hold my breath for five counts, and then exhale out my mouth for five counts. I continue with this breathing pattern the entire ten to twenty minutes of the exercise. I attempt to focus on my breathing. If I find my mind wandering around all over the place, I then also attempt to focus on a single point out in front of me in my "mind's eye."

When first starting to meditate (and even after doing it for a while), many discover they have "monkey brain." Monkey brain is when the mind wanders around from one thought to the next. When this happens, ever so gently focus on breathing or a single focal point. Don't worry too much about it. Training the mind to focus takes time—and everyone struggles in this area, especially in a culture of distraction we all live in.

In my journey into the world of non-"woo-woo," non-New Age meditation, I have found several helpful tools:

1. **Headspace App:** This is the first tool I started meditating with. There is a free side to the app that I used at the beginning. I enjoyed my experience so much that I attempted to buy a subscription. For some reason, I ran into a problem using my debit card for payment. I ended up abandoning Headspace for other available tools. Check out their website at https://www.headspace.com. They have various levels of paid subscriptions from a monthly plan all the way up to a lifetime plan.
2. **Calm App:** This application is like Headspace. Again, there is a free side and a paid subscription (they call it "unlocking Pro Access") side to the app. I do not own a subscription. I use the free part of the app if I have limited meditation time in the morning. I may also use this app to do any meditation in the middle of the day to de-stress and refocus my mind. Their website is http://www.calm.com. They have two paid subscription plans: monthly and yearly. All of this information is easy to access on their free app.
3. **Zen 12:** This is a series of twelve monthly mp3 files that can be purchased for a flat fee. The mp3 files come in four different types for each of the twelve months: relaxation music, a guided meditation, white noise, and sounds of nature. Use whatever version of each month's meditation mp3 file that you desire. I downloaded the 12 guided meditation versions and have them as a playlist in iTunes on my iPhone. This is the program I use each morning. Time commitment: recordings start out at twelve minutes for the first few months, and then increase with each passing

month. By month twelve, users are usually meditating for twenty minutes. The Zen 12 website is https://www.zen12.com. At the time of my writing this chapter, the current cost was $37 after plugging in their "special discount code."

I know some Christians will have issues with me on this particular section of the book about meditation. I understand the concern. Again, based on my own personal experience using the tools above, I do not view this style of meditation to be in conflict with Scripture. This version of meditation is non-spiritual. It is more like guided, deep breathing exercises to calm and focus a distracted mind. I believe everyone should be doing this each morning to prepare for a successful day. Try it. Experiment with the practice for a few weeks. I think it will be helpful.

### Scripture Reading and Prayer

After meditating for fifteen to twenty minutes, I move into a personal quiet time of Bible reading and prayer. Every Christian should have their own routine when it comes to Scripture reading and prayer. In this section, I will share what I have found helpful in my own life.

When it comes to Scripture reading, I'm a "read more and absorb more over long periods of time" type of reader. I have read through the entire Bible from Genesis to Revelation in one year a total of ten to twelve times. In the year I am writing this book, I'm attempting to read through the New Testament three times.

I know other pastor-types out there believe Christians should be selective on reading more "relevant" Bible passages (such as New Testament books). They believe Christians should read shorter sections and dig into the meaning of those sections. While I understand the logic of these suggestions, here are my reasons why I don't read the Bible in this manner.

First, it's difficult to obtain a comprehensive view of Scripture camping out on smaller passages of the Bible all the time. It's hard to grasp the breadth of the Genesis-to-Revelation storyline of the Bible on a steady diet of the Gospels alone or the Apostle Paul's epistles.

Second, there is the potential of developing faulty doctrine when not comparing Scripture to Scripture. Many times, people will research a specific verse or Bible story and come up with a much different doctrinal practice than if they were reading larger chunks of the entire Bible. In Acts 17:11 Paul speaks highly of the Berean Jews who examined the Scriptures: "Now the Berean Jews were of more noble character than those in Thessalonica, for they received the message with great eagerness and examined the Scriptures every day to see if what Paul said was true" (NIV).[xlviii]

Third, several "pillars of the Christian faith" were known to be avid practitioners of reading through their Bibles on a regular basis. The list of these believers includes Martin Luther, President John Quincy Adams, George Müller, President George W. Bush, and Billy Graham. Check out these famous quotes from some of these men regarding reading through the entire Bible:

"The Bible is a harp with a thousand strings. Play on one to the exclusion of its relationship to the others, and you will develop discord. Play on all of them, keeping them in their places in the divine scale, and you will hear heavenly music all the time." – William P. White

"For some years now I have read through the Bible twice every year. If you picture the Bible to be a mighty tree and every word a little branch, I have shaken every one of these branches because I wanted to know what it was and what it meant." – Martin Luther

"So great is my veneration for the Bible that the earlier my children begin to read it the more confident will be my hope that they will prove useful citizens of their country and respectable members of society. I have for many years made it a practice to read through the Bible once every year." – John Quincy Adams

Fourth, as I read more Scripture I absorb more Scripture. I am able to absorb key concepts as I read through my Bible many times over the years. As I journal, blog, and write about spiritual matters, I find these key concepts coming to mind as well as their general location in the Bible. I will then go back and search out a particular verse (or verses) and study the passage more carefully.

Fifth, I believe Bible reading should focus on the beginning of Genesis to the end of Revelation because the majority of Christians have never read all the way through their Bible. This is a sad statement about modern-day believers. I believe more Christians would have a solid understanding of their faith and theology if they took the time to read through their Bibles in one year.

The following are some excellent resources I have found extremely helpful in my own journey of reading through the Bible in a year:

1. *The Daily Bible In Chronological Order* (NIV), published by Harvest House: This was my "go to" Bible for several years. I'm a big fan of the chronological ordering of the Bible (it's not in your typical book-to-book, Genesis through Revelation format). You read through the Bible from creation to Revelation in the order the events actually occurred. This Bible also has devotional commentary and is arranged in a calendar passage format from January 1 through December 31 to make reading each day practical and easy. I recommend this Bible to begin your journey of reading through the Bible in one year.
2. *HCSB Study Bible,* published by Holman Bible Publishers: I purchased The Holman Christian Standard Bible as an app for my iPhone and iPad mini a couple of years ago. This is my default Bible when looking up various passages of Scripture.
3. *Bible Gateway* (www.biblegateway.com): This is an online Bible that has various translations available to read. There is also a Bible Gateway app available for download to your smart devices. One feature that I have found useful is the Chronological Bible Plan, which I used as my read through the Bible plan in 2014. A handy feature I discovered is the ability to sync up with Apple iCal so that I would receive daily reminders about my Bible reading for each day.
4. *The NIV Stewardship Study Bible*, published by Zondervan: I bought this several years ago when they had a Kindle version available (Note: I can no longer find a Kindle version on Amazon, only paperback).

5.  *CEV The Financial Stewardship Bible*, published by American Bible Society: I don't own a copy of this Bible, yet, but I have looked through one. I was impressed with the features and layout. Paperback seems to be the only version available.

Now, let's move on to the topic of prayer. Prayer is a personal experience. Mature believers in Christ should have their own specific methods, places, styles, and practices of prayer. In this section, I'll share my approach that I have developed over the last few years as a result of my own personal, unique circumstances. Perhaps my own prayer patterns will generate some ideas for others.

In a "perfect" Larry Jones morning habits world, I would pray immediately after reading my Bible in my home office early in the morning. Unfortunately, I no longer live in that "perfect" world. At the time of this writing, I have four daughters who range in ages from fifteen years old all the way down to two years old with a baby brother as well. My wife works a job in which she leaves early morning for work. Once she leaves the house, I become Mr. Mom as I help all my girls get ready for high school all the way down to preschool/childcare. In my current early morning schedule, I consider having an hour to myself from 4:30 to 5:30 a.m. to read my Bible and write a major blessing. This was the schedule in which I have written the majority of this book. It hasn't been easy, but you do what you need to do!

Because of my tight morning schedule with getting four girls up and ready for the day, I'm always looking for ways to spend my available time as wisely as I can and still accomplish what I need to accomplish. So, what I did was end up moving my prayer time to my daily commute time from home to work. This gives me about fifteen to twenty minutes of mostly focused time. In my car, I keep a small spiral-bound 3 x 5 card notebook as my prayer journal, and I flip through my cards and prayer requests as I'm driving. Again, this is not the ideal situation in a Larry Jones "perfect" world. I would love to have two to three hours of uninterrupted time in my home office each morning, but that "perfect" world left me a few years ago. I write this to communicate that creativity is almost always necessary in carving out time for prayer. Be intentional. It's not going to happen on accident.

Once a prayer time is established, what should be prayed for? There are several ways to go about creating a prayer plan. I would encourage doing a Google search for "prayer plan" and see all the wonderful ideas that come out of that web search. Here are some of the highlights from my own prayer plan. These are the key points I like to cover in my fifteen to twenty minutes of drive time each morning:

- ☐ **Worship God.** I praise Him for who He is. I pray through His attributes or characteristics—He is holy, righteous, omniscient (all-knowing), omnipresent (everywhere), omnipotent (all-powerful), and more . . . way more! In this opening part of my prayer time, I may even sing worship songs such as the hymn "Holy, Holy, Holy" or a praise chorus like "How Great Is Our God."
- ☐ **Confess sin.** I acknowledge my sinful state, my struggles of the flesh, my sins of omission and commission, and my failure to be the disciple that He desires me to be. I will often pray the psalm of King David, "Create in me a pure heart, O God, and renew a steadfast spirit within me. Do not cast me from your presence or take your Holy Spirit from me. Restore to me the joy of your salvation and grant me a willing spirit, to sustain me" (Psalm 51:10–12 NIV).[xlix]
- ☐ **Thank Him.** I thank God for all the amazing blessings He has poured out into my life: my salvation, my beautiful wife, my four amazing daughters, my son, a large home, two dependable cars, my calling into ministry, great jobs, health, and health insurance . . . the list goes on and on.
- ☐ **Prayer for Wisdom.** This is a "newer" prayer category for me, and here's why. I recently read the book *The Money Code: Become a Millionaire With the Ancient Jewish Code* by H. W. Charles. The number one key takeaway I came away with after reading this book is to pray for wisdom, just like King Solomon (who early in his reign could have asked God for untold wealth but instead asked Him for wisdom in leading His people). Proverbs 2:2–8 says, "...turning your ear to wisdom and applying your heart to understanding—indeed, if you call out for insight and cry aloud for understanding, and if you look for it as for silver and search for it

as for hidden treasure, then you will understand the fear of the Lord and find the knowledge of God. For the Lord gives wisdom; from his mouth come knowledge and understanding. He holds success in store for the upright, he is a shield to those whose walk is blameless, for he guards the course of the just and protects the way of his faithful ones."[1] My advice: spend more prayer time asking God to pour out His divine wisdom into one's mind, heart, and life.

**Specific Requests.** I vary my specific requests depending on the day of the week. On one day, I may spend more of my time praying for individual family members. On another day, I may focus more time praying specific prayers for my church family. But, here are some specific requests that I try to hit every day.

- First, I pray for more favor of the Lord to shine out upon my life and the lives of those around me. I pray for more blessing and greater opportunities. Does that sound selfish or self-serving? Yeah, maybe, but there is precedence in Scripture for this type of prayer. In 1 Samuel 1, Hannah prayed that God would bless her with a son, and He answered her request when she gave birth to the prophet Samuel. In 2 Kings 20:1–11, King Hezekiah asked God to spare his life and heal him. God granted him his request!
- Second, similar to the first, I pray the Prayer of Jabez (1 Chron. 4:10) over me and my family: "Lord, I pray that You would bless Larry, Jennifer, Jasmine, Nora, Katelynn, Addison, and Nathan indeed. I pray that You would do something so *huge* in all our lives that it is obviously from You. I pray that You would increase our influence and opportunities for You and give us a sense of Your continual presence and direction. Protect us and keep us from falling into Satan's traps. Amen" (paraphrased by me).
- Third, I pray for the salvation of a few of my family members whose spiritual condition I am concerned about.

- Fourth, I usually spend daily time praying through my current list of "BHAGs" (**B**ig **H**airy **A**udacious **G**oals) that I would like to see accomplished in God's time and in God's way.

Again, this prayer plan is my own. There is nothing inspired or divine about my plan. It's just a prayer outline that has developed over time. If this has helped inspire new ideas for personal prayer time, great! I'm glad I could help. I would encourage reading and researching other prayer plans. There are plenty of great ideas on the Internet and in other books.

**Affirmations**

Affirmations are another area similar to meditation that some Christians freak out about and claim to be too "woo-woo" and "New Age-y." I completely understand the concerns. There are some affirmations I have run across that have a New Age angle to them. I do think, though, there is a biblical model for doing affirmations in a way that honors the Lord. In Philippians 4:4–8 Paul writes, "Rejoice in the Lord always. I will say it again: Rejoice! Let your gentleness be evident to all. The Lord is near. Do not be anxious about anything, but in every situation, by prayer and petition, with thanksgiving, present your requests to God. And the peace of God, which transcends all understanding, will guard your hearts and your minds in Christ Jesus. Finally, brothers and sisters, whatever is true, whatever is noble, whatever is right, whatever is pure, whatever is lovely, whatever is admirable—if anything is excellent or praiseworthy—think about such things."[li]

In this Scripture passage, the apostle Paul is encouraging the members of the church at Philippi to rejoice in the Lord, to stay positive, to pray things through, to guard their hearts and minds, and to focus their thoughts on the positive and excellent.

I view well-written affirmations as a tool to reprogram the mind. All people talk to themselves at some level. However, this can turn into repetitious, harmful patterns when internal statements become habitual:

"I'm not smart enough."

"People don't like me."
"I'll never get that job I want."
"I'm not good with money."
"I'll never get married and have a family."
"I'll never get my stupid book written."

Talking to one's self in this manner is not healthy and will never bring about the desires hoped for. In fact, it will bring out exactly what a person doesn't want. A harmful phrase can evolve into a self-fulfilling prophecy as a result of repeating it all the time.

What does recent research say about the validity of affirmations? An article published by *psychologytoday.com* states the following:

*"... new research from Carnegie Mellon University provides the first evidence that self-affirmation can protect against the damaging effects of stress on problem-solving performance. Understanding that self-affirmation—the process of identifying and focusing on one's most important values—boosts stressed individuals' problem-solving abilities will help guide future research and the development of educational interventions.*

*'An emerging set of published studies suggest that a brief self-affirmation activity at the beginning of a school term can boost academic grade-point averages in underperforming kids at the end of the semester. This new work suggests a mechanism for these studies, showing self-affirmation effects on actual problem-solving performance under pressure,' said J. David Creswell, assistant professor of psychology in CMU's Dietrich College of Humanities and Social Sciences.*

*The results showed that participants who were under high levels of chronic stress during the past month had impaired problem-solving performance. In fact, they solved about 50 percent fewer problems in the task. But notably, this effect was qualified by whether participants had an opportunity to first complete the self-affirmation activity. Specifically, a brief self-affirmation was effective in eliminating the deleterious effects of chronic stress on problem-solving performance, such that chronically stressed self-affirmed participants performed under pressure at the same level as participants with low chronic stress levels.*

*'People under high stress can foster better problem-solving simply by taking a moment beforehand to think about something that is important to them,' Creswell said. 'It's an easy-to-use and portable strategy you can roll out before you enter that high-pressure performance situation.'*

*New research published in Psychological Science, a journal of the Association for Psychological Science, explores the neurophysiological reactions that could explain how self-affirmation helps us deal with threats to our self-integrity.*

*'Although we know that self-affirmation reduces threat and improves performance, we know very little about why this happens. And we know almost nothing about the neural correlates of this effect,' says lead researcher Lisa Legault of Clarkson University.'*[xlii]

Here are several positive affirmations I have used over the last few years. Or, you can steal ideas from others, write personal affirmations, or do a combination of both. You can write them for the various areas of your life from wealth to relationships to career to physical health. You can use Scripture as your foundation for specific affirmations.

## Health

- "I am healthy in mind, body, and spirit."
- "I am fit and healthy."
- "I perform well on six to eight hours of sleep a night."

## Money and Wealth

- "I am an excellent money manager" (Based on being a good steward of God's money).
- "My money works hard for me and makes me more and more money" (Based on the power of investing as seen in the Parable of the Bags of Gold).

## Relationships

- "Terrific people come into my life."
- "Today I choose to write a thank you note or two."
- "I choose to be generous to everyone in my world."
- "Raising happy, optimistic children is an important job."

## Career

- "Every day, I am doing what God has called me to do."
- "I relax into my future."
- "I can do anything I put my mind to."
- "Great opportunities fall into my lap today."

Here is how I work affirmations into my daily schedule. While I do believe this would be beneficial to work into my regular morning routine, I don't have that kind of time in the morning anymore as I mentioned in the previous section. Like my prayer time, I ended up pushing any of my affirmation time into my car as I drive from place to place. I have an extra spiral-bound 3 x 5 card notebook in which I have written down several different affirmations for various life areas. As I'm driving, I read the affirmations out loud to myself a number of times. I'm sure people driving next to me on the roadways think I'm crazy, but I have found this to be an excellent use of my drive time.

Doing consistent affirmations over the last couple of years has had a positive impact on my personal finances, career, and calling. I realize that this might come off as a sort of "name it and claim it" vibe. Here's the challenge, though. The manner in which a person thinks as well as what they say to one's self has a tremendous impact on a person's life—much more than they probably realize. The majority of people have horrible "self-talk." There is an old, well-known saying: "Garbage in, garbage out." To reprogram thinking, it's important to come up with new, positive scripts that will produce sought after outcomes.

They do work. Try it and see what happens.

## Journaling and Writing

Some of the greatest minds in human history have been writers. For example in biblical times, the most successful leaders such as Moses, King David, King Solomon, Daniel, and the apostle Paul were prolific thinkers and writers. In more recent history, these famous individuals kept journals: business leaders such as John D. Rockefeller; inventors like Ben Franklin and Thomas Edison; presidents such as John Adams and Ronald Reagan; and many authors like Mark Twain and Ernest Hemingway. These famous individuals left a personal history of their thoughts, life events, and decisions. They documented their legacy as well.

Let me state upfront that I am an inconsistent journal writer, but I do understand the value in keeping a journal. I have experienced the power of keeping a journal, especially over a specific period of two years when I was experiencing a difficult time in life. Lately, though, I have been inconsistent due to my tight time constraints in the morning hours. Since my available early morning writing time has been limited the last few years due to having young children in the house, I had to make choices. I can keep up with a journal and maybe have a little time left over to do some blog or book writing. Or, I can focus all my available writing time to complete one goal. For me, this is a no-brainer. I chose to focus on accomplishing one thing. This book is a result of stopping other writing to finish a single goal, but I digress.

As I mentioned, I have been an inconsistent journal writer, but there have been specific periods of time I have found great value in keeping a journal. When I go through periods of doubt and indecision, I find journaling to be helpful in getting my thoughts out on to paper or a computer screen as a method of thinking through the problem.

As I was going through a difficult time in life a few years ago, I found keeping a morning journal to be invaluable to dump my emotions out on paper and process what I was experiencing. The entire practice was therapeutic for me in my emotional and psychological healing.

There are various methods of journaling. Here are a few that I'm aware of and have used to some degree in the past:

1. **Diary:** Write down various things that are happening day to day. Private thoughts and feelings are usually what people document in a diary.
2. **Scripture and prayer journal:** In this format, people typically write down what they are learning in Bible reading, and/or prayer requests to pray through as well as answers to those prayers.
3. **Morning pages:** This type of journal is utilized first thing in the morning, right after waking up. The goal is to do a "brain dump"

of anything and everything one is currently obsessing about. Typically, it is good to set a time or a page goal on morning pages, such as writing for ten minutes or two pages straight without stopping. I found tremendous value in morning pages a few years ago when I was going through a rough time.

4. **Idea-processing journals:** These are the type of journals that Leonardo da Vinci and Thomas Edison kept. They kept a record of various ideas such as man-powered flight or the electric light bulb. They worked out the details of their ideas and inventions in their journals.
5. **Combinations:** No surprises here! In this type of journal the four styles above are mixed and matched. I do this from time to time.

Here's a listing of some wonderful tools for keeping some type of journal. Use one or a combination of all these tools depending on end goals:

1. **A physical blank paper book:** This type of journal is old school, but effective. Some options include nice paper journals from a stationary store, a 3-ring binder with loose-leaf paper, or a spiral notebook. Whatever floats the writer's boat! This type of tool is great for morning pages or idea processing journals, perfect for writing long hand or sketching out ideas.
2. **Evernote:** There are free versions of this app. I use this all the time for collecting ideas from the web or recording my own notes and thoughts. I recommend it!
3. **Day One:** Here's another app. This one is geared more toward the daily diary/journal format style. I have used this at various times when I'm struggling with a problem that I need to think through. I've also used Day One for a Scripture reading and prayer journal and even an idea generation depository.
4. **Blogging:** Over the last decade, this has become a popular method for many people to write their thoughts on specific topics such as leadership, relationships, personal finances, and more. Many of these blogs are written by one person, building a long-lasting online written legacy of their thoughts and ideas.

Journaling is a powerful tool in living a rich, rewarding, successful life. I recommend adding it to one's daily morning routine, as time allows.

Do you want to make a dent in your world? Do you want to have an impact for the kingdom of God? Do you want to attract resources and finances to your life to do what God has called you to do? Then, the best piece of advice I can give you is to read and write a lot. Journaling is a great place to start, so start writing today.

**Processing Big Ideas**

Ideas are important. *Big* ideas are even more valuable.

Consider that statement for a moment. Think back over the course of human history and the BIG ideas that have shaped the world such as the wheel, concrete, steel, steam power, gasoline engines, the telephone, the light bulb, airplanes, computers, the Internet and the smartphone. Great ideas combined with action on those ideas have tremendous power to change the world in incredible ways.

Wealthy, successful people deal in the world of big ideas and product creation around those ideas. People such as Bill Gates, the late Steve Jobs, Elon Musk, and even Dave Ramsey all deal in the world of big ideas. But they don't just think about these ideas. They process them. They take massive action on their ideas. Steve Jobs and Bill Gates had the big idea of taking personal computing to the masses, each in their own unique style. Elon Musk has been working in the area of several big ideas from electric cars to privatized space flight. Dave Ramsey has focused on changing the American culture when it comes to debt and how we handle money.

In the previous section, I mentioned the concept of keeping some type of journal for processing ideas, much like Leonardo da Vinci or Thomas Edison. Be like the great masters of yesterday and today! Get a digital app or paper notebook. Start writing down ideas each day. Start working through these ideas. Shape them. Refine them. Make them better.

Read like crazy within the arena of these ideas. If an idea is stirring about electric vehicles, then start reading and researching everything possible about that topic. If the idea is to better computing technology, then read and research everything on that subject. To make a dent in the world in the area of personal finances and wealth creation, read everything possible in that area of expertise. Work toward building credibility and expertise in that area of interest.

*Quick Tip: Looking for additional reading resources, especially in the area of personal finance? Sign-up for my financial book review email list at myfinancialbookreview.com. Each month, I'll email out at least one review of a relevant financial book.*

In addition to *researching* ideas, *record* notes and ideas. This is where I have found tools such as my Amazon Kindle app to be invaluable to me. Not only can I highlight book passages and type notes, but also I can go online and transfer all my digital notes over to Evernote for review later. This app is useful for recording unique thoughts and ideas to go along with research.

Exercise the brain—the idea creation machine! I recently read a great book titled *Become An Idea Machine Because Ideas Are The Currency Of The 21st Century* by Claudia Azula Altucher. This book is a wonderful way to execute a variety of daily exercises to train one's brain to work through ideas both big and small. I recommend reading this book.

Think about big ideas. Research and read on the ideas that seem most interesting—those that increase excitement in life—and write them down. Keep notes. Make sure to journal every thought. Take action on your ideas. Create a product. Write a book. Teach a class. Show others how to implement and use these big ideas.

One great idea acted upon with commitment and passion can be the passport in the 21st century to make an incredible impact in the world.

What's *your* one big idea?

*Quick Tip: For a FREE list of the Action Steps and Resources for each chapter of the book, simply go to:* http://www.heroicpersonalfinances.com/for-christians-book-action-steps/

# CHAPTER 4
# ENERGY MANAGEMENT

"He gives strength to the weary and increases the power of the weak."
— Isaiah 40:29 NIV[liii]

"It is only through labor and grim energy and resolute courage that we move on to better things."
— Theodore Roosevelt

"The energy of the mind is the essence of life."
— Aristotle

Several years ago, I turned forty. This was an age that caused me to stop and reflect on my physical health. I felt tired all the time. I was stressed out. I was moody and would get frustrated with any kind of problem, large and small. I was going through some of the most difficult changes in my personal life that one can experience. I wasn't happy with much of anything. I knew something had to change, and I took massive action as a result. Over the last six years, I have been on an amazing journey that has led to a healthier and happier level of living.

In the book *The Power of Full Engagement* (2003), authors Jim Loehr and Tony Schwartz assert people need to learn two new rules when it comes to energy and performance. First: recognize that energy is the fundamental currency of high performance. Second: performance, health, and happiness are grounded in the skillful management of energy. Later on, Jim Loehr added a third important rule: the stories a person tells one's self and others drives the way he or she gathers and spends energy.

In the previous chapter, the importance of morning routines as part of the journey into a richer life was encouraged. Establishing these life habits will help manage stress levels and daily energy better than the majority of people.

But energy management goes beyond establishing morning routines. It encompasses whole life management. The better a person treats their body through food fuels energy. A stronger body through aerobic exercise and strength training adds a quality of life that many don't understand. Better quality sleep allows the physical body to rest, recover, and repair itself which results in greater energy to do more.

In today's culture, people have taken on the mindset that burning the candle at both ends is a badge of honor to "get ahead." People go to bed late and wake up early; they eat junk food meals on the run. They sit in front of computer screens for twelve hours a day. Exercise is not prioritized, or non-existent. Is there any wonder there is an obesity epidemic in the modern age?

Conventional wisdom says sleep less to get ahead. Cut corners in health and wellness to climb to the top of the ladder faster than the guy in the cubical next door. Yeah, success might come faster, but so might a heart attack!

There is a better, healthier way to do things. The morning routines covered in Chapter 3 are an excellent starting point for energy management. Now, let's take a closer look at living a richer life through proper eating, exercise, sleep, and emotional habits.

## Eating

Eating the right foods at the right times has tremendous potential to create a good energy balance to live a high-quality life. The average American, though, wakes up in a rush, runs through a Starbucks drive-thru to grab a high sugar and cream combo coffee and a high-calorie pastry to go with it. At work, they grab other high carb and high sugar snacks to sustain them until lunch. At lunch, they eat fast food; they make more bad snack choices in the afternoon, and then they top it all off with a heavy dinner late at night.

But, with just a little bit of forethought on food intake, a healthier lifestyle can be achieved. It is possible to avoid putting so much bad stuff into one's body. These bad foods actually make people hungrier, bigger, and less energetic all at the same time.

One book that had a tremendous impact on my own personal eating habits has been *The 4-Hour Body* by Tim Ferriss.

*Disclaimer: As a Christian, there are certain aspects about sex in this book that I am in no way endorsing. Read at your own risk. You have been warned. No hate mail, please!*

The biggest takeaway for me from this book is the slow carb diet (SCD). After reading the book, I began a focus on consuming more protein at specific intervals throughout the day, especially first thing in the morning. I also try to avoid bad carbohydrates whenever possible.

I don't follow slow carb religiously, just a few of the basic tenets. But, with this diet plus exercising four days a week for twenty-five minutes each workout, I was able to sculpt my body. I dropped an extra twelve to fifteen pounds, moving from 175 pounds down to a consistent 160 pounds within a few months. I've never been a big guy, but even my family noticed a difference when I went on this food and exercise regimen.

Here are the basics of SCD as I understand them from Tim Ferriss and *The 4-Hour Body* book:

1. Focus meals on lean proteins such as eggs, egg whites, meats, nuts, etc. Eat the same few meals over and over again, especially for breakfast and lunch. You already repeat meals, anyway; now you're just picking new default meals.
2. Eat 30 in 30. Translation: Eat 30 grams of protein within 30 minutes of waking up. Tim Ferriss and others on SCD claim this is the biggest change in diet that will affect weight loss.
3. Eat plenty of veggies.
4. Don't eat fruit. (Fructose –> glycerol phosphate –> more body fat, more or less.) Avocado and tomatoes are exceptions to the rule.
5. Avoid "bad" carbs such as "white" starchy carbohydrates (or those that can be white). This means all bread, pasta, rice, potatoes, and grains.
6. Eat every three hours.
7. Enjoy one "cheat" day per week. This helps with plateauing weight issues when you are on the same diet every day.[liv]

As I mentioned above, I do not follow this plan to the letter. In our household with five kids, there's plenty of pasta eaten each week. But, my wife and I still try to focus a fair number of meals on lean meats and veggies whenever possible. Here's what my typical diet looks like each day:

1. Eat a 20-30-gram protein bar within thirty minutes of waking up. (I wake up around 4:15 am almost every day … my wife thinks I'm crazy!)
2. Eat 15–20 grams of protein in vanilla Greek yogurt plus a peanut bar between 7:00 and 7:30am.
3. Eat 2–3 heaping teaspoons of peanut butter around 10:00 am. Protein content is around 10 grams.
4. Drink a 13–26-gram protein shake immediately after a morning workout anywhere between 11:30 a.m. and 12:15 p.m. I double up on protein on days I do strength training.
5. Since I consume a lot of protein in the morning, I don't have a protein-focused lunch. My lunch choices are usually made on speed, ease of cooking, and cost. So, I'm eating simple microwavable soups and pasta to be able to move on to the rest of my day. Yes, I know. Not very SCD.
6. Eat 10–12 grams of protein by eating 10 to15 almonds between 2:30 and 3:00 p.m.
7. Eat 10–12 grams of protein in chicken, steak, or pork for dinner between 6:30 and 7:00 p.m.

This is a good thumbnail sketch of my protein-focused diet that I attempt to eat each day. In no way am I a model of clean eating that should be copied. I realize I could be eating better than what is represented above. Protein bars, yogurt, shakes, peanut butter, and almonds, these are super easy to consume because they require ZERO cooking time. I'd love to wake up in the morning and have the time luxury to make eggs, omelets, frittatas, and more. But with a busy family schedule, I just don't have that kind of time. I try to keep my diet simple and consistent so that it runs almost on autopilot. Over the last three years, this plan has worked well for me. I'd encourage trying to implement some of these, and other idea nuggets into a healthy eating routine.

## Exercise

A few years ago, I heard some wise advice that has stuck with me.

*Quick Note: I would like to say this is advice given by Michael Hyatt (MichaelHyatt.com), but I can't find the original source; otherwise I would reference it.*

"How well we live our lives in our forties and fifties will set us up for how healthy we will be in our sixties, seventies, and beyond." When I heard this advice, I had just turned forty. I had exercised some in the past, but nothing consistent. I was not a healthy eater. I mentioned earlier that I was tired a lot, as well as stressed out at work and home. I came to the realization that if I wanted to age well, I knew I needed to make some serious lifestyle changes.

I have zero excuses, too. My workplace has an excellent free workout facility for its employees. So, I began to develop an exercise routine that wasn't difficult or strenuous but got me into the gym at least four times every week. I also try to work out at the same time each day. I attempt to schedule my workouts in the late morning or early afternoon, right around my lunch hour. For whatever reason, I landed at this time due to my personal schedule and energy levels. It seems to have worked the best for me, so I've stuck with it.

*Quick Tip: Everyone is "too busy" to exercise. There's always more to do in a day than we have time to do. Because there are too many things on people's to-do lists that crowd out schedules, it is important to plan out each day with certain non-negotiable activities. This is one of my key points in this entire book. In Chapter 3, I referenced the "big rocks" illustration as made famous by the late Stephen Covey in his classic book The 7 Habits of Highly Effective People. Again, if to accomplish "big rocks" (in Covey terminology, the important but not urgent), fit the big things into schedules before all the smaller stuff crowds them out. Exercise is definitely one of those big rocks. It's not urgent, but it is important to stay healthy and energetic.*

Many people have physical goals they are trying to accomplish with their own unique exercise plan to get them there. For me, I strive for a balanced exercise routine of four to five days a week. I'm not interested in running marathons, half marathons, or even 5k's. I have no desire to look like Arnold Schwarzenegger or Paul Michael Levesque.[lv] With a large family and work responsibilities, I have time limitations. I have to keep my physical body "tight and right" in an optimal time frame.

I keep my exercise routine to twenty-five minutes and I'm done. I do cardio on an elliptical machine two to three times a week—Mondays, Wednesdays, and sometimes Fridays. On alternate days, Tuesdays and Thursdays, I do a cardio warm-up on an elliptical for ten minutes. Then, I spend the remaining twenty minutes weight training with nautilus-style machines.

This exercise routine, combined with my protein-eating habits described in the previous section, has produced results. I have been able to trim off ten to twelve pounds of excess weight, sculpt my body, and stay at this level for over three years. With this twenty-five minute routine, four days a week, I spend a minimal time working out, and it has increased my energy to a high degree. I also need less sleep than I ever have before.

Want more energy? A methodical, consistent, and focused exercise routine really is a game changer when it comes to energy management.

## Sleep

Sleep. Some don't get enough. Others get too much. Either way, the right amount is important for energy management. When I was younger, I didn't eat well. I didn't exercise much. My sleep patterns were inconsistent. As a result, my energy levels were all over the place during the day as well as from day to day.

Over the last few years, though, I have established better sleep patterns. I attempt to go to bed the same time each night, around 10:00 p.m. I wake up the same time each morning, close to 4:15 a.m. These sleep habits combined with better eating and exercise have led to higher energy levels. I don't need near the amount of sleep that I used to. I accomplish more at work. I'd also like to think that I'm a lot more pleasant person when I arrive home at the end of the day to greet my family in the evening. I have energy still left in the tank to pour out to the people I love the most.

I believe establishing good habits in the areas of food and exercise will result in six to eight hours of sleep. A person will wake up more rested. Of course, some people need more sleep than others. I get that part of it. I've always been on the low end of the sleep cycle. Others may need eight to ten hours of sleep. I'm sharing my own experience. This is what I have discovered in my own experiments in energy management.

The quality of sleep is an important factor for the greatest impact on minimal sleep. Here are a few sleep hacks I've picked up along the way to achieve better sleep quality:

- Be careful of caffeine intake during the day, especially any time later than mid-afternoon.
- Get 20–30 minutes of exercise each day, but don't exercise in the evening hours. That could energize you too much before bedtime.
- A short, 20-minute power nap in the early afternoon (if possible to get away with taking one!) can be a game changer for daily energy levels and mood.
- If possible, establish a consistent bedtime as well as wake up time. This is a lot bigger deal than people realize. Do this one thing and a lot of problems will disappear.
- Keep the room temperature on the cool side whenever possible.
- Keep the room as dark as possible.
- White noise generators or small fans help block out some of the background noises that may keep us awake or wake us up in the middle of the night.
- Keep cell phones in a different room, or at least turn on the "Do Not Disturb" feature so that email alerts, text messages, or phone calls won't disrupt sleep in the middle of the night.
- Avoid using bright screens before bed such as TVs, laptops, tablets, and smartphones. *Quick side note: In the latest version of Apple iOS, there is now a special "Night Shift" screen setting to help with this problem.*
- Consider melatonin supplements if needed.
- Establish a regular "getting ready for bed" routine that cues the body that it is time to sleep.

In my experience over the last three years, quality sleep (not always quantity) is one of the keys to having more energy.

**Emotional Control**

To most people, I'm sure I appear to be pretty stable and even-keeled when it comes to my emotions, at least in public anyway. I don't get crazy enthusiastic about anything (which could possibly be an issue). But, I don't grow upset about most anything, either. In public, I may not appear to struggle with emotional ups and downs, but in private, I do.

I don't like surprises. I don't like major, last-minute changes. I don't like unexpected problems. When I encounter these issues in my life, I tend to have a strong emotional response to them. I lose self-control. I become angry, upset, and judgmental. I want things my way or not at all. "How dare you turn my life upside down by bringing your problem into my world and handing me a headache to deal with?" This is the attitude and self-talk that tends to come out of me.

What happens, though, when people lose control of their emotions? Valuable energy is wasted on problems that are oftentimes out of the person's control anyway. Nothing can be done about them, but people tend to stew, fret, and be upset anyway. This type of emotional response results in exhaustion and energy-depletion. Joyce Meyer[lvi] says, "It's so important to realize that every time you get upset, it drains your emotional energy. Losing your cool makes you tired. Getting angry a lot messes with your health."

On almost any given day, there will be problems that trigger emotions that pull people away from where they need to be. Many have a tendency to overreact to these problems, losing valuable emotional energy on them. Instead of getting upset and angry, seek out solutions to those problems and take action. Make a shift in mindset and energy to seeking solutions and taking action—a much better way to control emotions. Lee Iacocca, the former CEO of Chrysler Motors said, "In times of great stress or adversity, it's always best to keep busy, to plow your anger and your energy into something positive."

For the Christian, prayer is always an excellent, positive first step in attempting to deal with problems in which you have zero control. In fact, prayer should always be our "go to" response when we encounter difficulties. I know I can always run to the Father when I feel like life is out of control. When nothing I am doing or could do will make a positive impact to turn the situation around, I know God can take care of it. We serve an awesome, all-powerful, all-knowing God. Nothing is too big for Him. Nothing catches Him by surprise. He promises those who seek Him will find Him. "Ask and it will be given to you" (Matt. 7:7 NIV).[lvii]

Another helpful suggestion I have about emotional control is the practice of meditation. I mentioned this in the previous chapter on morning routines. Deep breathing, mindfulness meditation has done wonders for me. Now, anytime I become stressed, I find myself doing these breathing exercises and not holding onto the stress within my body. I attempt to release it as fast as possible through these breathing exercises. A calm confidence replaces my stress and I am able to deal with problems in a positive way.

Successful people have learned how to handle their emotions. They have learned how to channel negative, energy-depleting emotions into positive action. This flips the whole equation around and gives them more energy. Gaining emotional control will result in more high-energy, high-impact days. Paulo Coelho[lviii] said, "When you are enthusiastic about what you do, you feel this positive energy. It's very simple."

## Sexual Energy

Sexual energy is a lot bigger deal than people realize. Or, they realize it's a big deal but don't want to discuss it. Sex is one of those weird issues people often don't want to meet head on within the Christian community.

I debated for quite some time if I should include this section in this chapter. The more I thought about it, though, the more I believe in the importance of sexual energy. How sexual energy is used impacts energy management. This section will not be for the faint of heart, but I will attempt to not be too graphic either. I do believe the topic needs to be discussed, though, in light of an overly sexualized culture. I have extended a warning!

God designed human beings as sexual creatures. He gave them a sex drive for specific reasons. He wants His people to "be fruitful and multiply" (Gen. 1:28 NLT[lix]). He created human beings with sexual desires for pleasing spouses, as well as for personal enjoyment.

However, western culture is over-sexed. Sex whenever and with whomever one wants has become the norm. Sex education begins at an early age in the public school system. Students can get free condoms at school. Because of the relative anonymity of online pornography, porn addiction has become a huge problem as well. Twenty-first-century technology combined with mankind's lust-driven sin nature has not been a good combination for anyone.

Unfortunately, Christians are not immune from this over-sexed culture, either. In many ways, I believe Christians may have more challenges in this area. The majority of believers *do* believe God's Word teaches sexual activity outside of marriage is sin. Whether they practice this belief, though, is a whole other issue. This is why so many believers carry around a lot of struggles, hang-ups, hurts, and guilt when it comes to sex, singleness, marriage, divorce, and re-marriage.

As a Christian man who has had his own unique challenges in this area, I have noticed a big difference in quality and quantity of sexual energy as I have moved into mid-life over the last several years. As this shift has occurred, I've also realized how high testosterone levels and enraging pent-up frustrations have drained me of much life energy I had when I was a teenager and young adult.

The challenge for younger Christian men and women who may be over-sexed is how to deal with their sexual energy in a positive way. From my own personal experience, I know it's a huge challenge. I may have more questions than answers in this area.

Now that I'm entrenched in mid-life (at the time of this writing I'm 45), the sexual energy/hormone issue is not as much of a challenge as it was when I was a younger man. My life energy is more calm, stable, and focused. This has been a freeing experience in and of itself.

Let me add here that sexual drive is important and vital to a productive, successful life, especially for men. A man's libido is the driving force that propels them to do anything and everything. A focused love/sex life in a monogamous relationship between a husband and wife is what has created thriving civilizations and cultures around the world. Comparing cultures that have thrived over a period of time versus those that have struggled, one key factor for those cultures that have flourished is **monogamous**

**marriages between men and women.**

In his classic book *Think and Grow Rich*, author Napoleon Hill talked about the "transmutation of sexual energy." He mentioned that men of genius used their sexual energy to fuel their creativity. Equally important, though, is the fact that the sexual relationship must include love.

Napoleon Hill says, "Sex, alone, is a mighty urge to action, but its forces are like a cyclone—they are often uncontrollable. When the emotion of love begins to mix itself with the emotion of sex, the result is calmness of purpose, poise, accuracy of judgment, and balance."[lx]

To be successful, happy, and fulfilled, figure out a way to channel all sexual energy into a focused path. The *best* and most focused path is to love a spouse and engage with them in a physical relationship on a regular basis. Be completely devoted to them in meeting their physical needs and not obsessed with meeting personal needs outside of this relationship.

For those who are unmarried, the challenge becomes greater but not impossible. I've known several people who have remained unmarried, yet (at least on the surface) appear successful because they have a singular, focused pursuit in which to release their sexual energy. This focused pursuit could be a hobby (such as music), their occupation, or a life goal accomplishment.

Control sexual urges. Marry the right person. Love that person wholeheartedly, and meet their needs. Transmute sexual energy to fuel creativity. Then, go out in the world and do amazing things with focused energy!

*Quick Tip: For a FREE list of the Action Steps and Resources for each chapter of the book, simply go to: http://www.heroicpersonalfinances.com/for-christians-book-action-steps/*

# CHAPTER 5
# TAKE ON THE WEALTHY MINDSET

"Do not conform to the pattern of this world, but be transformed by the renewing of your mind."
– Romans 12:2a NIV[lxi]

"Rich people think big.
Poor people think small."
– T. Harv Eker

Sara Blakely[lxii] may not be a familiar name in the average American home. Some of the products she has created for women, though, would be recognized through her company called Spanx. As a young woman, Sara pursued several different business opportunities that were not working out for her. Before starting her own company, she was selling fax machines door to door. Sara recalls that this time in her career was a great learning experience for her. She learned how to handle rejection through hearing lots of "no's." She also learned how to get to a "yes" as well. The art of the sale was a valuable lesson she learned as she finally launched her own company. She also learned another valuable lesson—visualizing becoming successful.

Blakey says she could see her business succeeding from the beginning. She visualized herself being the successful owner of Spanx. Blakely says, "I believe you can take mental snapshots of your future and what success looks like to you. If you mentally see yourself in a scenario, you'll start to make decisions in your life that get you there."

Sara Blakely thinks differently than most people. As a result, *Forbes Magazine* (forbes.com) has recognized her as the youngest self-made female billionaire in the world.

Wealthy people think differently at many different levels. I'm not talking about the NBA basketball player who has the $10 million crib with ten expensive cars parked out front, either. One could make the argument that many professional sports athletes handle their money like poor people who have won the lottery. But, I digress.

When I mention wealthy people, I'm talking about people who have learned to generate income through the purchase of assets and not liabilities. This is the classic Robert Kiyosaki definition that he outlines in his book *Rich Dad, Poor Dad*. The world has too many people running around today who appear wealthy. If one dug down into their finances, though, they would find they are actually quite poor. They have too many liabilities and not enough assets that generate income for their families.

Rich thinking doesn't mean driving a hoopty and living in a double-wide trailer while being the rental house king in our respective city with thousands of dollars in savings and investments. But before signing up for a book of payments on a $40,000 SUV or buying a $750,000 mortgage for the most expensive house in a great neighborhood, many questions should be asked. Wealthy people ask themselves money questions, such as:

- Am I buying assets or liabilities?
- Is this the best use of my money right now?
- Is there a better place or better opportunity to leverage my money?
- Do I need this particular item right now?
- Is this a true need or a want?
- What is the wisest thing I could do with this money, today?

For the Christian who is attempting to live according to these principles, this adds another layer of spiritual thinking. Additional questions could include:

- Would God be pleased with this purchase? Why or why not?
- Will this purchase impact my level of giving in the future?
- Have I prayed about this purchase, or am I engaged in a worldly mindset?
- Is this the absolute best use of God's money?
- If I make this purchase, would God be able to say to me, "Well done thou good and faithful servant"? Why or why not?

There are several key differences between the rich and poor concerning financial thinking. Wealthy people process money information, ask themselves a lot of questions, and seek the wise counsel of others they trust. Poor people follow the poor money habits of the majority of people around them. The poor make emotional purchases based on popular opinion and feelings instead of an overriding financial plan. This chapter will explore the wealthy mindset in greater detail.

### Focus On Quality Habits

A person's personal habits can make or break them. Poor mental, physical, emotional, and spiritual habits have the potential to create a poverty level of living. These habits could even send a person to an early grave!

Although there are no guarantees, quality personal habits can completely transform lives. They can take people to that next level of a wealthy and fulfilling life. According to statistics, the wealthy have much better habits over their middle class and poor counterparts. This is a big reason why they have become wealthy in the first place. I recently ran across a website called RichHabits.net, founded by Tom Corley. From his research, Tom outlines several of the key differences between the habits of the rich and the poor. So what do the rich do every day that the poor don't do?

**20 Things the Rich Do Every Day by Tom Corley:**

1. 70 percent of wealthy people eat less than 300 junk food calories per day. 97 percent of poor people eat more than 300 junk food calories per day. 23 percent of wealthy people gamble. 52 percent of poor people gamble.
2. 80 percent of wealthy people are focused on accomplishing some single goal. Only 12 percent of the poor do this.
3. 76 percent of wealthy exercise aerobically four days a week. 23 percent of poor do this.
4. 63 percent of wealthy people listen to audio books during commute to work versus 5 percent of poor people.

5. 81 percent of wealthy people maintain a to-do list versus 19 percent of poor.
6. 63 percent of wealthy parents make their children read two or more non-fiction books a month versus 3 percent of poor.
7. 70 percent of wealthy parents make their children volunteer ten hours or more a month versus 3 percent of poor.
8. 80 percent of wealthy people make Happy Birthday calls versus 11 percent of poor.
9. 67 percent of wealthy people write down their goals versus 17 percent of poor.
10. 88 percent of wealthy people read thirty minutes or more each day for education or career reasons versus 2 percent of poor.
11. 6 percent of wealthy people say what's on their mind versus 69 percent of poor.
12. 79 percent of wealthy people network five hours or more each month versus 16 percent of poor.
13. 67 percent of wealthy people watch one hour or less of TV every day versus 23 percent of poor.
14. 6 percent of wealthy people watch reality TV versus 78 percent of poor.
15. 44 percent of wealthy people wake up three hours before work starts versus 3 percent of poor.
16. 74 percent of wealthy people teach good daily success habits to their children versus 1 percent of poor.
17. 84 percent of wealthy people believe good habits create opportunity luck versus 4 percent of poor.
18. 76 percent of wealthy believe bad habits create detrimental luck versus 9 percent of poor.
19. 86 percent of wealthy people believe in lifelong educational self-improvement versus 5 percent of poor.
20. 86 percent of wealthy people love to read versus 26 of poor.[lxiii]

The late Zig Ziglar,[lxiv] the famous salesman-turned-motivational-speaker, has said, "Rich people have small TVs and big libraries, and poor people have small libraries and big TVs." We can see from the above list that there are clear differences between the rich and poor in their mental, physical, relational, and even recreational habits. According to information contained in this list, people who want to succeed would do well to read 30 to 60 minutes every day, watch less than one hour of TV a day, eat a lot less junk food, exercise four days a week, write down goals, and then focus on accomplishing one of those goals.

Time is the most precious commodity. A person can always make more money, but they can't create more time. Once it's gone, it's gone. It's important to exercise wisdom in making the best possible use of time. The wealthy understand this important principle. They leverage their time with high impact activities that will create even more money for them.

When people see this wealthy habits list, many will immediately attempt to make several changes in their habits all at one time. This is a recipe for failure. The best formula for success is to focus on one change at a time. Start small at first, and then take on more challenging changes later on. Spend at least three to four weeks implementing each new habit so that they will become habits you will continue for the rest of your life. Take your time and enjoy the process of changing you. This is the joy of the journey on the road to wealth.

Based on the wealthy habits list above, choose one habit to focus on and implement over the next few weeks that would have a tremendous impact on personal finances.

### Coaches, Mentors, and Counselors

Many poor and middle-class people think they have everything in life figured out. Why they think this, I'm not sure! Maybe, they are too proud to admit that they don't know what they don't know. They don't seem willing to expand their horizons. They aren't willing to crack open a book to gain more knowledge and wisdom in important life areas. They aren't willing to develop a relationship with someone at a higher level than they are. They aren't willing to spend money on counseling to help treat an addiction or psychological problem.

As a result, they remain poor or at least at a lower level of their potential. They stay stuck where they are. They can't achieve any forward momentum because they choose to remain ignorant in important life areas. They need to address these areas if they want to become successful.

According to God's Word, there is a strong connection between wisdom and wealth. The best example of this is when God came to King Solomon in 1 Kings 3. God told Solomon that he could have anything he asked for. Solomon asked for wisdom, and God was pleased with his answer. He not only gave Solomon wisdom, but He also made him wealthy and famous!

Physicist Albert Einstein once said, "Wisdom is not a product of schooling but the lifelong attempt to acquire it." The book of Proverbs has much to say about wisdom, too. In Proverbs 2:4, the writer (whom many theologians believe to be Solomon) encourages seeking out wisdom as if it was silver or a precious hidden treasure. Wisdom is found by practicing humility, reading books, and connecting with others.

Humility is the beginning point to increase in wisdom. Proverbs 11:2 says, "When pride comes, then comes disgrace, but with humility comes wisdom."[lxv] When believers remain humble, they accept that they don't know everything. They are open to learning more. They have a teachable spirit. They never stop learning until they take their final breath and a "dirt nap." Solomon writes in Proverbs 13:18 of the value of discipline and correction: "Refuse discipline and end up homeless; embrace correction and live an honored life" (MSG).[lxvi]

Those who are on the path to prosperity tend to seek out professional help on a variety of levels. They are secure enough in themselves to know if they want to reach that next level of development, whether it be in their business, physical health, or relationships, they need help from others. They are humble enough to recognize that they don't know it all. They know there are people out there in the world who are more accomplished than they are. They want to reach that higher level of success, so they seek out more successful people. This is one of those unique traits of the wealthy and successful.

The good news is that you can learn to be this way. If you struggle with pride and think you have life all figured out, it's not too late to make changes. In the beginning, it may not be easy. Over the long haul, though, it's definitely worthwhile to make these changes.

Depending on each person's situation and what he or she is trying to accomplish, consider seeking out help. A struggling small business owner could use a mentor who already has a thriving small business. Stuck in mid-life and want to make some type of career change? Look for a career coach. Struggling with teenage children? Seek the help of a professional counselor. When writing a book, consider finding an accountability partner.

When the wealthy get stuck, they look for solutions. They seek help. They don't just give up and bury their head in the sand. Many times, they don't even wait for a crisis before they look for help. They maintain professional relationships with coaches, counselors, and mentors to help them in both good and difficult times.

I don't know each of my reader's unique situations. Some may be thinking, "Larry, I don't have the money right now to hire professional help." If this is the case, I would encourage taking on a wealthy mindset by taking on a humble position and recognize the need for help. Then begin the process of seeking out a mentor or an accountability partner. These relationships shouldn't cost anything but time.

### Buy Assets and Avoid Liabilities

At the beginning of this chapter, I referenced Robert Kiyosaki's best-selling book *Rich Dad, Poor Dad*. In this book, Kiyosaki takes readers on a journey of what he learned from his biological father (his poor dad) as well as his friend's dad (his rich dad). His poor dad worked a steady job in the Hawaii State Department of Education. His rich dad owned several businesses. *Rich Dad, Poor Dad* is about completely rethinking how money works.

In his book, Kiyosaki outlines several lessons he learned as a young man. Here are three quick lessons from his rich dad. First, the rich don't always work for money. They work for good ideas. Second, an asset is redefined as something that generates cash flow, as opposed to something costing money to own. In the past, an asset for most people might be anything people owned that held value, such as a family's primary residence. In this new definition by Kiyosaki, though, a primary residence is now defined as a liability because it is a drain on personal cash flow. But owning a rental property would be considered an asset, assuming that cash flow outpaced expenses. Third, don't spend an entire paycheck on buying liabilities. Invest as much as possible on assets. Pay off debt fast, keep expenses low, and pour as much money as possible into property, investments, and businesses that generate even more income.

*Rich Dad, Poor Dad* is not a perfect book and has issues. But the book's main premise of the wealthy buying assets and avoiding liabilities is a great concept to integrate into a person's financial life.

As I mentioned earlier in the book, this is where Dave Ramsey's financial plan in Financial Peace University can be too simplistic when arriving at Baby Steps 4 through 7. Wealthy people don't just put 15 percent of their income into their 401(k) or Roth IRA, invest for college, pay off the house, and give a bunch of stuff away because they are now considered "rich." Don't get me wrong, though, I want to accomplish this stuff too!

Wealthy people are making strategic financial decisions like Dave Ramsey has been doing for more than twenty-five years. The wealthy figure out ways to leverage time and money so that they are not slaves to a J-O-B and a 401(k). They are building great businesses. They are creating quality intellectual property. They are building cash-generating websites. They are writing books and on the public speaking circuit.

This is exactly where I am right now. This book was created out of a desire to go to the next level in my professional career and personal finances. At the time of my writing this chapter, my family is right in the middle of Baby Step 4 (invest 15 percent) and 5 (college funding). We're getting a lot of traction in our finances right now. But, I can also see many other options out there beyond working 40+ hours a week, investing 15 percent of our money into retirement accounts, paying off the house early, and then waiting around for retirement at age 70. Unfortunately, that's the assumed, best wealth action plan you receive when going through Financial Peace University.

While investing money is a part of the equation of leveraging time and money, there are many other options out there. These options go beyond stock market investing for decades until retirement. In Part Two of this book, I will dig deeper into these strategies. For now, here is a quick thumbnail sketch of a world of possibilities when it comes to leveraging time and money:

- Create a small business focused on passive streams of income (Chapter 6)

- Become your own private bank through special life insurance strategies (Chapter 10)
- Peer-to-peer lending strategies (Chapter 10)
- Buy virtual property, such as web domains and income generating websites (Chapter 11)
- Buy physical property, such as duplexes, 3/2 homes, apartment buildings, commercial properties, and raw land (Chapter 11)
- Dividend investing in specific stocks (Chapter 12)

This list reveals there are many possibilities when it comes to banking, saving, creating, and investing opportunities outside of the cookie-cutter Baby Step of "save 15 percent for retirement." Counting on my 401(k) to make me wealthy twenty-five years down the road seems way too risky to me, especially with all the crazy fluctuations in today's stock market. Surely there is a better way, and Part Two of this book will dive deeper into these strategies.

### Automation and Delegation

Wealthy people value their time. They also leverage their time. I alluded to this a few pages back when I mentioned Tom Corley's list of rich habits. The wealthy understand the monetary value of one hour of the work they produce. Any activity they perform that is of less value than their hourly production they will delegate to a process or person. To leverage time, focus, passion, and calling as the wealthy do, consider leveraging these activities through automation and delegation.

Let's begin with automation. With today's technology, it's possible to automate a few areas to eliminate time and energy capital to keep up with everything. Personal finance is the first area that comes to mind. Several years ago, I read two books that had a tremendous impact on me in this area. The first book was *Automatic Millionaire* by David Bach. The second was *I Will Teach You To Be Rich* by Ramit Sethi. With the information shared in these two books, I automated almost my entire financial life from tithing, mortgage payments, utility bills, and retirement savings accounts. All I do is check my bank accounts through my Mint.com app on my smartphone every few days. Because the majority of my family's financial life is on autopilot, I spend little personal energy in this area. Yes, we have financial goals and dreams that we're working toward. But, I also know that we need to focus as much of our time and energy where we can "get our biggest bang for the buck" and spend less time on less important areas. There is no "bills night" or "bills fight" at the Jones' home. We automate everything, and as a result, our home is peaceful and stress-free.

Another area of automation that I have heard others use but haven't attempted yet, is automating specific purchases that need to be made on a continuous basis. For example, a young family with babies at home could set up a scheduled delivery of diapers and wipes every month. Or a specific dietary supplement could be set-up to be auto-delivered by mail each month. Maybe there are other regular household items needed on an ongoing basis such as toilet paper, toothpaste, cleaning supplies, and even grocery items. Using a service such as Subscribe & Save on Amazon.com could be a way to automate many different purchases to save trips to the grocery store each month.

*Quick Tip: The variety of choices to delegate and automate can be overwhelming. Here are my recommendations to help move people in the right direction. First, calculate personal income per hour. It's pretty easy to get a rough estimate of per hour earnings. Take total salary plus any and all benefits received within a year and divide that total salary package by a rough estimate of hours worked in a year. For example, if a person makes a salary of $50,000 per year and receives a benefits package (insurance, retirement, etc.) on top of that valued around $12,000, they make $62,000 per year. If that person works fifty weeks out of the year at forty hours per week, they work approximately 2000 hours in a year. $62,000 divided by 2,000 reveals their hourly rate is around $31.00 per hour.*

*Knowing this, think through any current lists of home duties and chores. This list may include items such as lawn mowing, yard maintenance, house cleaning, grocery shopping, laundry, ironing, and home repair. For these various duties that are a drain on time and energy, how much would it cost to hire someone to do these activities? Would it cost less than $31.00 per hour? If so, then I would come up with a prioritized list of activities to delegate. Begin looking for a team of people to take care of chores, and work toward delegating all these tasks to others. This is how the wealthy think.*

In the modern world with a variety of possibilities, delegation is key.

The kid down the street can be hired do yard work. A college student can run errands such as weekly grocery trips, dry-cleaning drop offs, and putting gas in the car. A cleaning service can be scheduled every other week to perform a thorough house cleaning. A virtual assistant can help with a variety of tasks from booking airline flights to editing a book.[lxvii] There is much potential for excellent help in the area of delegation.

Why delegate, though? What's the end goal? No, it's not about hiring help to free up time to sit around watching TV or play video games and brag about all the fun, free time that has opened up. The true purpose of hiring help is to leverage time, energy, and focus to be even more productive in areas of expertise. As a result, it will be possible to make even more money in the process.

In the book *Good to Great* by Jim Collins, Mr. Collins talks about the "Fly Wheel Effect." I'll spend more time at the end of the book discussing this concept, but here's a quick explanation. A flywheel is "a heavy revolving wheel in a machine that is used to increase the machine's momentum and thereby provide greater stability or a reserve of available power during interruptions in the delivery of power to the machine." As in a machine, the same is true in a person's personal life. Focusing on strengths and performing at a high level over a period of time, in essence, cranks "the flywheel of our lives." As a result, a tremendous amount of momentum is built.

Some might be scratching their heads thinking, "Larry, this is all great to talk about in theory, but it's going to take a bunch of time and money for me to set these kinds of systems all up. It's not worth it." When first cranking on that "flywheel," it will seem difficult and take a tremendous amount of time and effort. Hiring and training extra help such as someone to mow the lawn, run errands, or be a virtual assistant may seem like a waste of money and not worth it on the front end. But, maximizing the free time and energy this help provides will generate more income per hour—greater than what is going out to pay these people to help. It will be worth it in the long run. Hang in there, and keep cranking on the work/life flywheel hard enough and it will happen. Potential will be maximized! I've included some additional resources in the area of automation and delegation at the end of this chapter.

## Legal Matters

I am not an attorney, nor do I play one as an author. I didn't write this chapter to offer specific advice in my readers' unique situations. I did write it, though, to encourage each person to think like the wealthy and seek out the expertise of legal professionals. The following is for informational purposes only. Do not receive this as legal instructions. Refer to the disclaimer I placed at the beginning of this book.

The wealthy understand the importance of taking care of business, especially when it comes to legal matters. They seek out excellent legal help and are willing to pay quite well for that help as needed.

Unfortunately, the United States is a litigious society. People, corporations, governments, and hospitals are being sued at an alarming rate. As I was doing research in this area, I discovered some disturbing statistics. In the United States alone, some fifteen million civil cases are filed each year. The percentage of the world's lawyers that live in the United States is 80 percent! The majority of lawsuits brought by individuals fall under tort law. A tort is a wrongful personal injury that merits legal compensation. Statistically, the plaintiff (the party who filed the lawsuit) wins 55 percent of all tort trials in the United States. In 2010, the states with the most torts were: New York, Pennsylvania, New Jersey, Florida, Michigan, Illinois, Missouri, Montana, and California. The amount of US Gross Domestic Product that went to these tort costs was 2.2 percent of GDP, which equaled $251 billion! Americans spend more on civil litigation than other industrialized countries—twice as much as what is spent on new cars. Of all the lawsuits filed in the world, 94 percent are filed right here in the United States. Yes, that isn't a mistake . . . 94 percent![lxviii]

Approximately one out of four people will be sued in a given year. Worse yet, the average number of lawsuits an individual may expect in their lifetime is five! Expect one of these five lawsuits to have the potential to be financially devastating. One nasty lawsuit could completely wipe out a family's finances. The best offense is a good defense. Be prepared, and be protected legally.

An excellent first step for a family's legal foundation is to make sure to have excellent insurance coverage. Be sure insurance covers vehicles adequately. A horrible injury resulting from a car wreck that's your fault could result in a lawsuit—and losing one's shirt for being underinsured. Another wise insurance product to consider is an umbrella policy. Umbrella insurance is another layer of liability insurance to cover any losses that are not covered in primary insurance policies in the event a person is sued. Insurance agents will be able to discuss these policy details, coverage, and costs over the phone. My wife and I recently made some changes to our auto and home coverage as well as added an umbrella liability policy on top of the rest of our policies. In my opinion, you can't go wrong with the cost. They are relatively inexpensive and a wise insurance coverage to have.

Business owners should be sure to purchase important business insurances to protect the business. These types of insurances include but are not limited to professional liability, property insurance, worker's compensation, and vehicle insurance. This is a quick thumbnail sketch of what should be considered. Be sure to discuss specific individual needs with other business owners, insurance brokers, and attorneys.

Next, the wealthy understand the importance of wise financial estate planning. They establish a firm legal foundation by having all their key, important legal documents in place for their family. They have wills, living trusts, durable power of attorney, health care proxy, and life insurance. Consult an attorney on what documents should be completed for each state.

The wealthy also establish legal entities around their business endeavors to protect themselves and their financial assets against sue-happy people. I admit upfront that I am not an expert in this particular area. Right now, my family's finances are not complex enough to warrant financial fortress strategies. But, families who have several different streams of income (and those who have a corporation, LLC, or any other type of legal business entity) should consider wise, legal strategies to protect the business, family, and business assets from frivolous lawsuits. The wealthier a person appears, the greater the possibility of being taken advantage of.

An excellent starting point to learn about these strategies is the book *Multiple Streams of Income: How To Generate a Lifetime of Unlimited Wealth, Second Edition* by Robert G. Allen. Check out Chapter 16, "Financial Fortress Strategies: Shielding Your Multiple Streams of Income." In this chapter, Allen outlines the plan by his own financial fortress strategist, J.J. Childers. He is an attorney and owner of Profit Publishing Group, Inc. Childers' strategy, called "Secret Millionaire," utilizes a combination of the following legal entities:

- The Nevada corporation
- The family limited partnership
- The limited liability company
- The retirement plan
- The living trust

Why is all this necessary? Does it seem like a whole lot of trouble to shield assets? Yes, in many ways it does seem complicated. But, as I mentioned above, it's paramount to protect family assets on the off chance of being involved in a losing lawsuit. Plus, this will help the family estate from going to probate, should death occur unexpectedly. Probate costs are expensive and on average take fourteen months to complete. Take some time and investigate options. Consult legal experts and seek out the best course of action. Then, create a plan and take action. Make sure all family assets are well protected.

*Quick Tip: For a FREE list of the Action Steps and Resources for each chapter of the book, simply go to:* http://www.heroicpersonalfinances.com/for-christians-book-action-steps/

# PART TWO:
# NEXT LEVEL FINANCIAL STRATEGIES

# Part Two
## Introduction
### (An Explanation and Framework)

Part One of *Heroic Personal Finances for Christians* looked at the spiritual, emotional, and intellectual aspects of personal finances. God is the ultimate source of wealth, and Part One uncovered the secret to living is giving. Next, meditation and affirmations were revealed as important morning routines on the path to abundance. Next, the importance of energy management in everyday living was discussed. And finally, the mindset of the wealthy and how the wealthy think was considered.

Part Two will dig into more *practical* aspects of money. Let's dive into areas that other Christian personal finance experts do not explore, at least in any kind of depth. This was my motivation to write *Heroic Personal Finances for Christians* in the first place. This is the book I wanted to read when I started gaining traction in my personal finance journey.

Before launching into the remaining chapters, I need to add some context—a framework—that will help guide readers through the second part of the book. The Investment Pyramid is that framework.

In the book *Financial Fitness: The Offense, Defense, and Playing Field of Personal Finance* by LIFE Leadership (Brady and Woodward), the authors include a recommended investment strategy they call the "investment pyramid." The plan starts at the bottom of the pyramid with what the authors view as the safest form of investing. Then, they encourage readers to work their way to the top of the pyramid to what they view as riskier forms of investing. There is validity to the investment pyramid concept, and it is definitely a unique way of looking at investing. This step-by-step investing approach is not taught in other Christian personal finance courses. After a fully-funded emergency fund is established, many experts jump into stock market 401(k) and IRA investing. If you charted this action on the investment pyramid, you would move from a Level Two emergency fund directly to Level Six stock market investing. You would completely bypasses Levels Three, Four, and Five. Other financial experts would appear to have a lot more risk tolerance than Brady and Woodward.

Diagram Source: You, Inc. Investment Hierarchy from *Financial Fitness: The Offense, Defense, and Playing Field of Personal Finance* by LIFE Leadership[lxix]. Used by permission.

Level One, the bottom of the pyramid and the safest part of this investment strategy, is to invest in one's self. What Brady and Woodward are referring to at this level is what I mention at the end of Part One of this book: learning to think wealthy thoughts. Investing in education and training will take a person further in their careers as they believe they can go. This investment into personal growth may even take a person into another career or area of expertise. I'm not talking about spending a bunch of money to go back to college and finish another degree, either; I'm talking about educational investment through reading relevant books, magazines, and blogs. Or, it can be as simple as listening to audio books, training programs, and podcasts, or attending conferences. Allow other leaders in the industry to be mentors! There are many ways to invest in one's self that will cost more in time than in money. Investing time and money at the base of the financial pyramid will lay a firm foundation before advancing into other complex forms of financial investing.

Steve Siebold is a former professional athlete and national coach. He has spent the past twenty-six years studying the thought processes, habits, and philosophies of world-class performers. Steve has interviewed more than 1,200 of the world's wealthiest people. According to Siebold's research, "Self-made millionaires get rich because they're willing to bet on themselves and project their dreams, goals, and ideas into an unknown future."[lxx]

Level Two—the next level of the pyramid in which to invest—is an emergency fund. I will spend more time talking about this level in a few chapters. This level is equal to what Financial Peace University™ teaches in Baby Steps 1 and 3. Baby Step 1 is to get $1,000 in savings as fast as possible and then get out of debt as fast as possible. After completing the debt snowball in Baby Step 2, the next goal is to establish a fully funded emergency fund of three to six months of expense money in Baby Step 3. Depending on income, expenses, and needs, this could equal out to a range of approximately $10,000 to $30,000.

Level Three advances to investing in survival preparation. I will spend more time fleshing out this level in a few chapters, so I won't dive into details here. An important point to consider when it comes to this level is that survival preparation is a form of savings. It is translating money into purchasing important goods such as food, water, generators, fuel, guns, and ammo. This is to protect the family during a worst-case scenario and an important part of a sound investment strategy.

Level Four focuses on investing in long-term and targeted savings. Brady and Woodward recommend that regularly saving 10 percent of total income into typical savings accounts. They favor safer investment strategies than most Christian personal finance experts. At this level, they also recommend people have targeted savings accounts (sinking funds) to save for car replacement, new furniture, and so on.

Levels One through Four are conservative levels of investing in one's self with little risk. They are basic levels of savings. Brady and Woodward contend that if people focused only on these four levels of the investment pyramid, people would do well, financially. The authors reserve the final three levels for what they consider more speculative investing.

But in Level Five, people should begin investing money into secure investments such as CDs, money market accounts, and municipal bonds. Many financial experts undervalue these investments because they pay lower interest, but they also carry lower risk.

Brady and Woodward consider Level Six and Seven to be highly speculative investing. In fact, their recommendation is to avoid the top of the pyramid altogether, unless the investor is knowledgeable in the areas of real estate, the stock market, ventures, and start-ups. Deciding to invest in Level Six and Seven involves a willingness to put money in these areas that wouldn't be missed if it were lost completely.

Keep these seven levels of the Investment Pyramid in mind while reading the remaining chapters of this book. Although not all the steps in this book line up with the investment pyramid, there are many similarities. The investment pyramid is an excellent tool to use when evaluating various investment strategies. Now, let's look at the foundation layer of the pyramid: investing in yourself.

## CHAPTER 6
## INVEST IN YOURSELF

"Whatever your hand finds to do, do it with all your might."
– Ecclesiastes 9:10a NIV[lxxi]

"There is something about giving everything to your profession. In Italian, an obsession is not necessarily negative. It's the art of putting all your energy into one thing; it's the art of transforming even what you eat for lunch into architecture."
– Renzo Piano[lxxii]

Several years ago, I found myself at somewhat of the beginning of a career crossroad in life. Unknown to me at the time, I was moving into a secondary role as stewardship pastor while working in the worship and fine arts area at my church. Before this transition took place, I had limited knowledge and experience in the area of stewardship. The only knowledge I had was what I learned through a Crown Financial[lxxiii] Bible Study class as well as reading Dave Ramsey's original *Financial Peace* book. What made me unique in this specific area of stewardship, though, is that I applied and lived out the principles I was learning. I developed a budget. I built up a little emergency fund. I paid off all my debts—$30,000 worth of debt in approximately nineteen months using the Financial Peace University™ baby steps. I even sold a nice house to get out of debt as fast as possible. I was that committed to sound, biblical stewardship principles. I wasn't doing any of this to become a stewardship pastor. I was doing it because I believe what God's Word says about this important area of our lives.

In early 2008, I began coordinating Financial Peace University™ classes at my church. I wanted to help people get out of debt and be better managers of God's stuff. For our first class, we had eighty-nine people register! It was evident that God was up to something. My debt-free story began circulating around the church. My story combined with the success of that first FPU class grabbed the attention of our former senior pastor. It was at this time he asked me to take on a second role as stewardship pastor. In many ways, I felt completely inadequate to take on the role. So, I started reading as many books as I could get my hands on related to stewardship ministry. I went to conferences. I met with other church leaders and parachurch leaders who worked in the stewardship space. I immersed myself in learning this new position because I have a passion for it. I could see the potential of investing in myself in a new area of expertise for my long-term career trajectory. In fact, this book was birthed out of the desire to invest in myself to place me as an expert in stewardship.

To my knowledge, there is no college or university degree program to attend to learn what I needed to learn in this area. I needed to invest time, energy, and a small amount of money to develop myself to the level of competency and then excellence.

The best "bang for the buck" for investing according to the book *Financial Fitness* is to invest heavily in one's self and one's own business. How did Dave Ramsey become successful? Dave invested a lot of time, energy, and money into his original Lampo Group business. He created his two signature products: the *Financial Peace* book and Financial Peace University™ classes. Now called Ramsey Solutions, Dave's company has many divisions. He will continue making an impact in people's lives even after he has gone on to be with the Lord.

In FPU, Dave spends a little time discussing the idea of investing in one's self through personal growth to maximize earning potential. In my opinion, though, the *Financial Fitness* investment approach is much more intentional than Dave's approach. This chapter will dig a little deeper in what it means to spend more time, energy, and money at the base of the investment pyramid.

The majority of people are not good at creating efficient, productive work in the modern era. They work too much at all the wrong times, attempting to multi-task and accomplishing little. They allow personal problems from home to distract them at work. And at home, work projects in turn distract them. As a result, families suffer from neglect. There is little time to rest and reflect in people's personal lives. There is little joy or satisfaction in the current work model.

Because of advances in technology over the last 100 years, the pace of society has increased in exponential ways. In people's work lives, these advances have caused employers to expect employees to accomplish more with fewer and fewer resources. Technology has also chained people to their jobs; people can never escape. Due to email and text notifications on smartphones, the expectation can become that employees are "on call" and always available whenever they are needed.

The majority of work situations are completely unhealthy and unsustainable. People are either going to have a nervous breakdown or a heart attack at some point. It's time to stop the insanity when it comes to work and personal lives. There is a better way to invest in work. Some common work misconceptions will be explored in this chapter, and some new ideas about work will be considered. First, let's analyze the history of work and work hours.

## A Brief History of Work Hours

Before the Industrial Revolution in the 18th and 19th centuries, life was difficult for most people. Many lived on farms in rural communities and eeked out a living by farming the land, raising a few farm animals, and making their own clothing.

With the invention of new manufacturing processes in a transitional period from 1760–1820, the industrial revolution began. Soon after, factories and urbanization were introduced. While this led to increases in advancement and prosperity, many in the lower to middle class struggled with difficult work hours and work conditions. For example, it was common for men, women, and even children to work twelve-hour days in hot factories with dangerous machinery moving all around them.

As the industrial revolution continued to evolve, work employee unions formed to push back against horrendous, unsafe work conditions and long work hours. Governments also stepped in to legislate work hours and working conditions, especially for women and children. Over time, many workplaces adopted an eight-hour day, which continues today.

There is nothing sacred about an eight, ten, or twelve-hour workday. People work long hours all the time, and yet don't always accomplish a lot in their profession. The law of diminishing returns[lxxiv] does come into play when it comes to work. Working more hours does not always lead to a higher output of work accomplished.

For example, let's say two individuals named John and Adam work in the same office and have an equal skill level. They both arrive at work at 8:00 am and leave at 6:00 p.m.

John works almost without stopping, attempting to multi-task in-between meetings all day long. He will usually eat lunch at his desk to save time.

Adam, though, has a different approach. He is highly focused in his work for about 90 minutes and then takes a 15-minute break before resuming his work. Around noon, he will go out to lunch for 45 minutes. He may even squeeze in a quick workout at a nearby gym. In the middle of the afternoon, he will close his eyes for a quick ten-to-fifteen-minute executive power nap. A little later, he might take a brisk walk outside if the weather is nice.

John and Adam have two opposite approaches. Their resulting personal energy levels and work accomplishment is noticeably different.

John spends ten hours at work. He begins his work at seventy-five percent capacity because he knows he needs to pace himself for a very long day. Right after lunch at his desk, he is beginning to feel fatigued. John's energy level has dropped to approximately 60 percent capacity, and slowly losing more with each passing minute. Between 3:00 and 6:00 p.m. he has dropped to 40 percent capacity (his last three work hours of the day). John makes many mistakes throughout his final half of the day and returns home exhausted with little energy to give to his family in the evening.

Adam also puts in ten hours at work. His approach, though, is quite different. He feels comfortable starting work at 90 percent capacity because he knows that he will take a break soon. After lunch, he has the same mid-afternoon slow down as John. Because he takes a power nap and a couple of other breaks, Adam is able to maintain a higher afternoon work capacity around 70 percent. He makes fewer mistakes than John and even has energy left for his family when he arrives home later that evening.

The number of work hours clocked in each day doesn't matter quite as much as people think they do. We generate more value through the physical, mental, emotional, and spiritual energy we are able to bring and sustain at work. I referenced these concepts in Part One of this book, so I won't spend too much more time on it in this chapter.

Certain work strategies help focus time, energy, passion, and calling.

These strategies result in producing more in a shorter amount of time; workers will be successful in what God has called them to do, and still have an enjoyable, fulfilling life. Let's unpack how to achieve this.

## The Power of Focus

As I mentioned earlier, many have a mindset that working more hours equals a better, more productive employee. A person can work eighty hours a week and be an unproductive employee or business owner who doesn't produce much. Or, he or she can work twenty-five hours a week and be the best employee at the company.

Don't believe me? Impossible? Not in the least. I've seen it happen on many occasions in the right work environment. I've even observed this up close and personal by observing a personal friend grab a hold of this principle and work fewer hours than she did in the past. She even received more compensation as the result of her productivity.

My friend's intense work focus journey began right after her second child was born a few years ago. She took her full twelve-week maternity leave and then returned to her position at a reduced hours level for a few months. Her direct supervisor agreed to this arrangement with the understanding that she would return to a full-time schedule within three months. My friend loves what she does and the company she works for, but she had zero desire to return to full-time status. Her desire was to be closer in work hours to a part-time employee so she can spend more time with her young family. She wants to relish and enjoy being a young mom before this time passes her by.

My friend knew from the beginning that because of the group she worked in, the "part-time, I only work 6:30 a.m. to 12:30 p.m. at the office, do a little work from home, and that's it," wasn't going to fly. She set out to prove that she could be just as or maybe even more productive than a full-time employee through part-time work office hours. She started going to work earlier in the morning. She became clear on what she does best and what adds the most value in her work. She tracked all her metrics along the way. She even had meetings with various executives in her specific work group and included all her personal work metrics in a PowerPoint presentation. Although her supervisors seemed impressed with her work output, they weren't budging on the work hours. They wanted her to go back to full-time, 9:00 a.m. to 5:00 p.m. work hours. I guess they assumed they could double her output if they forced more work hours. The reality, though, is that she was trying to prove a point. If they forced the time issue, she had the option to "throttle back" her work energy and not be as focused and productive. Or, she would be on a continuous hunt for a better work situation for herself and her family.

This is the main problem with many workplace environments. They equate longer work hours with higher productivity. Depending on the type of job and work environment, this isn't always the case.

Fortunately for my friend, she was able to attract the attention of another executive in a different department and work out a great deal on time, money, and benefits. She's in a much better situation now because of her laser-like focus on time and results. At the end of the day, her incredible work metrics continue to speak for her personal productivity and success in her work.

The key to working fewer hours and producing more is the power of focus. Focusing the best working time (generally morning hours) on the work that produces the best results will result in a superstar employee or business executive. The problems that many people have at work are the following: first, people are distracted with lots of stupid stuff in the modern era. With hundreds of email messages to sift through, constant social media updates, web surfing, text messages, and phone calls, it's amazing that anybody gets anything accomplished! Also, employees are forced to attend ineffective meetings that waste energy in prime working hours. Companies end up shooting themselves in the foot on a regular basis through poor planning.

Second, people aren't sure which work actions produce the greatest results—or at least they have never given it much thought. The Pareto Principle—or 80/20 Rule—states "Eighty percent of the effects come from 20 percent of the causes."[lxxv] Or put another way, 80 percent of a company's profits come from 20 percent of its customers. Eighty percent of a company's sales are made from 20 percent of its products. Eighty percent of a company's profits come from 20 percent of the time and actions of the staff. What is the key to a greater business? Time and energy focused on the 20 percent that produces the 80 percent.

Third, employees aren't sure or haven't given much thought to prime working hours and how to leverage their best working time for the greatest benefit. It is a known fact that most people work best first thing in the morning. But when do most corporate meetings take place? Morning hours. There's something wrong with this schedule. Most employers would be better off encouraging their employees to determine their top 20 percent of activities that lead to the 80 percent profitability of their company and do that 20 percent every morning! Then, employers should place meetings in the afternoon hours (or at least late morning) when staff members tend to be less productive anyway.

Fourth, employees don't focus their top 20 percent activities into their top 20 percent of the time that ultimately results in 80 percent of desired best results. Working through this list should be a no-brainer at this point. **The specific work tasks that one does that lead to the best results for the company should be accomplished during a person's most productive work hours.**

Employees and business owners should take the Pareto Principle and apply these specific concepts to work life. Employees will transform in their supervisor's eyes. Supervisors will notice a measurable difference in an employee's work quality and output as compared to the other employees around them. Those who put themselves out there and do excellent work will begin producing great stuff in the workplace. Based on my own personal experience as well as my observation of others in the workplace, I know this to be true. Try it and see what happens.

### The Power of Passion

The late Nelson Mandela, former President of South Africa, once said the following: "There is no passion to be found playing small—in settling for a life that is less than the one you are capable of living." Anyone who wants their work—their calling in life—to count for something in this life and the life to come must have passion!

The Urban Dictionary defines passion as, " ... when you put more energy into something than is required to do it. It is more than just enthusiasm or excitement, passion is ambition that is materialized into action to put as much heart, mind, body, and soul into something as possible."[lxxvi]

Do you love what you do? Why or why not? Are you passionate about part of your work, but unhappy with another part? Why is that? If you are struggling with passion in your current work situation, you might be the source of the problem.

Yes, I realize this sounds harsh. Everyone to some degree or another has parts of their job they enjoy and other parts of their position that they loathe. Been there. Done that. Got the t-shirt. Anyone who desires passion back in his or her J-O-B has to bring it. No amount of money or change in duties is going to change it. Sure, on the front end, the excitement of more money and greater responsibility could bring a temporary surge of passion back into one's work life. Sooner or later, though, they will become bored and restless. Passion will wane because the necessary ingredients of passion are forgotten; each person has to bring their own, and they have to play big!

Of course, passion will only take a person so far. Research, study, common sense, leadership, and plain old hard work united with passion will create the correct chemistry to achieve greatness.

Will every aspect of work be fantastic? No, of course not. There are nitty-gritty details and responsibilities I'm sure every employee on earth would love to kick to the curb. I know I struggle in this area from time to time. Focusing on the big picture—the end goal—and moving the "vision ball" forward to the next place is necessary at this point. Focus on the journey while on the way to the destination. Think about growing and learning, even if daily activities feel mundane. Get passionate about what has developed as a result of personal involvement in a job. Celebrate all the successes, even though they may be small ones right now.

Always keep the big picture in mind for the entire organization, not just what's been assigned in a respective niche. Understand how one person's small cog fits in with the other cogs to drive the machine of the company. If help is needed in someone else's part of the work machine, give them a hand because one person's help benefits everybody else.

Only the person can bring the passion to his or her work. No one else can do this. It needs to come from within. Martin Luther King, Jr., the great civil rights leader, once said, "If a man is called to be a street sweeper, he should sweep streets even as Michelangelo painted, or Beethoven composed music, or Shakespeare wrote poetry. He should sweep streets so well that all the hosts of heaven and earth will pause to say, here lived a great street sweeper who did his job well." Success comes from doing a job well (passion), not from what is actually done (the job).

Passion is the enthusiasm, drive, and energy that one brings to life in general—relationships, hobbies, chores, challenges, and routines. People notice passion. People respect passion. People reward passion. If you're passionate about life and all that you do, that passion will be rewarded. It may not be today. It may not be tomorrow. But it will happen sooner or later.

Simon Sinek, the author of *Start With Why* and *Leaders Eat Last*, said this: "Work ethic is giving great effort to complete a task. Passion is giving great energy to achieve an outcome." Trying to check tasks off a to-do list? Instead, attempt to achieve an incredible outcome. Passion is the difference maker!

So if passion makes the difference, can one get it back if it has been lost somewhere along the line?

First, you need motivation. Passion is simply an emotion, which can be triggered by other emotions. Are you mad at yourself, your boss, or your co-workers? Use that emotion of anger to figure out a way to turn things around and improve a situation. Transmute anger and frustration into passion!

Second, see the big picture of what you do in your organization. How does your work role and responsibilities fit in with everyone else? Do you understand the importance your part gives to all the other parts? Do you understand the ultimate outcome you are all trying to achieve together?

Third, live out the Law of the Harvest when it comes to passion in your work. The Law of the Harvest states what a person sows they will reap. If I plant corn, I will harvest corn—not soybeans. If I plant an apple tree, I will harvest apples—not pears. If you need an infusion of passion in your work, you're going to have to bring some level of passion with you, cultivate it, let it grow, and then you will receive more passion. The great principle of the Law of the Harvest is that a person will always receive more than they put in at the beginning of the process. Rick Warren, pastor of Saddleback Church in California, states it this way: "This is the principle of the harvest: Whenever you have a need, plant a seed. When a farmer looks at his barren fields, he doesn't gripe about it. He just goes out and starts planting some seed. If he only has a little bit of seed, he has a choice. He can either hoard it, or he can give it away. If he holds onto it, that's all he's got. If he gives it away, God will multiply it. The amazing thing is this: You don't just reap what you sow. You always reap more than you sow!"[lxxvii]

## The Power of Calling

I think many Christians have come to believe that God has a unique, special calling on their lives and their job is to wait around for Him to reveal it. In my personal opinion, this is flawed, dangerous thinking.

In the Bible, there were maybe 100 people who were individually called upon by God to a specific task. In mid-life, Noah was called upon by God to build an ark for more than 100 years to save his family from the pending flood. At age eighty, two-thirds of the way through his life, Moses was called to lead the Israelites out of Egypt and into the Promised Land. God called specific judges to help lead the nation of Israel after Joshua's death. God anointed David to be king of Israel. God allowed David to prepare the materials for the first temple, and David's son Solomon was commissioned to oversee its construction.

The Lord spoke through individual prophets such as Elijah, Elisha, and Jeremiah to speak to the nations of Israel and Judah to bring them back into a right relationship with God. Jesus Christ called the twelve disciples to be the founding members of the universal church and spread the gospel around the known world. He also called the apostle Paul to take the gospel to the Gentiles in Europe.

God's calling is unique. He may or may not have a specific, "special" calling on every person's life as He had for the biblical examples I have cited above. I know many pastors and other church leaders who live in complete certainty that there was a specific time and place in which God called them into the ministry. I would be hard pressed to dispute their belief.

With a specific calling or not, though, God has wired each person and shaped them to do some specific work with excellence within their sphere of influence that will make an eternal impact for the kingdom of God. He places people in a specific place at a specific time. He has poured out talents, abilities, interests, passions, and opportunities. He has allowed every person on earth to be shaped by family, friends, mentors, environments, circumstances, and challenges. Because of this, each person views the world in a unique way.

You, too, bring something special to the table as a result. Your challenge as a Christian is to determine how you can best fulfill God's mission with what He has given you.

When I was a younger man, the buzz phrase for this was "the will of God." I heard many Sunday School lessons and sermons on it. Everybody was concerned whether they and other believers were in the perfect or permissive will of God. The result of this concern was that no one took action. Christians were waiting around in an attempt to make sure they were in God's perfect will before they would move forward to do anything.

Here's the problem with this type of thinking, though. God's Holy Word is the primary vehicle in which He uses to communicate to His people. His will is clearly spelled out in many areas in His Word. The believer's job is to read His Word, understand His will from Scripture, and then obey what He says.

For example, in 1 Thessalonians 5:18 Paul instructs believers to "give thanks in all circumstances, for this is God's will for you in Christ Jesus."[lxxviii] In this verse, the apostle Paul states that God's will for the Christian's life is to give thanks in all things—not only when everything is "puppy dogs and rainbows," but even in the difficult times. God wants an attitude of continual thankfulness.

In another passage on the will of God, in 1 Thessalonians 4:3–5 Paul writes, "It is God's will that you should be sanctified: that you should avoid sexual immorality; that each of you should learn to control your own body in a way that is holy and honorable, not in passionate lust like the pagans, who do not know God" (NIV).[lxxix] In these verses, God's will for the life of His followers is sexual purity.

In these two examples, God gives clear instruction for what His will is. There is no praying about these things. There is no seeking God's face for answers to these questions. God states exactly what He wants from His children—and the response should be obedience. In other areas that may not be so clear, God asks believers to pray for wisdom, to walk out in faith and act, and then be willing to change course if needed.

The apostle Paul is an excellent example of walking out in faith with action, and his willingness to change course when asked to by God. Acts 16 describes his desire to move into the province of Asia to preach the gospel. God through the Holy Spirit redirects Paul and his companions in the opposite direction—into Macedonia: "Paul and his companions traveled throughout the region of Phrygia and Galatia, having been kept by the Holy Spirit from preaching the word in the province of Asia. When they came to the border of Mysia, they tried to enter Bithynia, but the Spirit of Jesus would not allow them to. So they passed by Mysia and went down to Troas. During the night Paul had a vision of a man of Macedonia standing and begging him, 'Come over to Macedonia and help us.' After Paul had seen the vision, we got ready at once to leave for Macedonia, concluding that God had called us to preach the gospel to them" (Acts 16:6–10).[lxxx]

Eric Liddell was a Scottish athlete and missionary who lived in the early 1900's. The movie *Chariots of Fire* is a beautiful portrayal of Eric's story. As an athlete, Eric was best known as the fastest runner in Scotland. He had the opportunity to compete in the 1924 Summer Olympics in Paris. As a devout Christian, Eric had decided in advance he would not run on Sundays to honor the Lord. Because of his personal conviction, this took him out of his favorite and best race (the 100-meter) but he could still compete in the 400-meter. Even though the 400-meter race was not his strongest race, he prepared his best and was able to achieve a world record, gold medal run which stood as a European record for twelve years!

When people asked Liddell about how he could justify running in the Olympics versus going to the mission field, he is often quoted as saying, "I believe God made me for a purpose, but he also made me fast! And when I run I feel his pleasure … It has been a wonderful experience to compete in the Olympic Games and to bring home a gold medal. But since I have been a young lad, I have had my eyes on a different prize. You see, each one of us is in a greater race than any I have run in Paris, and this race ends when God gives out the medals … believe in God the Father, Almighty, Creator, infinitely holy and loving, who has a plan for the world, a plan for my life, and some daily work for me to do …"

After the Olympics, Eric went on to missions work in China. The core of his belief was that everything he did should give God pleasure, whether that was running in the Olympics or being a missionary in China. As a missionary in China, he was known to work with poor people, rescuing victims of war, teaching school children, and becoming a shining example of Christian love to the enemy while being imprisoned in a Japanese internment camp. He died in China in 1945.

As a Christian, do you have a calling on your life? Do you sense that God through His Holy Spirit has called you to do something specific and unique for Him through your life? I'm not sure that God the Father has a specific, unique calling on your life. If He does, though, if you sense there is something specific He has called you to do or be, then you definitely need to be obedient to that calling.

Assuming you have not sensed a specific calling, then you need to be obedient to what you know God's will to be according to Scripture. Then, take action based on that knowledge. Don't wait around for some mystical, magical, mountaintop experience. Be like Paul who had a plan to travel into the province of Asia to preach the Gospel, and then God redirected his travel plans. Paul took action and remained flexible.

You were created for a purpose, perhaps even a few purposes. Your purpose may change as you move from one stage of life to another stage. The key is to know your purpose at whatever life stage you are currently in. For example, when a person first enters adulthood in their late teens and early twenties, they are still in the learning and preparation phase of life. It is a stage of attempting to determine what one is good at and where he or she should direct their energy best to have a successful career. At this stage of life, it's okay not to have everything completely figured out. Keep learning, growing, and preparing for what God has planned! Once you do figure it out, though, embrace your new phase and become the best you can be in your field. But being the best doesn't necessarily mean working 80 hours a week and hating life.

Colossians 3:17 states, "And whatever you do, whether in word or deed, do it all in the name of the Lord Jesus, giving thanks to God the Father through him."[lxxxi]

## Career

How many people love what they do for a living? Are you one of those people? I've heard all the arguments from both sides of career and business experts about following passion versus finding a need and filling it. But what if both sides could be achieved with excellence? What if it was possible to discover what a person is passionate about in this life as well as find a need inside that passion that desperately needs to be filled? And what if many people are willing to pay lots of money for that need to be filled? That would definitely accomplish the best of both worlds.

Most adults dread Mondays and celebrate Fridays because they are in work careers they hate. They've ended up trapped in job positions that have paid the bills and put food on the table for their family, but they aren't passionate about their work. They would love the opportunity to break out and do something that makes their heart sing.

Many times this isn't always obvious. A little introspection and research might reveal a general direction to follow. This is why I believe the earlier chapters of this book in Part One are so important. Focusing on a stronger spiritual walk with the Lord, and acknowledging that He is the only source and that His people are managers of whatever He has given them is paramount. Living a life of joyful generosity will open up hands to receive more of the blessings of God. Giving moves people into a place of abundance in their lives. Consistent morning routines such as meditation, Scripture reading, prayer, affirmations, writing, and processing big ideas begin to mold and shape people into the life managers God wants them to be. Then there will be growth! As people learn more about themselves, they will begin to see more life potential and possibilities. They will manage their life energy at a higher level with better sleep, eating, and exercise, as well as greater emotional and sexual control.

In this chapter, I've focused on "investing in yourself," but what does that mean, exactly? While each person is on a unique financial journey, each person also needs to discover what they enjoy doing. They need to figure out their passions. They need to determine what they want to invest their life and energy into.

Are you unhappy with your current work environment? Do you feel like God has called you to a higher purpose, but maybe you lack the skills and experience to go that next level? Then you need to invest in yourself.

When you hear this phrase, you may think you may need to go back to college and get another degree so that you will be considered "competent" in the area you would like to move into. In my own personal experience, though, I don't know if this is always the best option.

The foundation, the most important part of the investment pyramid as proposed in *Financial Fitness*, is investing time, energy, and money into one's self. View yourself as a private corporation—You, Inc. As the owner of You, Inc., you need to be one of the best in your career field. Be well read in your work area. Become an expert. Attend conferences and workshops. Better yet, what if you were to become one of the keynote speakers at a conference in your career field? How could you establish the credibility necessary to get you to this place? A good place to start may be to begin a blog, write a book, teach a class, and network with others in your area.

Consider starting some type of part-time business related to one's field of knowledge—maybe a consulting-type business to help other companies that could use that expertise?

In this area of personal investment, start thinking bigger. Dig deeper. Look for problems that no one else is addressing well. Try to come up with creative solutions that people will happily pay money for.

Solve more problems. Help more people. Invest even more time and resources into yourself. See if you can grow and expand your part-time business into a full-time venture. This is exactly what people like Dave Ramsey and other experts have accomplished. Work hard but also work smart. Invest in yourself so that you have a firm financial foundation that will supply the other levels of the investment pyramid.

## Time Flexibility and Lifestyle Design

If you are currently working in a job position that has any kind of time flexibility, you are blessed. If you are in a work environment where you can come and go as needed and don't have your direct supervisor looking over your shoulder, then you definitely have a "perk" that few people enjoy.

If your work position doesn't require your physical presence on the job site on a continuous basis, and you have the capability to work remotely, then you are a lot wealthier than you may realize. You are blessed. You have a multitude of possibilities over those who are stuck in a career in which they physically need to present at the work site, such as people flipping burgers at the local burger shack, building houses, mowing lawns, or performing twelve-hour brain surgeries at the Mayo Clinic!

The information age combined with today's amazing technology has opened up an entire world of endless possibilities that people have only begun to explore. Depending on the career, there is the potential to live halfway around the world and still complete work for employers or a business.

Now, consider combining flexible work time and working remotely with the power of focus, passion, and calling. It's possible to break out of the mold of punching time clocks from 9:00 a.m. to 5:00 p.m. every day, even when working for an employer. Greater flexibility is possible by owning a business instead of working for someone else, whether as a consultant or perhaps owner of a website that sells a product that is drop-shipped directly to the customer. There are plenty of options out there for those who are creative and determined.

Lifestyle design is a big "buzz word" in today's society. Because of the amazing technological advances available in today's modern world, it is possible to design a life with greater time and activity flexibility. In fact, many of today's employees prefer the ability to integrate work around a flexible schedule rather than receiving a higher salary.

The millennial generation was recently surveyed about these issues. Forty-five percent of millennials prefer flexibility versus pay. This generation has made a decision that stockpiling wealth isn't their number one goal. Do they want to make a decent living? Sure. Everyone does, but this isn't this generation's primary goal or passion. Instead, these folks are driven by the flexibility to live life and enjoy those things that can't be bought. They prefer life balance to burn out.

Anyone can always make more money, somehow and somewhere. It is a renewable resource. What no one can create is more time. God has established a fixed, yet unknown amount. I could drop dead of a heart attack tomorrow or I could live until age 120. God has ordained every person's steps here on earth. Job 14:5 says, "Since his days are determined, The number of his months is with You; And his limits You have set so that he cannot pass."[lxxxii] Also James 4:14 says, "Yet you do not know what your life will be like tomorrow. You are just a vapor that appears for a little while and then vanishes away."[lxxxiii]

Since no one knows how much time they have left here on this earth, what would be the better choice? To work sixty-, seventy-, or eighty-hour weeks in pursuit of a bigger paycheck but with zero personal life? Or, a more balanced work/life integration where life and relationships can truly be enjoyed over being a slave to the workplace? This is something to consider for the long-term trajectory of life.

If you have time flexibility in your current work position, then the next question to ask is what do you do with any extra time you may have? In a lifestyle design mindset, there are endless possibilities: spend time with your family, learn a new hobby, or maybe even travel the world while working remotely. These are noble pursuits in the world of lifestyle design, but let's return to the mindset of investing in one's self. We will dig deeper in this area over the next two sections.

## Reading, Writing, and Public Speaking

Let's assume you have created some extra, flexible time in your work schedule and personal life. Be an excellent manager of that extra time. Understand the importance of investing in You, Inc., to reach your greatest potential. This kind of time mindset would be somewhat like a "re-investing dividends for an even greater return on investment" in the financial investing world. In the same way, take any extra time, double down on that, and invest the majority of extra time into yourself.

In the world of horse race betting, there is a term known as a "trifecta." No, I'm not advocating betting here. Just go with me right now on my weird line of thinking. A trifecta is defined as "a bet in which the person betting forecasts the first three finishers in a race in the correct order."

In my opinion, there is a trifecta of sorts as related to investing in one's self. There are three specific areas to pursue in a specific order that are the best ways to invest in one's self and create a solid foundation in *you* as a business. The three areas in this "trifecta" ordering include information consumption, writing, and public speaking. Let's dig deeper and unpack all three of these areas in more detail.

First, begin with consuming more information. To be an effective leader and communicator in an area of specialty, be knowledgeable through reading a variety of material such as books, blogs, magazines, as well as consuming vast quantities of other information sources such as audio programs, podcasts, and videos. Develop a hunger for your chosen area of expertise and become an expert through absorbing as much information as possible. This is also known as immersion.

I know from personal experience in growing in the stewardship/Christian personal finance area, that the more books I read, the more podcasts I listen to, and the more videos I watch, the more I realize what I don't know. This develops a desire within me to learn even more.

There is a well-known phrase, "readers are leaders." In the modern era, this could be rephrased into something like, "Information consumers are leaders." A great way to keep track of all this information consumption is a simple tool called Evernote. Evernote offers the ability to write individual notes and tag information on things learned. The "web clipper" tool can clip helpful blog posts and articles. Users can save photos of paper book pages and write notes. It is even possible to migrate Amazon Kindle book highlights and notes to Evernote for further review. Evernote is a useful tool for this first level of personal investing. The best way to begin investing today is to become a voracious consumer of information in an area of expertise. Start reading, listening, watching, and then watch personal growth take off.

Second, once arriving at a level of information consumption in which you feel knowledgeable about your field, start writing about your area of expertise. Don't start writing garbage, though. Learn how to write *well*. Branch out and read books and blogs on writing. Read the blogs and writing of other great writers. I know for myself, reading the blogs of people such as Michael Hyatt[lxxxiv] and Tim Ferriss[lxxxv] helped me grow in my early days as a writer. All great writers have a unique writer's voice, and these great writers placed a desire within me to find my voice as well. Consume more information on the writing process itself. Write as much as possible on a daily basis and learn to "find your voice" as a writer. Find a mentor. Maybe join a writers' Meetup[lxxxvi] group.

I know from personal experience that journaling and blogging are excellent avenues to find one's voice as a writer. I realized I was starting to "make it" as a writer when one of my first blogs on personal finance drew more and more daily page views, and then a small media company offered me money for my blog. When talking with the owners of the media company, they remarked that they liked my writer's voice. They could see my development as a writer over the eighteen months that I had been producing the blog. Write something every day. Practice, and then practice some more. This has been my approach writing this book. I just keep plugging away on it a little or a lot around the same time each day until I can finally finish it.

Third, the arena of public speaking is a natural outgrowth from writing. No one will be a good speaker until they first become a decent writer. Develop content through writing and then learn how to deliver that content in a speech. Just like writing, learn the craft of being an excellent public speaker. Get busy listening and watching other great public speakers. TED Talks are a great place to start. A few of my favorite TED speakers are Amy Cuddy, Simon Sinek, Tony Robbins, and Elizabeth Gilbert. You can also go to Youtube.com and do a search on "best public speakers in the world." A great list of videos will appear to help educate and grow speakers. Read books on communication and speaking. Listen to podcasts. Consume as much information as possible, and then find avenues to put everything learned into practice. Several years ago, I heard about Toastmasters International[lxxxvii] and their reputation for developing people to become better communicators. I knew this was an area that I needed to invest more time and energy into. Like many things, though, I kept pushing off into the future what could be the most important investment I could make in my life. Finally, in March 2013, I visited my first Toastmasters club[lxxxviii] meeting, and I was hooked. I could see the immediate value of pursuing this kind of training. Groups like Toastmasters provide opportunities to practice and develop speaking skills on a regular basis. Plus, peers in the club usually evaluate others' speaking projects and provide immediate feedback on speaking skills with practical advice on how to become a more effective communicator.

The early decades of the 21st Century were an amazing time in human history. This has been called the Information Age, also now known as the New Media Age. In this period of time, more and more people are valued for their ability to communicate and relate at a high level. Some of the wealthiest people in today's world are the best communicators in their profession. They are brilliant thinkers, and their thinking has led them to create valuable content in blogs, books, podcasts, and speeches. All three of these areas are interconnected. Information consumption leads to better writing, and writing leads to better speaking skills.

Take a couple of minutes and create a quick list of highly successful, business people in recent history. Who's made that list? My list includes people such as Steve Jobs, Tim Ferriss, Michael Hyatt, Oprah, Dave Ramsey, and Bill Gates. What do the majority of these successful people have in common other than having extreme wisdom and knowledge when it comes to business and money? These people are all effective communicators (writers, content creators, public speakers). As a result, they are the leaders in their respective fields. This is the true currency of the modern era. Strive to be an effective writer, public speaker, and leader, and employment will always be within reach in today's information age.

Let's go back to Steve Jobs for a second. Was Steve Jobs an innovator with an incredible drive to make Apple, Inc., one of the greatest companies in the world? Yes, most definitely. Steve Jobs excelled in having a vision for his company and then learning how to communicate that vision to the world so people could understand and buy into his vision.

For example, when Jobs introduced the Apple iPod to the marketplace back in 2001, was this mp3 player something completely new and revolutionary? No, not exactly. The little "wheel" user interface was new to consumers, but there had been other mp3 players before the iPod. What made the iPod unique to the general public was the whole marketing and branding concept from Jobs when he described this iPod mp3 player as "1,000 songs in your pocket." Now, that resonated with people. They understood the value and the power of having the ability to carry around a large amount of music on one device. Sales went through the roof as a result. Steve Jobs became a wealthy man because he learned how to become an effective communicator to the people he was attempting to reach through Apple.

In the same way that Jobs invested the time and energy to become a more effective communicator in the Information Age, consider investing in the areas of information consumption, writing, and public speaking.

### Multiple Streams of Income

Long gone are the days when a family had one source of income, usually generated by the father. Dad would work in the same company his entire life, make a decent salary with good benefits, and then receive a pension for the rest of his life after his retirement. This is actually my dad's story. This is the home I grew up in. My mom was a stay-at-home mom until my brothers and I were in school full-time; she then felt able to step out and find part-time work that interested her. I don't think we ever completely depended on her source of income.

In the new economy, though, things are a bit different, especially in the early decades of the 2000s. Work salaries have not kept pace with the cost of living. Employees have had to take on more of the burden of healthcare costs, and these costs keep rising at an alarming rate. Because of these issues, more and more families have been dependent on both parents having the ability to work and provide at least two full-time incomes and even a couple of other part-time incomes thrown in on top as well. Multiple streams of income within a family are more of a necessity today than the desired goal. Are there still families out there who can survive and even thrive on one income stream. Sure, I've known several who have been able to pull it off and kudos to them. But, in today's uncertain economy, wisdom says pursuing multiple streams of income is a smart decision for most people.

The challenge for families juggling multiple streams of income is the time element. Are there enough hours in the day? Do we have enough energy? Can we create enough life balance to be able to spend time with our families, accomplish chores around the house, and complete jobs with excellence all at the same time?

Let's camp out here for a minute and discuss three different types of income. First, there is linear income in which a person is paid to show up and perform a variety of tasks—with a paycheck for work at a predetermined time. When the employee stops working, except for in the case of paid time off, they stop receiving an income. The majority of people have a least one (sometimes more) source of linear income. In a nutshell, the employee shows up for work, performs tasks for a set amount of time, and is paid. As I mentioned earlier in the chapter, this type of work can range from the hamburger flipper at the local burger shack all the way up to the brain surgeon in the operating room. The pay scales are completely different, but the concept is the same. These people are paid to be on location to perform a specific task. Of course, there are various levels of linear work, where a person may be able to work less but benefit from a bigger payout at the end. For the sake of simplicity, though, I won't chase down the multitude of ways to earn linear income.

The second type of income is passive income. Passive income is income generated from money working for a person via investments. Money may be in CDs, money market accounts, higher-yield savings accounts, various types of bonds, and then, of course, the stock market. Real estate investing could be in this mix as well. If all the markets are behaving, passive investment income is great. However, if riding the stock market roller coaster, it's not so much fun. Passive income usually requires little extra work depending on the investment strategy. The person earns the money, and the money is then put to work. A passive income strategy is great for building retirement savings, but not always the best way to support a family financially (unless there are millions of dollars at work).

The third and perhaps most interesting type of income is residual income. Residual income is defined as income that continues to be generated after initial effort has been expended. Do the work once, and then receive income from that work spread out over time. Types of residual income would include the following: affiliate marketing, subscription services, book sales, drop ship websites, pay-per-click online ads, and vending machines. Pat Flynn from SmartPassiveIncome.com is a great example of someone who has created residual income products that provide well for his family. Pat's journey to residual income all started from being laid off from his architecture job in 2008. He then created a website to help himself pass an architecture industry exam called the LEED exam. Little did Pat know that his little website was generating thousands of visits per day. People were interested in his content and expressed their desire for some type of eBook of his LEED material. This is when the "lights came on" for Pat. He created the eBook, and within the first month of being for sale, he made $7,008.55! Since that time, Pat has not turned back. He has created even more residual streams of income. In 2014, he made almost $1,000,000 in revenue from all his residual/passive income streams.

This should be the ultimate goal in investing in one's self—creating multiple streams of income and no longer be dependent on one or two linear incomes. Let's play a little game of "what if …" when it comes to this idea of passive, residual, multiple streams of income:

- What if you came up with ONE big idea that could translate into a bunch of different income streams. Here are some examples: Pat Flynn and Smart Passive Income that I referenced earlier. Tim Ferriss and the 4-Hour Work Week. Jack Canfield, Mark Victor Hansen and Chicken Soup for the Soul.
- What if you created one main website that supported that ONE big idea such as SmartPassiveIncome.com, FourHourWorkWeek.com, etc.?
- What if you wrote many books around that ONE big idea?
- What if you had all those books in multiple forms such as print, eBook, and audio; as well as in different languages?
- What if you had a blog?
- What if you had a podcast?
- What if you had a vlog on your own YouTube channel?
- What if you created a membership website connected to your big idea?
- What if you created larger, more in-depth informational products to go along with your ONE big idea?
- What if you had paid advertising on your website?
- What if your website contained affiliate links that earned lots of passive income?

When I reflect on people such as Jack Canfield, Tim Ferriss, Pat Flynn, Michael Hyatt, and yes, even Dave Ramsey, I can't help but grow excited about the possibilities for the future! The key is investing the time and energy into that ONE big idea that is going to be the catalyst for all the other ideas and revenue that come from that idea.

Invest more time, energy, and money into what could be your ONE big idea that has the potential to set you up to be the next passive and residual income expert.

*Quick Tip: For a FREE list of the Action Steps and Resources for each chapter of the book, simply go to: http://www.heroicpersonalfinances.com/for-christians-book-action-steps/*

# CHAPTER 7
# EMERGENCY PREPAREDNESS

> "The wise store up choice food and olive oil, but fools gulp theirs down."
> – Proverbs 21:20 NIV[lxxxix]

> "Be prepared . . . the meaning of the motto is that a scout must prepare himself by previous thinking out and practicing how to act on any accident or emergency so that he is never taken by surprise."
> – Robert Baden-Powell, founder of the Boy Scouts[xc]

On January 30, 2002, one of the worst ice storms in recent memory hit the Kansas City Metro area, my current hometown. At the time, we owned a house in an older neighborhood that boasted large trees and above ground electrical power lines. This is definitely not a good recipe to have during an ice storm. Hundreds of thousands of us in Kansas City were without power for several days.

One large tree in our backyard lost a limb that ripped out the power line that was running from the pole directly into the back of our house. We had zero backup plan. We had no fireplace in this older home to burn any wood to keep warm. We didn't own a generator. We had no emergency food or water. We ended up improvising an emergency plan for fourteen days. This plan included staying in a hotel ninety minutes north of the city while we waited for the power company to get to our house and repair our main power line. My young family survived, but we definitely could have been better prepared for that emergency.

In Financial Peace University™, Dave Ramsey does a great job of preparing people for financial emergencies. Baby Step 1 consists of putting $1,000 in the bank. Dave calls this the baby emergency fund. Its purpose is to be a hedge against going into any more debt. The baby emergency fund is there to use instead of a credit card whenever an unexpected, emergency-type of event arises—like replacing the alternator in the car or the water heater in the house.

After paying off all consumer debt (credit cards, car loans, personal loans, college loans, etc.) through the debt snowball in Baby Step 2, the next step is to advance to a fully funded emergency fund of three to six months worth of expense money. Set aside the necessary funds for this longer time frame to pay any main bills such as mortgage payments, utility bills, and food in case of job loss or other extreme situation. In Financial Peace University, this would seem to end the discussion on any type of emergency preparedness.

Now, I don't want anyone to freak out! Don't be scared that Armageddon is right around the corner, or that it's necessary to construct an underground shelter as soon as possible. I'm neither a conspiracy theorist nor a doomsday "prepper." I do think, though, that everyone should be prepared at a reasonable level when emergency situations come up such as severe winter storms, tornados, hurricanes, floods, brownouts and blackouts, as well as for other weather, utility, and government problems that could arise.

In this chapter, I'm going to dig deeper than FPU Baby Steps 1 and 3—beyond $10,000 to $30,000 in an emergency fund. I'm going to challenge my readers to think, act, and prepare *bigger* for an emergency crisis that goes beyond having extra money in the bank.

Are you and your family prepared at all levels for a local, national, or maybe even a worldwide crisis? Let's dig into this chapter and find out.

## The Emergency Fund: Cash and Savings

Many personal finance experts teach the basic emergency fund concept of "three to six month's worth of expenses in a good money market account." But the preparation ends there for an emergency fund – a big pile of money in a bank account. I'm not knocking this advice because I think it is good advice. My family has a rainy day fund such as this for unexpected financial problems.

What happens, though, if for some reason that stash of cash is inaccessible and it is needed sooner than later? What if there is a run on banks? What if there is a global computer virus that turns digital money in online savings accounts into a big fat zero? Lots of weird stuff can happen, especially in today's unstable world.

Let me present another potential way to put together a rainy day fund. In my own personal plan, I have several layers of emergency funding. And just like Dave talks about, remember that an emergency fund is more in line with an insurance policy—not a way to do something "big" with money. Yes, piles of money will be lying around not growing as fast as they could be, and that's okay.

**Step 1 for a Financial Emergency Fund:** Buy a decent safe. Depending on how many items need to be stored and how big the safe needs to be, costs for a good safe range from $200 to $1,000. I realize that may seem like a lot of money, but from personal experience, a safe is well worth the investment. Another personal note on safes: always go a little bigger than you think you need to. I bought my family's current 1.2 cubic-foot safe around ten years ago. This size has been too small for our needs for the last four to five years. I recently added an extra safe about twice as large as the first, primarily to hold all the various Jones family legal documents. Be sure to buy a safe that is well built and has a high fire rating.

**Step 2:** Depending on personal comfort level and "prepper" attitude, I would put anywhere between $3,000 to $5,000 cash in a safe. This is the first level of an emergency fund. And no, this isn't pizza money for dinner or a, "I need to go buy something on Craigslist right now" fund either. Pull together a decent-sized collection of $5s, $10s, and $20s for this first level of an emergency fund. In this way, if a bank account can't be accessed in a crisis, there is cash at hand that will carry a family through a minor emergency for at least a few weeks.

*Quick Tip: The Federal government with the help of local banks (that's so helpful of banks, isn't it?) tracks people who take out large amounts of cash. Most banks will definitely "flag" transactions if a withdrawal of more than $3,000 occurs in one transaction. Be sure to keep copies of checks and withdrawal slips with cash in the safe. This is proof to the government that you are not a drug dealer, money launder, or terrorist if they should ever come knocking on the front door. If you don't have proof of withdrawal, the government could possibly confiscate all your money—not a good thing. Keep the paperwork. You could also show the guys in the black helicopters that show up to your house this chapter of the book and blame me for your stash of cash!*

**Step 3:** Set aside around $2,000 to $5,000 in a savings account at the same bank you have your checking account. Be sure you have both accounts linked together to move money back and forth as needed. This is your second level of an emergency fund. In this way, when you have a financial problem, you can immediately transfer the money you need from savings to checking to spend it immediately via check or debit card. This third step is most likely adequate for the majority of your "regular" emergencies such as car repairs, smaller home repairs, and minor medical emergencies. The next two steps will be the "icing on the cake" for your major, abnormal life emergencies.

**Step 4:** Set aside anywhere between $10,000 to $30,000 in a "higher yield" savings account that will take a few days to transfer your money into your checking account. This account will be your largest savings account, closer to your three to six months of expenses. I recently found one of the highest percentage yield online accounts over at MySavingsDirect.com. At the time of this writing, it is 1.00% APR. There are many online banks like this. Check out: Nerd Wallet at https://www.nerdwallet.com/rates/savings-account.

*Quick Tip: Interest rates have been historically low for quite some time. At the time of this writing, there is now talk about the potential of negative interest rates. If this happens, banks would actually charge customers to have them hold their money (crazy, right?) If this becomes a reality, refer to my earlier quick tip on getting cash money out of the bank. One final thought: word on the street in the financial world is that we are moving closer and closer to a cashless society. There is talk of removing $100 and $50 bills out of circulation. At some point soon, it may be illegal to use cash. Stay alert and informed about what the Federal government is planning to do with your money and work your financial plan accordingly.*

**Step 5:** This next step is going to seem completely "geeky," but to fight a yearly inflation rate of anywhere between 3 to 5 percent on your primary emergency fund in step four, I would take the high number of 5 percent and subtract the bank account interest gain of 1 percent, leaving you with 4 percent that you are "losing" out with your financial purchase power in your emergency savings due to inflation. Next, I would set up a small recurring deposit into this account to cover inflation losses. So, if a base emergency savings is $10,000, that amount times 5 percent inflation means a loss of around $500 per year. You are making 1 percent ($100) in interest and will need to cover the remaining $400 lost due to inflation. $400 divided by twelve months equals about $33 that would need to be deposited into the account each month. In this way, the three to six months of cash reserves will not lose its purchasing power in the event of a large emergency. Put this small deposit on autopilot between bank accounts. In the words of the great Ron Popeil,[xci] "set it and forget it!"

*Quick Note: I have this "inflation busting" strategy set up with all our layers of emergency funding. Every month, I add $20 cash to our cash pile in our home safe (Step 2). I also have a small recurring transfer/deposit that automatically moves from our bank's checking account over to our savings account (Step 3). All of our emergency money sources now keep pace with inflation.*

**Step 6:** This final step is for those who have high deductible health insurance with an HSA account. Max this account out every year. In the year 2015 (you will need to check these numbers for the current year), a single person can contribute up to $3,350 per year. A family can contribute up to $6,650 per year. These amounts are 100 percent tax deductible (at least for now!) because they are withdrawn in pre-tax dollars. Medical emergencies are the number one reason people end up declaring bankruptcy. I would treat my HSA account as another layer of an emergency fund to protect my family against this bankruptcy statistic. Don't be tempted after a good health year to cut back the amount deducted from each paycheck toward HSA the following year. Keep on plunking in the maximum amount and treat that HSA account as another layer of emergency funding in the area of health care. At some point, it will be needed, so you may as well plan and prepare for a health care emergency.

This six-step approach is a more deliberate, organized plan than just sticking "three to six month's worth of expense money in a money market account." A good emergency plan prepares for the worst-case scenario occurring to the banking system. Because this is a debt-laden economy completely run by susceptible computer systems, trouble is inevitable if relying solely on the government and computers to be 100 percent reliable

every day. Prepare for the worst and pray for the best!
## Precious Metals

Let me state upfront that I am not an expert in the area of precious metals. I would take this section of the book for informational purposes only. I have a basic understanding of the material myself, and I am in the beginning stages of acquiring my own precious metals.

The first precious metal items I am considering are small silver coins. I'm sure many of my readers are asking, "Why silver coins?" There are a few reasons. First, gold is too valuable to have on hand for emergency or catastrophic survival purposes. Gold is difficult to separate into portions to buy what is needed in emergencies. Because silver is a smaller unit of value, it's a lot more portable and practical to carry around. Second, silver is less expensive and easier to buy in coin format.

The second precious metal items I am considering are small gold bars. These gold bars, though, would not be for any type of emergency preparedness due to the reasons I listed earlier. The main reason to buy gold in any form would be as a hedge against inflation.

The historical significance of purchasing gold as an inflation hedge is a deep topic that I don't have time to go through in this book. I will give a quick explanation here about the basic concept. In the early 20th century, the United States government made several significant changes to its monetary policy. First, the government moved to paper fiat currency.[xcii] Second, it established a central banking system. Third, it banished the ownership of private gold for several decades. Fourth, the government moved monetary policy completely off the gold standard. As a result of these four main financial changes, this country has experienced runaway inflation for more than 100 years.

Compare the cost of a car produced in 1915 to a car produced in 2015. Yes, at some level there are natural price increases for certain items, but by in large, the value of $1.00 in 1915 is worth $23.63 in 2015. This is a cumulative rate of inflation of 2262.8%. Crazy, right? Be even more depressed about inflation by checking out this website: http://www.usinflationcalculator.com.

The reason gold is an excellent hedge against inflation is that gold (usually) retains its value over time. So factoring for inflation, an ounce of gold back in 1915 roughly equals an ounce of gold today. Gold is not considered a great investment because of this specific quality. The monetary value of gold only grows at the rate of inflation.

In the book *Financial Fitness* by LIFE Leadership the authors recommend buying gold to bring about what they call "freezing your fruit." This action addresses the issue of inflation. Buying a few gold bars and placing them in a home safe "freezes" a specific amount of monetary value. Several years later, it's possible to reclaim that monetary value as needed, especially during times of high inflation.

I am currently considering buying silver coins for emergency preparedness. The main purpose is if the "grid" goes down resulting in a barter/cash economy. I am also considering purchasing gold bars as a hedge against inflation. However, be careful of getting caught up in the precious metals hype advertised on the radio and seen in TV commercials. Purchasing precious metals as some type of great investment in a down economy is a bad idea. In my opinion, I don't believe the numbers add up to these being great investment vehicles. However, they do make sense for emergency preparedness and as an inflation hedge. Research before buying anything!

## Food and Water

The next level of emergency preparedness includes food and water. To survive any type of disaster, food and water supplies are necessary for you and your family.

The polls are all over the map on how many people are prepared for an emergency situation. Some polls say that 20 to 30 percent of Americans are ready. Jim McKay, editor of *Emergency Management*[xxiii] believes those numbers are way off, and states the preparedness level is around 10 percent. Needless to say, the vast majority of Americans are not prepared at all. Apparently, people don't believe anything bad can happen.

There are several companies that sell emergency food supplies. These come as non-perishable, freeze-dried "just add hot water" food packets. They also come in various supply quantities such as one month, three-month, six-month, or even a twelve-month supply. These companies include:

- Wise Company ([wisefoodstorage.com](wisefoodstorage.com))
- My Patriot Supply ([mypatriotsupply.com](mypatriotsupply.com))
- Nitro-Pak ([nitro-pak.com](nitro-pak.com))
- Augason Farms ([www.augasonfarms.com](www.augasonfarms.com))
- The Ready Store ([www.thereadystore.com](www.thereadystore.com))
- Preparewise ([www.preparewise.com](www.preparewise.com))
- Food Insurance ([www.foodinsurance.com](www.foodinsurance.com))
- My Food Storage ([www.myfoodstorage.com](www.myfoodstorage.com))
- Emergency Essentials ([www.beprepared.com](www.beprepared.com))
- eFoods Direct ([efoodsdirect.com](efoodsdirect.com))

There are several ways to have a ready supply of drinking water available. The easiest way is to purchase standard plastic water bottles at the grocery store. Anytime our family goes to the grocery store, we try to remember to grab a couple cases of water bottles. This helps build up our supply in our basement storage room. Since water bottles are sealed containers, this type of water storage should remain potable for several years. To keep the water drinkable, these water bottles must be stored in a cool, dark place away from other chemicals.

*Quick Tip: The plastic on these water bottles can still allow some odors and chemicals in through the thin container. Avoid storing these water bottles in places like the garage near gas cans, lawnmowers, or other vehicles that might emit strong odors.*

How much water should a typical family store? The recommended daily amount is one gallon per person—a half-gallon to drink and a half-gallon for hygiene. For a family of four, this means four gallons per day. A one-month supply would be approximately 120 gallons. A 35-count package of plastic water bottles is around 4.5 gallons—so 27 packages would be a safe one-month supply. This may or may not be the most practical solution.

The same food companies listed earlier also sell emergency water supplies and related materials. These include water filters, "water bricks," or even large water tanks for tap water storage. One note on storing tap water: many "prepper" websites recommend treating this water at some point with bleach. Here is a list from the website newjerusalem.com about water purification guidelines:

## WATER PURIFICATION

1. Clear water is a sign of pure water. Always drain long-standing pipes for thirty seconds to one minute before drinking! (Cheap remote motels?)
2. One gallon of water can be disinfected with eight to sixteen drops of regular household bleach (visually about 1/4 of a teaspoon)—double that for cloudy water. Shake and let stand thirty minutes. One teaspoon will disinfect five gallons. Immediately after treating, water must initially have a slight smell of chlorine. If it does not, repeat the process.
3. Household bleach is relatively harmless. The smell or "waft" of chlorine is not bad: it indicates that water is treated and germ-free. Once treated and disinfected, the chlorine smell will go away in a few days.
4. Regularly used water from large tanks may be treated once or twice a month with one ounce of bleach per 200 gallons or five ounces of bleach per 1000 gallons.
5. Long-standing water in tanks can be disinfected with one pint of household bleach per 1000 gallons (2500 gal tanks are fine with three pints.)
6. Bleach effectively kills bacteria and viruses and stops smells, before breaking down. Its effective germ killing alkaline property is completely neutralized very quickly. It does not stay chemically active in tanks for more than a few days. Most germs require sunlight to grow. Store water in the dark.
7. If water is relatively clear but has a noticeable smell of chlorine, it is drinkable, disinfected, and harmless. Humans need two quarts per day.[xciv]

Having a decent long-term supply of food and water is important for you and your family in the event of a serious emergency. You never know when a serious enough event could take place that knocks out your regular food and water supply. When you are prepared and an emergency does occur, you will be safely huddled in your home while the outside world is in chaos. They will be fighting over whatever food and water supplies are even available. You will ride out the storm. Don't neglect this vital part of emergency preparedness.

## Power

Those who live in the United States or other industrialized countries are spoiled. Most people take technological advancements for granted—HVAC systems will always work, providing cold air in the summer and warm air in the winter. There will always be hot water to take a shower, wash clothes, and wash dishes. The power grid is reliable, providing power to do whatever *whenever*—unless there is a bad weather event that knocks out power lines.

People are blessed in the United States and rarely go without power. But as I mentioned in my ice storm story at the beginning of this chapter, bad weather events do happen. They can shut down power for longer periods than expected. Homes get too cold or hot depending on the season. Food spoils in refrigerators and freezers. Charging electronic devices becomes a problem. People are almost unable to "survive" without power in today's world. When a lengthy power outage occurs, consider "bugging out" and living in another location such as a hotel until power can be restored.

Another power grid concern many people have is cyber terrorism. An event such as this could leave millions of Americans without power for a long time. Your family needs a good backup plan for just such an emergency.

At the time of my writing this particular chapter, my family has been preparing for such a loss of power. We recently purchased a heavy-duty generator and all the accessories needed to have power for select items in the house for a few days. We have several large gas cans filled with gas and Stabil. We have extra extension cords to run through the house as needed. We also had our furnace air handler unit "pigtailed" with a power cord to accept an extension cord to hook up to the generator. In this way, we can at least keep the house warm in cold weather. If we ration the time we run the generator, we should be able to keep the generator going for at least several days on our current gasoline supply.

A larger budget would allow for some better emergency power sources. There are solar, battery-powered generators. There are larger professional-grade generators made by companies such as Generac (Generac.com) that can run whole house electrical systems. Here are some choices to consider:

*Fuel*. First, make a decision on a source of fuel—gasoline, diesel, LP (natural gas), and solar/battery. Second, determine how much power needs to be generated to take care of emergency energy—enough power for the entire house? Or, maybe power is needed for only a few items such as the furnace, refrigerator/freezer, a few lights, and some smaller electronics items? Third, once power needs are decided, determine how many output watts and amps the generator will need to deliver. For our large family of seven, I stumbled across a good deal for a higher output portable generator of 8,400 watts for $550.00. Based on our estimated potential emergency power consumption, I believe this should be adequate for our needs.

For cold weather heat sources, consider also the option of a wood burning stove or fireplace to save generator fuel. It's possible to switch back and forth between fireplace and furnace depending on the length of a power outage. If wood-burning, make sure to store an adequate supply of emergency firewood. A natural gas log insert for the fireplace is another option. There are no guarantees, though, that the utility gas supply won't be interrupted at some point in a catastrophic event. Keep a few electric space heaters around as well, just in case, to plug into a backup generator. A few small portable fans might come in handy during warm weather months.

Don't be like my family in the winter of 2002 running all over the Kansas City metro area trying to find a place to survive for two weeks. Have a power back-up plan.

## Guns and Ammo

Hey, if the zombie apocalypse happens soon, everyone will need some weapons, right?

Unfortunately, times are challenging and difficult right now. There is a lot of political unrest in many cities around the country and even more so around the world. When I was writing this part of the book, the city of Paris was just attacked with ISIS terrorist bombs and gunfire in November

2015. A month later, in December 2015, a Muslim extremist husband and wife opened fire at a county workers' Christmas Party in San Bernardino, California. While I was in the middle of editing this chapter in June 2016, a Muslim extremist walked into an Orlando, Florida nightclub and opened fire, killing forty-nine and wounding at least fifty-three.

The wisdom of a wealthy mindset says to protect one's self and family from riots, political unrest, terror attacks, extremists, or someone attempting to break into the house.

I will admit upfront that I am not a gun or weapon expert. Presently, a gun purchase is on my emergency preparedness "To do" list to protect my family. When I arrive at the point of purchasing some guns and ammo, I know exactly how I'm going to approach this next step on my list. I plan on doing the following:

1. **Talk to family members, friends, and those I know in law enforcement.** I have several family members and friends who own guns and ammo. I also know a few law enforcement officers. They stay current with the best equipment and prices. They will be my first step of information and learning before I make any purchases.
2. **Online research.** Hey, it's a Google world now. I'm going to spend time on the inter webs trying to find the best deals on the best equipment. I will research how to fire weapons to protect myself and my family in an emergency survival situation.
3. **Books.** I have a Kindle Unlimited subscription. I just did a quick check over on my Amazon.com account. I can do some book reading and research on the topic before making my purchases.
4. **Visit specialty stores.** It never hurts to consult the "brick and mortar" stores that specialize in guns, ammo, and personal protection. Talk to the people who own as well as those who visit these stores.
5. **Conceal and carry class training.** The next stop after my purchase will be to become certified by my state so I can carry a handgun with me to protect my family.

Many who prepare for the worst-case scenario don't just have cash, silver coins, and emergency food and water supplies. They also plan ahead to protect their families if they are ever under assault. I wish the world were all peace, love, doves, puppy dogs and rainbows. This side of heaven and before the millennial reign of Christ, this is definitely not reality. The world is dark, sinful, aggressive, violent, and dangerous. Every day of the news tells stories of rioting in the streets of different major cities or home invasions in some of the best and safest neighborhoods. There are no guarantees in life.

There's an old expression "bad things happen to good people." The best thing to do is prepare for the worst and pray for the best. Have a decent amount of extra cash and precious metals socked away in a well-built safe. Have at least three to six months worth of emergency food, water, and extra emergency supplies in storage. Buy a reliable generator and have extra fuel on hand to run it. Own some guns and ammo to protect your family. It's certainly not necessary to go to the extreme lengths of a doomsday prepper, but people who bury their head in the sand are ignoring some very real emergency possibilities that could become problematic. Create a plan. Put together an emergency supply checklist. Execute that plan.

*Quick Tip: For a FREE list of the Action Steps and Resources for each chapter of the book, simply go to: http://www.heroicpersonalfinances.com/for-christians-book-action-steps/*

# CHAPTER 8
# INTERLUDE: TAX STRATEGIES

"Then Jesus said to them, 'Give back to Caesar what is Caesar's and to God what is God's.'"
– Mark 12:17 NIV[xcv]

"Collecting more taxes than is absolutely necessary is legalized robbery."
– President Calvin Coolidge

In the book *Multiple Streams of Income: How to Generate a Lifetime of Unlimited Wealth*, author Robert G. Allen discusses plugging the various "leaks" in our income streams. One of the biggest leaks in people's personal finances is taxes. Here are a few quick excerpts from that book related to plugging up tax leaks:

*You see, money is a game, albeit a very important one. If you know the rules, you win; if you don't know the rules, you lose. As physician George David said: Wealth is when small efforts produce big results. Poverty is when big efforts produce small results...*

*All told, on average, the millionaire spends about a minute or two more per transaction than the poor person. This takes no more than ten minutes per day. But what a savings in time and money! ... By investing an extra minute to record the transaction and to file it properly, you have at your fingertips a vast source of information. You know your current account balances. You can compare your spending to previous months, and you'll notice trends. You are more aware of your actual spending. This gives you much greater control of your finances. You can calculate your tax consequences in minutes, not days. You can back up your tax decisions with instant documentation. In case of dispute, you know where, when, and how you spent your money, and you have a receipt to prove it. You are in control. And the resulting peace of mind creates a feeling of power. This increases your confidence, creativity, and judgment. You make fast, correct, decisive decisions. This gives you that secret millionaire's advantage. From now on, every time you spend money, take a few extra minutes during that money event to practice the millionaire minute: Plan your purchase. Get a discount. Get a receipt. Examine your receipt. Categorize your receipt. Balance your account. File your receipt ... At the end of the year, doing their taxes is a real chore, taking time and extra money for their accountant to sort out—more lost money. Just how much are those lost receipts worth? Suppose you buy a pen and instead of throwing away the receipt you actually keep it, categorize it, and file it for tax time. Now you have proof of a tax-deductible expense for your home-based business. You can deduct this expense from your income before you calculate your taxes. What is this worth to you? An immediate 30 percent return on your money! If you're in the 30 percent tax bracket, every dollar you categorize as a tax deduction gives you a 30 percent return on your money. Did you get that? Hello? Where can you today get an instant 30 percent guaranteed return on your money? When you get and keep the receipt for a tax-deductible expense and then deduct that expenditure on your taxes, you're making 30 percent on your money. This 30 percent return on your money is the kind of thing that turns ordinary people into millionaires. Start today to gain greater control over your money by doing the millionaire minute . . . You'll be amazed.*[xcvi]

Talking taxes isn't everyone's favorite subject, so I won't dwell on this too long. I'll offer some thoughts, ideas, and resources for lowering tax obligations. Writing on the topic of tax strategies was an afterthought for me as I was putting together this second part of the book. In my first draft, I did not plan on including this topic. Since I'm currently dealing with some tax issues in my own personal finances, I thought this chapter would be a good reminder of the importance of an excellent tax strategy. As we come out of the chapter on emergency preparedness and before we embark on various investing strategies, I believe now would be a good time for a bit of "interlude" and talk taxes.

Taxes. Nobody likes them, but they are one of those necessary evils in life that must be dealt with. Christians should be obedient to Scripture and the government authorities God has established. The Bible says believers should "render unto Caesar what is Caesar's" (Mark 12:17), but I don't believe Jesus' intent in that verse is to pay more than each person's fair share. That would be bad stewardship on the believer's part, *and* violate additional stewardship principles contained in other verses in the Bible. It is wise stewardship to take every legal tax deduction available.

Everyone's tax situation is different. In fact, my tax situation is out of the "norm" for most people, which led me to even include this chapter in the book. My family's current financial situation is in the middle of several changes in which we have the possibility to save thousands of dollars a year in taxes for the next decade or more. I didn't grasp the real potential of this tax savings until I started experimenting with various numbers in my tax preparation software. I set up an "experimental" tax form just to see how my family's tax liability changed when certain variables were altered. I was shocked by our potential changes in tax savings. It was bigger than I first thought!

Let me pause here and say that I am not a CPA, tax advisor, or financial planner. I don't play one on the Internet, either. For the most part, I'm just a regular guy with a few tax advantages than the normal taxpayer who does his own taxes each year with downloaded software. I am also required to pay quarterly estimated taxes instead of having taxes deducted from my paychecks. Maybe that's a good thing or a bad thing. All I know is that I feel the "pain" of paying taxes, and I'm always on the lookout for credible, legal ways to lower my family's tax obligations.

Don't discount the importance of having an intelligent, strategic, and implemented tax strategy. A wise tax plan has the long-term potential to put tens of thousands and maybe even hundreds of thousands of dollars in a person's pocket. If doing taxes is not a personal strength, consider hiring a tax professional to help. Ask people for recommendations. This is money well worth spending and will save money in the long run.

Here's a good rule of thumb in dealing with tax strategies: use whatever tax strategies are available in a given year to reduce adjusted gross taxable income as low as possible. The goal is (hopefully) to move down into lower tax brackets and, of course, pay a lower percentage in taxes. This is exactly what wealthy people do. Perhaps, this is why they are wealthy?

In the book *How to Pay Zero Taxes 2015: Your Guide to Every Tax Break the IRS Allows* by Jeff Schnepper, the author writes the following:

> *Tax planning is not for the timid. The laws are constantly changing and you have to keep up to minimize your tax liability. You have to know the rules. That's what "How to Pay Zero Taxes" is for. If you don't know the rules, you can't win the game.*[xcvii]

Okay, let's talk deductions to move into those lower tax brackets. Here's a listing of various deductions to be aware of when using tax software or a tax professional to determine eligibility for the deductions. This is not a comprehensive list, but I've listed the biggest ones. I've also separated these by category. Most on this list I found through a GoBankingRates/TaxAct online article[xcviii] as well as from my own personal experience.

**Family Deductions:**
1. **Standard Deduction.** In 2014, single filers could deduct $6,200 from earned income, $12,400 for married couples filing jointly, and $9,100 for heads of households.
2. **Personal Exemptions.** You, your spouse and your kids all qualify as exemptions on your taxes unless someone else can claim them ahead of you (such as an ex-spouse, etc.). For the year 2014, you could claim $3,950 for each individual.
3. **Dependent Care Flex Spending.** If you take advantage of a FSA through your workplace, you can contribute up to $5,000 pre-tax toward dependent care expenses. As long as the expenses qualify, you won't be taxed on that money.
4. **Childcare Expenses.** If you don't use flex spending, you can still deduct childcare expenses on your tax forms. All deductible expenses must be necessary to keep you and/or your spouse employed.

**Home Deductions:** (You can only claim these deductions if you own your home and have a mortgage.)
1. **Mortgage Insurance Premiums Deduction.** If you itemize your taxes (and not do the EZ forms!), you may be able to deduct your PMI premiums paid on your home.
2. **Home Mortgage Interest.** If you itemize, then you can take this deduction.
3. **Mortgage Points.** If you itemize, then you can take this deduction on your primary residence.
4. **Points Paid on Home Improvement Loans.** If you itemize, then you may be able to take this deduction on points paid on a loan to improve your primary residence.

5. **Casualty, Disaster, and Theft Loss.** Any type of losses related to your home, items in your home, or vehicles that were not covered by insurance could be deductible.

## Taxes Paid Deductions:
1. **State and Local Real Estate Taxes.** If you itemize your tax forms, you may be able to deduct any local or state real estate taxes that you pay each year.
2. **State and Local Sales Tax.** You have the option to deduct either state and local income taxes or sales taxes. If you live in a state with no income tax, deduct sales taxes.
3. **Tax Preparation Fees.** If you paid someone to do your taxes or you purchased software to do it yourself, then you can deduct that expense on your tax form.
4. **Vehicle Registration Fees.** You may be able to deduct some vehicle registration fees based on the value of the vehicle. In my home state of Missouri, these are known as personal property taxes that we must pay each December on cars, trucks, SUV's, motorcycles, RV's, boats, and more.
5. **State Taxes Due.** If you were behind in your state taxes from a previous year, you may be eligible to deduct that money from your federal taxes.

## Non-Profit Donation Deductions:
1. **Cash Donations.** If you donate $250 or more to specific charities or non-profits that are IRS approved, you should receive a year-end statement listing your donations. If you itemize your taxes, then you can deduct these financial donations.
2. **Non-Cash Donations.** If you itemize, you can also deduct the fair market value of clothes and other household items that you donate. Be sure to keep receipts and pictures of the items that you donate each year.
3. **Unreimbursed Expenses for Charity Work.** If you use your vehicle to help a charity, you can take the standard mileage deduction ($.14/mile), plus any tolls or parking expenses. Be sure to keep some type of mileage log and any receipts.

### Education and Work Deductions:

1. **Tuition and Fees Deduction.** In the year 2014, you could deduct up to $4,000 in qualifying tuition and fees as long as you aren't claiming these expenses for another tax break.
2. **Student Loan Interest.** Any student loans you're paying on, you can deduct up to $2,500 of interest paid on those loans in the year 2014.
3. **Job Search Expenses.** If you itemize, then there are certain expenses you can deduct if you conduct a job search in your current career in a given year. Keep logs and receipts.
4. **Moving Expenses.** Similar to #3, if you have to move to take a new job position, you may be eligible to deduct certain expenses if you meet certain IRS qualifications. Again, keep good detailed logs and receipts.
5. **Military Reserves Travel Expenses.** For those who serve in the military reserves and need to travel more than 100 miles from home to serve, you can deduct certain travel expenses. Keep good records.

### Medical Deductions:

1. **Some Medical and Dental Expenses.** This would be a somewhat unusual situation, but after you pay out certain percentages (7.5 - 10% based on age and income) on health care expenses in a given year, then you may be eligible to deduct expenses beyond those amounts.
2. **Health Savings Account (HSA) Contributions.** Not everyone can take advantage of an HSA. If you can, though, do it. Then, assuming you contribute pre-tax to your HSA, you will receive pre-tax savings on your healthcare money. HSA's are much better than FSA's because you don't have to spend all the money each year. Even if you don't use it all, you won't lose it. You can let this money build up in your HSA account. Speaking from our own personal experience, my wife and I have had an HSA for the last three years. We use ours as an extra layer of emergency funds for

medical expenses. We have definitely experienced the financial benefits they give to the "average" family.

**Business Deductions:**
1. **Business Use of Your Home.** If you employ many of the strategies contained in Part Two of this book, I would encourage you to form a business, either a Sole Proprietorship or better yet, an LLC. Carve out some space in your home to serve as a home office to take care of business and then you can deduct certain expenses as result. Win-win!
2. **Business Use of Your Car.** Be sure to keep good mileage logs and receipts to use this deduction.
3. **Business Travel Expenses.** Again, keep good records to take advantage of any potential tax savings.
4. **Self-Employed Health Insurance.** If you are self-employed having to buy your own coverage for medical and dental, then you can deduct premiums paid for you and your family on your taxes.

**Investing Deductions:**
1. **Investment Fees and Expenses.** Fees paid to manage investments that generate taxable income are deductible.
2. **IRA Contributions.** In the year 2014, it was possible to deduct for IRA contributions up to $5,500 to $6,500, depending on age.
3. **Safe Deposit Box Rental Fees.** You can deduct the cost if you use a safe deposit box for storing important paperwork related to your investments.

Here are some final thoughts outside of the realm of year-to-year tax deductions. When nearing retirement, around age 55, consider long-term strategies regarding taxes. It is best to be in a decent tax position when in retirement age and taking certain disbursements from retirement accounts. Consider what tax bracket is best once this all takes place. Also, consider what role Social Security plays into retirement as well. Retirement tax planning strategies should be discussed with a professional who could potentially help a retired person save a lot of money. Talk with people who have already gone through the process of maximizing their tax situation for retirement planning. Find out what tax professionals they have used. Never pay more to the government than should be paid!

*Quick Tip: For a FREE list of the Action Steps and Resources for each chapter of the book, simply go to:* [http://www.heroicpersonalfinances.com/for-christians-book-action-steps/](http://www.heroicpersonalfinances.com/for-christians-book-action-steps/)

# CHAPTER 9
# STOCK MARKET INVESTING: PART 1

"Invest in seven ventures, yes, in eight;
you do not know what disaster may come upon the land."
– Ecclesiastes 11:2 NIV[xcix]

"I will tell you how to become rich. Close the doors. Be fearful when others are greedy. Be greedy when others are fearful."
– Warren Buffett

I recently ran across the following story online that gives a humorous explanation on how the stock market works.

*Once upon a time in a village, a man appeared and announced to the villagers that he would buy monkeys for $10.*

*The villagers seeing that there were many monkeys around, went out to the forest and started catching them. The man bought thousands at $10, and as supply started to diminish, the villagers stopped their effort. He further announced that he would now buy at $20. This renewed the efforts of the villagers and they started catching monkeys again.*

*Soon the supply diminished even further and people started going back to their farms. The offer rate increased to $25, and the supply of monkeys became so little that it was an effort to even see a monkey, let alone catch it! The man now announced that he would buy monkeys at $50! However, since he had to go to the city on some business, his assistant would now buy on behalf of him.*

*In the absence of the man, the assistant told the villagers. Look at all these monkeys in the big cage that the man has collected. I will sell them to you at $35 and when the man returns from the city, you can sell it to him for $50.*

*The villagers squeezed up with all their savings and bought all the monkeys. Then they never saw the man nor his assistant, only monkeys everywhere!! !*
*Welcome to the 'Stock' Market!*[c]

In Financial Peace University™, once you complete Baby Step 3, three to six months of expense money in savings, you move on to Baby Step 4, invest 15 percent. Dave and the Ramsey Solutions team give you the basic investing rule of "invest 15 percent of your household income into Roth IRAs and pre-tax retirement plans."

Dave Ramsey and retirement investment advice. In the opinion of many, this is not his strongest area of expertise in the world of personal finance. In an online Motley Fool article by Brian Stoffel titled "Criticizing Financial Guru Dave Ramsey for This Advice Misses the Point Entirely: While his investing advice is suspect, naysayers are ignoring the bigger picture on debt reduction," Brian writes:

*Dave Ramsey and I have a brief— but very colorful—history with each another [sic]. Back in 2013, I penned an article on why I considered some of his retirement advice to be dangerous. Specifically, I called him out for telling investors to expect a 12 percent return on their investments using a metric (average annual return) he knows isn't suited to make such predictions. (It should instead be the compounded annual growth rate, or CAGR, that is used, and is just over 9 percent historically, since 1871.)*

*He had me on his radio show to discuss the article. It wasn't pretty. In fact, a lot of ink was spilled afterwards [sic] based on the interaction.*

*I followed up with an article showing how following Ramsey's retirement advice would give you a 50 percent chance of running out of money by age ninety. Finance expert Felix Salmon reached much the same conclusion in a piece for Money Magazine.*

*Suffice it to say, then, that I don't shed too many tears when I read others' thoughtful disagreements with Ramsey's investing advice*[i] ...

While I agree people should all be saving and investing wisely for retirement, I have my own concerns about the current stock market system. Based on the investment pyramid discussed earlier in the book, consider the stock market as speculative investing. There is too much emotional trading that takes place. That's why all these wild swings have taken place in the market for the last few years.

Limiting stock market investing is somewhat of a "Catch-22," though. The goal is for money to be "working hard" and generating more and more money for retirement. But, it's also important to shield as much income as possible from taxes. Or, in the case of the Roth IRA, paying taxes up front (maybe a better approach), and growing this invested money tax-free.

In this chapter, I will share about investing in the stock market. Many who are employed with companies, non-profits, or the government have the potential of receiving FREE money for retirement investing through employer matching.

## 401(k)s and 403(b)s

Dave gives a simplistic sketch in Financial Peace University of investing in employer plans such as 401(k)s, 403(b)s, Keogh plans, and Thrift Savings Plans. Quick research performed on these retirement options reveal they all have several issues that should be considered. In fact, the more I read about them, the more I question the wisdom of putting the majority of my retirement money into any of these plans. As I have already mentioned at the beginning of Part Two, Brady and Woodward place stock market investing at the top of the investment pyramid. They consider it risky. Their advice is to put a small percentage of retirement savings money into these plans. Here are several concerns I see in these types of stock market retirement plans:

First, these retirement vehicles are all relatively new options. As I was doing research on 401(k)s and 403(b)s for this chapter, I was reminded how "new" these plans are in historical terms. The legislation that created these retirement arrangements dates back to 1978. At the time of this writing, we are approaching the 40th anniversary when these plans were added to the tax code. The youngest employees who took advantage of the tax code with the 401(k) or 403(b) are now entering retirement age. Performance reviews for the last 38 years are mixed for these types of retirement plans.

Second, I have a tendency to be a little suspicious of anything the government "creates" for the so-called benefit of the people. I realize this sounds paranoid and borderline conspiracy theorist, but ask the question: when has the government acted in the best interest of the people it serves? There's always a political angle in policy and legislation somewhere. I would say the likelihood of these retirement accounts benefiting the government more than the people is pretty high.

Third, there are many who are concerned that the US Government could tax these plans out of existence or worse, confiscate them outright. This has already been attempted in some European nations experiencing financial problems such as Ireland, France, Hungary, Bulgaria, and Poland. Would the United States government outright take privately held retirement money? Probably not, because it would be political suicide for career politicians, but it's well known that they are very aware of the huge pool of money that is currently sitting in private citizens' retirement accounts. As the government continues to struggle financially, these accounts become even more attractive to out-of-control bureaucrats.

Fourth, the plans offered by companies typically are not quality plans. There are limited options in which to invest money. At the end of the day, this means earning potential is lower than if a person has complete control and more options in which to invest.

Fifth, because these are stock market based plans, there is the potential for a lot of volatility. My 403(b) is a decent mix of moderately conservative to semi-aggressive right now. At the time that I'm writing these chapters in the fall of 2015 and early months of 2016, the Dow has been taking several hundred point drops one day, and then several hundred point swings back up the next day. I can see these swings reflected as I daily track my retirement account. I have gotten to the point that I am doubting my retirement planning strategy. For the last several years, I have had my 403(b) allocated in funds according to what Dave teaches in FPU. In Lesson 7 on Retirement and College Planning, Dave advises structuring retirement accounts in the following way: 25 percent in Growth (Mid Cap), 25 percent in Growth and Income (Large Cap), 25 percent in Aggressive Growth (Small Cap), and 25 percent in International. My 403(b) is set-up like this allocation. The only modification I made was to only place 10 percent in Small Cap, since this is the highest risk investment. The remaining 15 percent I placed in Real Estate Securities (REITs) because I wanted to have the option of investing real money in real estate without owning a property outright, at least up to this point in my investing experience.

*Quick Tip: Due to my concerns with the stock market roller coaster ride in late 2015 into early 2016, I began a journey of investment research especially in the area of bond funds. As a result, I ended up changing my entire approach to both my wife's and my retirement accounts. I'll address this new allocation in Chapter 12.*

Because of these five concerns, I believe there are some better investing strategies that should be considered. But 401(k) or 403(b) investing is still step one of many in investment planning.

Before continuing in this area of stock market investing, let me remind readers that I am not a certified financial planner. I'm just a guy that has gotten out of a lot of debt on two separate occasions, coordinated Financial Peace University classes, and read hundreds of personal finance books. In fact, this book is a synthesis of my own personal experience and research. I'm going to write things in the following chapters on investing that run counter to traditional retirement advice. I could be 100 percent wrong on this advice. Please, don't take my word for it. Read and research before attempting any strategy. Consult with professionals. My goal in this book is to expand my readers' thinking on potential financial strategies they may not have ever heard about or considered.

### Start Here, Then Stop!

Step 1 in retirement planning should be to take advantage of employer matches in the company 401(k) or non-profit 403(b), and then stop here for a while on stock market investing. Wisdom would seem to say if "free money" is being offered in the form of a match, that money should be matched and saved for retirement.

In my experience, most companies match in the 2–3 percent range, so even if that limited amount is matched, it shouldn't break the bank. Plus, this money will be tax-deferred, anyway. The impact won't be felt too much in family finances. Taking the match will at least be a step toward saving for retirement—around 6 percent (3 percent employer, 3 employee) of personal income. This is a great starting point for wealth building.

So, once an employer has matched funds, what's next? Step 1: investigate available investing choices. Employer 401(k) or 403(b) will have a certain number of limited options through an investment company such as Fidelity, Vanguard, or Charles Schwab. Take inventory on how to invest this retirement money.

Step 2: Look for any and all possible index funds to invest in. In Chapter 12, I'll give solid, concrete reasons regarding why index funds are a superior product over mutual funds. For now, just be on the lookout for good index funds to invest workplace retirement accounts.

Step 3: Find index funds in the four categories that Dave Ramsey recommends: International, Large Cap, Mid-Cap, and Small Cap.

Step 4: invest 25 percent of all incoming money into each of these four categories of index funds.

Step 5: Be sure to set-up investments to automatically rebalance portfolios each year. If not, these four categories will become more and more unbalanced over time due to changes in the market. Annual rebalancing will keep each category around 25 percent.

Step 6: More conservative investors than Dave Ramsey might consider different options then this 4-slices-of-the-pie or 25 percent each. Adding bonds and cash equivalents to an investment mix might be a better option. I'll discuss these additional options in more detail in Chapter 12, Stock Market Investing: Part Two. For example, the two categories in the Dave Ramsey pie that carry the most risk are international funds and aggressive growth funds. To minimize risk, consider the following investment breakdown:

- 25 percent in Growth and Income Funds
- 25 percent in Growth Funds
- 15 percent in International Funds
- 15 percent in Aggressive Growth Funds.
- 20 percent in Bond Funds

*Quick Tip: This could be a good investment allocation for a younger person in their 20s or early 30s.*

Or, consider another more conservative breakdown that looks like this:

- 20 percent in Growth and Income Funds
- 20 percent in Growth Funds
- 10 percent in International Funds
- 10 percent in Aggressive Growth Funds.
- 40 percent in Bond Funds

*Quick Tip: This could be a good investment allocation for someone in their 40s.*

I am personally not convinced that a simplistic retirement plan of "invest 15 percent of your income in these four ways" as taught by Dave in FPU is the best approach. I think there are some better strategies available to us in planning for retirement. But, if a company is offering "free money" through an employer match, take the match and stop there for now in stock market investing—and come back to stock market investing depending on the other investment strategies available.

I might sound totally crazy (and I probably am!) in proposing such a low level of initial stock market investing. If so, consider the following alternative investing strategy. Invest up to 10 percent of total income into a conservative allocation as I proposed above. This would still be less than Dave's proposed 15 percent. Then, a person has the option to take the remaining 5 percent and invest this money in a personal business or other investment strategies I will discuss in the next two chapters.

My overriding concern regarding investing is falling into a perceived FPU mindset of "keep working your J-O-B, and invest 15 percent into Dave's four-part allocation." According to Dave, this will result in a "12 percent return from the stock market and the ability to retire with millions of dollars in the bank, all because you did it his way." In a perfect world, maybe, but I have serious doubts that is going to happen in today's tumultuous economic climate. Most experts say that a 12 percent return statistic is a pipe dream and not reality. Historic stock market returns are more in the 9 percent range over the long term.

In the next few chapters, I will explore a different investing mindset—one that includes investment choices offering safer, more consistent returns than stock market index funds.

*Quick Tip: For a FREE list of the Action Steps and Resources for each chapter of the book, simply go to:* [http://www.heroicpersonalfinances.com/for-christians-book-action-steps/](http://www.heroicpersonalfinances.com/for-christians-book-action-steps/)

## CHAPTER 10
## PUT YOUR MONEY TO WORK LIKE BANKS, INSURANCE COMPANIES, AND THE WEALTHY

"The Lord will open the heavens, the storehouse of his bounty, to send rain on your land in season and to bless all the work of your hands. ***You will lend to many nations but will borrow from none***. The Lord will make you the head, not the tail. If you pay attention to the commands of the Lord your God that I give you this day and carefully follow them, ***you will always be at the top, never at the bottom***."
– Deuteronomy 28:12-13 NIV,[cii] *Emphasis mine*

"If you want to continue to be slaves of the bankers and pay for the cost of your own slavery, allow them to continue to create money and control credit.'"
– Josiah Stamp, Former Director of the Bank of England

Remember the classic game of monopoly? If so, think of a favorite token to play—the dog, thimble, top hat, iron, or race car. My dad always liked to play the dog, and my two younger brothers and I always fought over who would get to play the race car. The best role to play in the game of Monopoly, however, could be the banker. The banker has a few advantages over the other players. The investors (the primary game players) have their set of rules. The banker has his own set of rules that are advantageous in the game of money. The same is true in real life. The banks make all the rules for people as consumers, producers, and investors.

In the online article *Re-Thinking the Game of Monopoly* writer K. Mike Merrill says this about Monopoly and banking:

*In the original rules the role of the banker is simply a chore—the board game equivalent of taking out the trash. But in real life the banker is no passive entity. The banker is the center of the universe.*

*The Libor scandal, the UBS money laundering scandal, the SAC Capital scandal,*

*FINRA suing Wells Fargo and Bank of America, TD Bank paying to settle charges of a ponzi scheme, Galleon Group's insider trading scandal. This list could go on. The point is that banking is exciting work!*

*The role of the banker is special. The banker should have no piece on the Monopoly board, but this person is in charge of the bank's money. The success of the banker is judged the same as any other player: Whoever accumulates the most wealth is the winner. Of course, as in life, the banker has some advantages (like control of all the money).[ciii]*

Think about the following two questions for a moment. First: what are some of the wealthiest institutions in this country? Second: who are some of the wealthiest people?

The institutions that are the wealthiest tend to be in the financial services industry, such as banks and insurance companies. They know how to put money to work to achieve the greatest leverage. Banks can borrow money at low-interest rates (using their customers checking and savings deposits that pay low interest), and then charge much higher interest rates as they loan it back out in the form of credit cards, auto loans, and home loans. Banks also make a lot of money through high bank fees from bounced checks and overdrafts because many people don't know how to manage their personal finances. It pays well to be the bank.

Being in the position of a real-life bank is a great place to be. The bank sets all the financial rules. The bank can create more money. The bank has the cash flow. Banks and insurance companies put their money to work at the lowest levels of risk. When the majority of a person's money is in high risk, stock market investments, they are gambling with retirement savings. Banks and insurance companies don't take that bet. The key to making money with money is to diversify investments at lower levels of risk, and at the same time maximizing return.

I recently read an article about former Federal Reserve chairman Ben Bernanke and his own personal investment strategy. Before he could become the Fed chairman, Mr. Bernanke had to disclose his investments. Interestingly enough, his disclosure showed that he held only a few stocks and bonds. The majority of his money was held in annuities (I will dig into annuities a bit later in this chapter). Here we have one of the most influential men in finance, and even he doesn't ride the roller coaster of the stock market. Hmm, he must know a bunch of financial stuff that the general population doesn't. He's running his finances much differently than the majority of Americans and contrary to the "invest 15 percent in good growth stock mutual funds" approach. Perhaps there is a better way.

The wealthiest people and institutions around the world understand these principles. Bill Gates is the wealthiest man on the planet today, and his wealth is growing exponentially each year, even after giving more money away. For example, in the fall of 2014, Gates was worth almost $82 billion, which was actually $6 billion wealthier than the year before. Now, here's the kicker. In the same year his money grew, he also gave away $38 billion to his charitable foundation, the Bill and Melinda Gates Foundation. The only way this is possible is by putting money to work and making more and more money. Bill Gates hires intelligent people to put his billions to work in smarter investment strategies such as real estate and non-tech companies like the Canadian National Railway Co., AutoNation Inc., and Republic Services Inc.[civ] Again, this is an example of wealthy, intelligent people investing their money with a different, better strategy then what other money experts talk about.

This chapter will explore a few strategies to put money to work that perhaps might be new information. Before diving into a world of exciting financial possibilities, I just want to remind readers that I am not a trained financial expert, especially in the areas of insurance and tax law. Please take the information I share in this chapter as that—basic information. Buyer beware. Take time to research and perform due diligence on the concepts I mention in putting money to work like a bank. At the end of this chapter, I will recommend several books to read and website links to check out on the various methods of putting money to work. Please take the time to read and ponder the information shared in these resources before pulling the trigger on any of these suggestions. In this chapter, I will share my own positive and negative research. I encourage my readers to do their own research in these areas. Don't take my word as gospel truth.

### Maybe We Should Worship At The Altar Of The Great FICO®?

In early 2015, I asked a real estate agent friend of mine (I'll call him "Joe") out to lunch to discuss a couple of items. One of the main topics I wanted to speak with him about was buying a home. My wife and I were gearing up to be homeowners, once again. We wanted to use him as our agent when we were ready to get out and look at properties. We had gone through a period of ten years where we had both been renting to pay off a sizable amount of debt. That debt was paid off by October 2014. Now we were furiously saving for a down payment to make a home purchase by summer or fall of 2015. We were tired of renting and ready to put down roots in the community for our family.

As we discussed more details, I explained to Joe one challenge we might have in a future home mortgage application is that I did not have a credit score at all. I have been doing all the Dave Ramsey, Financial Peace University™ stuff religiously over the last decade. My credit score looked like Dave's score— FICO® can't calculate one, just as if I were deceased!

Although I don't believe Joe operates his personal finances according to the seven Baby Steps, he is very much aware of the credit score issue as taught by Dave and his team. Joe wishes that Dave wouldn't press the credit card/credit score thing so hard with his debt-free disciples because it does cause problems when applying for home mortgages.

So, within a couple of days of having lunch with Joe, I went online and applied for a couple of credit cards I wouldn't have any difficulty getting approval. I received the cards in the mail within a week or two. After receiving them, I established my online accounts on both cards and set up auto pay for the entire balance each billing cycle. I gave my wife one of the two cards, and we only use them to make purchases that we need to make on a regular basis such as gas for our cars or online purchases that we would be making with our debit cards anyway.

*Quick Tip: Set-up credit card usage for success by doing the following: first, create an online account as soon as you receive the card; second, turn on auto pay for each billing cycle and be sure to have the card balance pay off automatically each cycle; third, use credit cards for "regular" purchases that normally on debit cards anyway (such as buying gas at the pump).*

Within a month or two of using these two new credit cards, my credit score went from "can't calculate" to 740, which is in the lower range of excellent. Fortunately for me, I had only been off the credit rating grid for about seven years. I believe this helped me quickly boost my score back up.

If it had been longer than a full ten years, I believe I would have had more difficulty re-establishing my credit.

Because I listened to the advice of my real estate agent, my wife and I had no difficulty getting a quality, conventional home loan with the lender of our choice. Now, let me say that I do understand why people such as Dave and others out there don't like the whole FICO® "I love debt" score. I hate it too. I wish banks and other institutions would do a more thorough investigation into someone's finances than just pressing a few buttons to get a score number. Some lending institutions will do manual underwriting, and that's fantastic. The majority won't, though.

In today's world, this is how the financial system currently works. Even in the "macro" economic world, there is an emphasis placed on nations to have a good credit rating. Recall a few years ago when the media made a big deal about the United States credit rating being lowered by Standard and Poor's. Nations rely on good ratings to deal with their debt issues. Banks and other financial institutions also rely on their own quality credit ratings to do business each day. If credit ratings are a big deal for nations and banks, then maybe everyday people need to reconsider their stance on credit ratings when it comes to personal finances?

I wish Dave all the best in changing that system; fighting it opens up the possibility of running into problems in personal finances. Manipulating the system to achieve what is needed is the only other option. I'm not on a crusade like Dave is. My solution was to re-establish my credit score responsibly with two credit cards, paying for only those things that my family buys on a regular basis anyway, and then turn on automatic bill pay so that those funds are automatically drafted out of our checking account. We've done this for over a year now with no difficulties.

I do understand the other side of the credit card/FICO® score debate. There are many people who cannot handle credit cards responsibly. If personal discipline is a problem, then these people need to close all their accounts, strive to be completely debt free, and not worry about their credit rating. Our home buying experience caused me to re-evaluate the whole credit score issue. Perhaps worshipping at the altar of the great FICO® is necessary?

## Bank On Yourself: The Infinite Banking Concept

Many personal finance experts make it clear that they hate whole life insurance products. They encourage everyone to buy term life insurance and then invest the difference normally paid for a whole life policy. I get it. I understand most of the reasoning behind the debate.

When I first heard about the whole versus term life insurance debate around 2004, I immediately bought a decent amount of term life insurance to protect my family. Then, I turned around and canceled my variable universal life (VUL) policy that I had been suckered into by a "friend" and his buddy life insurance guy a few years earlier. I was too ignorant back then and didn't understand the various forms of life insurance. I had no clue on "good" and "bad" forms of life insurance. Fast forward a few years. I now have in place a newer, larger, quality, twenty-year term life policy. I have peace of mind knowing my wife, four daughters, and son will have the resources they need if something happens to me.

A few years after buying this latest term policy, I ran across several books and blogs recommending a new financial product (which is really an older way of doing life insurance) called the Infinite Banking Concept (IBC). The basic idea behind IBC is the reality that most American families will finance large ticket items such as cars, college, and homes. When financing these items through conventional banking methods, borrowers are throwing away thousands of dollars in interest that they could be recapturing for their own personal benefit. When properly set up, an IBC utilizes a form of permanent, whole life insurance to create a personal "bank" of money to borrow from, that also has some tax advantages tied to it (assuming that the Federal government doesn't mess with these policies in the future).

Let me say upfront that I currently do not have an IBC. At the time of my writing this book, I'm still in the research and investigation phase. My first impression after reading several books and web articles on IBC is that the concept and its application in this way are intriguing. The idea of building up a storehouse of wealth over several years in which the person, in theory, becomes his or her own bank seems rather ingenious to me. But, because I have heard the whole Dave Ramsey rant on whole versus term life insurance for so long, it has taken me a while to process the concept.

*Quick Tip: If healthy and relatively young (30s to 40s), I would still consider having a term policy in place for 20 to 25 years at the level of 10 to 15X one's annual income, even if deciding to go with an IBC policy. For the money (rates are inexpensive), I think it's a great layer of added protection for a person's family while working through Baby Steps and building up assets.*

In the article "My History With IBC," economist Robert P. Murphy, Ph.D. addresses the problems that Dave brings up about whole life policies:

*… Dave Ramsey is a radio talk show host who (admirably) counsels people on how to get out from their crushing debt load, through obvious but crucial things like making out a budget, communicating with one's spouse on financial affairs, etc. Ramsey is very entertaining and I can certainly understand why his show is so popular. However, Ramsey absolutely has it out for whole life (and other types of permanent life insurance) policies, advocating instead that people "buy term and invest the difference." For example, in a post from his website, Ramsey implies that you won't have any cash value for the first three years of a new policy. He goes on to explicitly say that the rate of return on your money is much higher in mutual funds, that you won't need life insurance after 20 years if you follow his plan, and that the insurance company keeps your cash values when you die, giving your beneficiary only the death benefit.*

*Every one of these (typical) objections is either misleading or downright false, at least when it comes to Nelson Nash's IBC approach of using whole life policies. First, if you set up the policy properly with a "Paid Up Additions (PUA) rider," then right off the bat, a portion of your periodic payment is buying a chunk of fully paid-up life insurance. Thus, your cash value begins rising immediately, and you can begin borrowing against your policy right away (if you need to).*

*As far as comparing rates of return, again the problem is that Ramsey is viewing permanent life insurance as an investment, rather than a cash flow management strategy. Yet even if we use the standard tools of financial analysis, it is a non-sequitur to point out that a mutual fund is expected to have a higher 30-year (say) average annualized rate of return, compared to the internal rate of return on an insurance policy's projected cash value growth. Such a bald statement ignores the difference in risk between the two strategies. (Whole life insurance policies have guaranteed minimum rates of return. Do equity-based mutual funds have that?) Ramsey could just as easily "prove" that nobody should ever buy a corporate bond, because stock issued from the same company will always have a higher expected return ...*

*By making these comments, I'm not "proving" that more life insurance is always the best thing to buy, from a conventional "asset class" allocation perspective; otherwise we would have the absurd result that everybody should put every last dollar of his wealth into life insurance policies, with nobody owning stocks, bonds, real estate, or precious metals. (Obviously somebody has to own a share of corporate stock or a piece of real estate, and that ownership must be voluntary. So their prices adjust to make it attractive for someone to acquire and hold.) All I'm making is the modest point that in Ramsey's critique of whole life and related insurance policies—when he compares them very unfavorably with "buy term and invest the difference in mutual funds"—he isn't even attempting to set up an apples-to-apples comparison of the two strategies. He's pulling one set of statistics—internal rates of return—out of context and trumpeting them as if they're decisive, when the actual situation is much more nuanced.*[cv]

When IBC policyholders take out a policy loan to personally finance large sums of money, they must set up terms of repayment with interest. The purpose of repayment with interest is in order for the policy to generate the benefits of the storehouse of wealth system. The good news here is that policy owners are paying themselves back with interest. They are able to bypass the greedy, overpaid executives in the large corporate banks in New York City. This is the beauty of IBC.

As I continue doing research on IBC over the last several months, I've been asking myself a bunch of "what if" questions such as:

- What if I established an IBC, let that policy mature for a few years, build up a storehouse of wealth, and then put this money to work creating more streams of income that create more streams of income?
- What if took out a policy loan for a decent amount of money, used it as a down payment for a bargain rental property, and started some new streams of income this way?
- What if I took out a policy loan to buy an existing business that had decent cash flow to it already?
- What if I used a policy loan to do some peer-to-peer lending?

I do see the potential to use an IBC as a personal storehouse of wealth to create even more wealth. This money could be put to work at higher interest percentage rates and create multiple streams of income. My own next step in the process is to speak directly to a trained professional in setting up an IBC policy.

Here are some of the core details of what I understand about the Infinite Banking Concept. First, the policy (or policies—multiples can be set up for family members) must be established in **mutual insurance companies**. Second, these policies are not the "run of the mill" whole life policies. They are a very specific, specialty product: high-premium, dividend-paying, whole life insurance policies. Third, <u>seek out trained professionals who know the specific mutual insurance companies as well as the technicalities to set up an IBC properly.</u> Check out the resources at the end of this chapter to find these professionals. Fourth, it will take a few years (perhaps 3 to 5) of premium payments to establish a policy in a position to be a storehouse of wealth. There are methods to speed up the cash value of a policy to tap into these benefits earlier than this. I recommend speaking with a certified professional in IBC to uncover all the many options.

Fifth, when requesting a policy loan, it is just a matter of filling out a form to request the money—and it will be available in a few days. The insurance company won't ask a bunch of personal financial questions or check credit scores like most lending institutions. The insurance company administers and guarantees the value of the collateral. The company actually doesn't even care if you repay the policy loan. They will simply deduct that amount from the cash value/death benefit of the policy. But, the policyholder cares if it's repaid, because repayment with the terms chosen accelerates the growth of the policy. Sixth, an IBC policy shouldn't be viewed as an investment vehicle. It should be viewed as a cash flow management strategy with many unique benefits. Seven, creating an IBC policy (or policies) in a family is a way to move away from the corrupt, fiat money system of a central bank. It creates a personal privatized banking system. This is the key distinction and benefit of the IBC. Conventional, commercial banks create money "out of thin air" as well as create all sorts of national financial problems. A privatized banking system such as IBC is based on actual cash values created within the policy.

Next, let's take a look at another method of behaving like bankers through the process of making money with money by lending to others.

## Peer-to-Peer Lending

Although financial lending between individuals has been around since the dawn of time, there are many exciting opportunities available to us today to leverage money with technology just like banks do. The modern day form of peer-to-peer lending began in the United States with the launch of Prosper (Prosper.com) in February 2006. A similar company called Lending Club (LendingClub.com) followed shortly after. Companies such as Prosper and Lending Club had several struggles in the first few years of their existence. Today, though, these companies are prospering (no pun intended, really!) as more people have accepted the practice of lending their money or borrowing other people's money through online websites. In my limited personal research and knowledge into this topic, I have come to understand that Lending Club is the superior of the two web-based companies. The primary reason Lending Club is better is because there is greater potential to make higher rates of interest on money. When I'm ready to dive into peer-to-peer lending, I will definitely start my journey with Lending Club. Based on that fact alone, I will focus the rest of this section on what I have learned about this one company.

Most peer-to-peer loans are unsecured personal loans. There is a risk to this type of financial investing. Depending on how one invests in these loans, though, risk can be minimized and returns maximized. This is the same way that banks operate when doing personal, auto, and home loans. They assess the potential borrower's financial situation through filling out paperwork. They run a credit check. They determine the percentage chance that the borrower will ever miss a payment and default on the loan. Banks take risks loaning out money to the least risky individuals possible. They follow the golden rule of investing: *never lose money!*

Peer-to-peer lending companies such as Lending Club not only assess their potential borrowers for their creditworthiness, but they also grade them for their financial risk in lending them money. The best and least risky borrowers receive a score of A1 and are able to borrow the most money at a lower interest rate. The riskiest borrowers receive a rating of G5 and are able to borrow the least amount of money at the highest interest rate.

Peer-to-peer lending is an "easy" way to make money with money, without the volatility of the stock market. My initial research into peer-to-peer lending is telling me to get in as soon as I can.

*Quick Tip: Most investing experts agree that peer-to-peer lending investing is considered a medium-term investing strategy. 401(k)s, 403(b)s, and IRAs focus more on long-term investment strategy. But a peer-to-peer lending investing strategy could be good for medium term purchase planning such as cars, college, and weddings.*

There are a couple of different ways to invest money in a company such as Lending Club. First, plug into one of their pre-produced investment packages. They do all the work upfront, kind of like investing in a Lifecycle Fund such as the Fidelity Freedom Fund 2035.[cvi] These pre-produced investment packages range from super safe to ultra-risky depending on risk tolerance.

The recommended approach by experts in peer-to-peer lending is to pick out each individual loan using a strict set of criteria. Then, diversify investments in each of these loans by spreading the money out in small, $25.00 investments.

The challenge with investing in individual loans on these websites is that there is the real potential that some of these loans will go bad. The borrower may be unable to completely repay the loan. This is why experts recommend screening these loans on important criteria, and then only investing a small amount in each loan. This is a similar strategy the majority of people are already doing with stock market-based retirement plans.

When assessing borrowers and potential loans to invest in, here are a few criteria to follow. Set these as filters on the Lending Club website while searching for loans to invest in:

1. **Loan Purpose:** Look for traditional-type purpose loans such as home, auto, etc. Other non-traditional loans such as renewal energy loans, small business loans, and education loans are a higher risk because the default rate is over 5 percent on these loans. It would be wiser to steer clear of these.
2. **Review Status:** Look for loans that are already approved. Don't speculate on borrowers who are still in the approval process.

3. **Credit Score:** the recommendation is to filter out anyone lower than a 679 credit rating. Lower scores than this result in a higher default percentage.
4. **Max Debt-to-Income Ratio:** The best borrowers who are least likely to default on their loans are in the 15 percent to 34 percent debt-to-income ratio.
5. **Inquiries in the Last Six Months:** Use this filter to find borrowers who aren't on any kind of credit binge/spending spree. Look for loans in which the borrowers have less than three credit inquiries in the last six months.
6. **Months Since Last Delinquency:** It would be wise to select borrowers who have at least a period of thirty-six months since their last delinquency. Again, this is an attempt to minimize the chance of ending up with a loan in which the borrower will default.
7. **Public Records:** Use this filter to screen out any borrowers with any public records on their credit report such as judgments, foreclosures, lawsuits, tax liens, and past-due child support.
8. **Exclude Loans Already Invested In:** Use this filter to screen out any loans already invested in. It's best not to have too much money in one loan. Diversification is key when investing in peer-to-peer lending.

There are other filters available on Lending Club. These eight are the key filters to check first, however, to avoid investing in some risky loans. The goal in using this filters is to lower the loan default rate (the average is 3.33 percent) and maximize the interest rate (the average is 12.55 percent). Hitting the sweet spot between these two key criteria will earn a healthy rate of return on a peer-to-peer investment strategy.

I could write even more on the subject, but this section of the chapter is meant to be a broad overview. An eBook I found extremely informative as I was doing my research is called *How to Profit from Peer-to-Peer Lending - Earn 9% to 33% with Small Loans,* by Scott Todd.[cvii] Scott seems knowledgeable and experienced with this type of investing. This book is on Amazon.com. Check it out!

## Tax Deeds and Tax Lien Certificates

Banks put money to work. This is how they make money, and they're good at it. The bank takes people's money. They offer them a tiny percentage rate of interest to place their money into a savings account. Then, they invest that money in other creative, higher percentage paying ways. In doing my research on tax liens, this is a product that banks DO like to invest people's money in. Based on the premise of putting money to work like banks do, tax lien certificates must be a secure investment with a decent rate of return. Like any financial product, there are positives and negatives to tax liens.

Let's back up a minute and define what a tax lien certificate is. According to Investopedia,[cviii] a tax lien certificate is "a certificate of claim against property that has a lien placed upon it as a result of unpaid property taxes. Tax lien certificates are generally sold to investors by most counties and municipalities in the United States through an auction process. Subsequent to a winning bid made by an investor for a specific tax lien certificate, a lien is placed on the property and a certificate issued to the investor detailing the outstanding taxes and penalties on the property. The tax lien certificate, therefore, enables the investor to collect unpaid taxes plus the prevailing rate of interest applicable to such certificates, which can range from eight to more than 30 percent, depending on the jurisdiction. The term of tax lien certificates typically ranges from one to three years."[cix]

Let me pause here and mention that not every state, county, or municipality do tax liens as a result of unpaid property taxes. Many states are "tax lien states," while others are "tax deed states." What's the difference between states that operate with tax liens versus tax deeds? Great question!

A tax lien is a lien against the property that takes precedence over any and all other liens against the property. When buying a tax lien, the buyer has an interest in that property, but still does not own the property . . . at least not yet. Buying tax deeds, though, is a different story. A tax deed according to Investopedia is defined as "a legal document that grants ownership of a property to a government body when the property owner does not pay the taxes due on the property. A tax deed gives the government the authority to sell the property to collect the delinquent taxes and transfer the property to the purchaser. Such sales are called 'tax deed sales' and are usually held as auctions where the minimum bid is the amount of back taxes and fees owed."[cx] When a tax deed is purchased, the buyer owns the property at a steep discount. Now, there are some rules surrounding many tax deeds such as a right of redemption of the previous property owner. It's not always super clean and easy to buy tax deeds. There are specific rules and laws for each county and state in which they are bought.

Based on my initial research, there seem to be several positive aspects to investing in tax liens or deeds. First, there exists the potential to achieve a high rate of return on money (anywhere between 8 to 36 percent) outside the roller coaster of the stock market. Second, the investment is secured by real estate. Third, there are no "third party fees" associated with tax liens or deeds. Buyers buy direct from the local government at the auction. Fourth, a lot of upfront money isn't necessary to get started in these investments. Fifth, a high credit score isn't needed, nor a special account to get started. Buyers don't even need to be a US citizens to invest. Sixth, there are some online options to buy tax liens. Seven, a self-directed IRA can be used to invest in tax liens.

On the flip side, there are some drawbacks to investing in tax liens and deeds.

First, it's important to do some homework on these properties. There's no showing up at an auction and plunking down some cash for a winning investment every time. If it were only that easy! Based on my research up to this point, ample investigation on the front end will help prevent bad investments.

Second, the buyer must stay current on property taxes each year. If not, the result may be a lien against the lien. The buyer must remain current on each year's taxes until the property is finally redeemed. Also, determine if a particular property is worth the extra cash outlay to hold on to over the span of a few years. And, it's possible to overspend what the property is really worth.

Third, depending on which counties and states invested in, it's important to factor in more time and travel expenses.

Fourth, because tax liens and deeds are in the realm of real estate, there are always going to be some market issues in which to be aware.

Fifth, there will be lots of paperwork to keep track of and store in a secure location. Buyers who are not highly organized and systematic with government paperwork trails might not want to become involved in this type of investing.

*Quick Tip: In theory, I like the concept of bank liens and deeds. It seems like a (potentially) great way to get a decent return on investment. The one thing that concerns me about them, at least in my initial research on the topic, is the amount of time needed to invest in researching auctions and properties. There's an old saying "time is money," and I plan on setting tax lien investing on the "back burner" while I pursue less time-consuming opportunities, first.*

According to Joanne Musa in her book *Tax Lien Investing Secrets: How You Can Get Double Digit Returns On Your Money Without The Risk of the Stock Market*, there are five steps in which to buy profitable tax liens. As a side note, I have found this book to be very informative and reality based. The author gives both the good and bad sides to this type of investing. Other books I have read paint too rosy a picture of investing in tax liens. Anyway, back to the five steps:

- **Step 1:** Select the right place to invest. Pick counties and states that either do tax deeds or tax liens (depending on the investment plan). Look for locations that have more potential for a good return on time and money invested.
- **Step 2:** Track down the tax sale information. In today's Internet world, much of this can be found online. If it's difficult to find out exactly what is needed, simply find the contact information on the county website and make a phone call.
- **Step 3:** Evaluate the tax sale properties. This will be the most challenging and time-consuming part of the process. Definitely, don't bid on houses or properties that could turn into lemons immediately after the auction.
- **Step 4:** Prepare to bid at the tax sale.
- **Step 5:** Show up and bid at the tax sale!

This section on tax lien certificates and deeds has been a quick overview from a guy who has an initial interest with this type of investing in the future. There is a lot more to tax liens and tax deeds than what I have laid out here in this quick summary. My goal is to list some potential strategies, and then let my readers take it from here and run with it.

The best piece of advice I have received on tax liens so far is to attend one or two auctions just to get a feel for the process, but definitely don't invest right away. Learn what takes place and do a fair amount of homework on the front end to avoid making a bad investment that will end up costing big time in the future.

**Annuities**

One of the keys in putting money to work for one's self and not for other people is in the strategy of creating income streams. An annuity could be considered a potential, future stream of income with a guaranteed, decent rate of return. I'm all about income streams. The more money flowing into a person's life with the least amount of work, the better off they will be in the long run. I referenced the power of many streams of income back in Chapter 6, "Invest In Yourself." But annuities tend to be confusing investment strategies that have several risks tied to them, especially if you buy the wrong product.

In the older 13-week version of Financial Peace University™, Dave does talk a little about annuities in the investment lesson. He doesn't emphasize them much, though. From what I remember about that particular lesson, he seems to come at annuities from the angle that they are an "okay" product in which to invest in when someone has maxed out their 401(k), 403(b), Roth IRA, and anywhere else you can invest money. I believe Dave's recommendation is to consider annuities only if wealthy with additional money to invest. Based on individual risk tolerance along with the Brady and Woodward investment pyramid, an annuity could be a viable product to invest in. Again, let me stress that I am not a certified financial planner. I'm sharing my own personal finance journey as I investigate and consider next level financial strategies. Each person should perform their own due diligence on whether annuities are the best product for them personally, and for their family.

*Quick Tip: The majority of taxpayers in the United States are already paying into an annuity of sorts. It's called Social Security. Every US citizen, for their entire working life, has been legally forced into contributing FICA taxes to a large pool of money. At some point in the future—at retirement—those contributions will become a regular, monthly income (at whatever age the person decides to turn on this income stream from Uncle Sam).*

The definition of an annuity is "simply a contract between you and an insurance carrier. When purchased for income, the contract is for a stated amount of income (payout) in the future (even if that future is just thirty days away) for a stated amount of purchase price right now. Think of it as buying/locking in a future income stream ... the traditional primary use of an annuity is as a transfer-of-risk product (as befits an insurance product). Purchasers are transferring their risk of an uncertain income stream to an insurance carrier for a known, guaranteed income stream. This transfer-of-risk is made possible by the guarantees in the product. In general, the more guarantees an annuity offers, the better the transfer-of-risk and the stronger the product. Therefore, when looking at an annuity, the focus should be primarily on the guarantees and the only reason to buy an annuity is for the guarantees it contains."[cxi]

With an understanding of the basics of annuities, the challenge comes when faced with the multiple variations of annuities. Companies create varied annuities to differentiate their product from the others. This is when the confusion begins for everyone.

Here is a quick overview of four steps to take when comparing various annuity products. I recommend reading Alessandra Derniat's book *How to NOT Get Ripped Off when Buying an Annuity*. She provides a lot of nitty-gritty details on these four steps. I found her book to be the most useful in my research on the topic.

**Step 1:** Identify the key characteristics of the annuity.

- Is it a **variable annuity** or a **fixed annuity**? A **variable annuity** is an investment product wrapped into the guarantees of an insurance product. Only people who are licensed to sell both mutual funds and insurance can sell variable annuities. A **fixed annuity** is an insurance product. Any licensed insurance agent can sell fixed annuities. The key difference between a variable or fixed annuity is who carries the majority of the risk. In a **variable annuity**, the purchaser carries the risk in the increase of cash value because it is an investment product in mutual funds. In a **fixed annuity**, the insurance company takes the bulk of the risk because it is an insurance product. *When looking for a product that transfers risk, buy a fixed annuity and steer clear of variable annuities.*

- Is the annuity **immediate** or **deferred**? This refers to when the income stream of the annuity will begin. An **immediate annuity** will begin either thirty days after the product has been purchased or one year, depending on if the buyer signed up for either monthly or yearly payouts. A **deferred annuity** begins payouts after a specific amount of time, usually several years into the future. If time is on the person's side (i.e., they are younger), they should go with a **deferred annuity** to benefit from a bigger and better income stream later on in the future.

**Step 2:** Identify the four critical comparison points.

- Critical Comparison Point 1: **Guaranteed Income Base.** Here is the question necessary to answer when researching an annuity: "Does this annuity have a guaranteed number that income will be based on when deciding to take the income?" This number should be as high as possible! Sometimes special riders need to be attached to the policy to set this language in stone. Don't be afraid to speak with an agent. Ask lots of questions. Make them identify where all these guarantees are spelled out in writing in the policy.
- Critical Comparison Point 2: **Guaranteed Percentage Payout.** This is the percentage of the guaranteed income base the insurance company is willing to pay out each year.

- Critical Comparison Point 3: **Guaranteed Payout Amount.** This is the guaranteed amount of income that will be paid out each month or each year.
- Critical Comparison Point 4: **Guaranteed Fees.** All financial products come with fees. Either they are built in the final price or spelled out in the contract. Go through the contract carefully to make sure there is no hidden overpayment.

**Step 3**: Look at additional considerations in the policy's fine print.

- Additional Consideration #1: **Single or Joint Life.** Payouts can be selected based on either one life (single) or two lives (joint). Joint life payouts will be based on the younger of the two lives, and these payouts will be less because the insurance company is on the hook for two individuals. If either annuitant dies, though, the other will continue to receive payments for the rest of their natural life.
- Additional Consideration #2: **Surrender Charges.** The majority of all deferred annuities have a surrender charge period. Because of this, the majority of these polices are not considered to have good liquidity. Guaranteed income streams come with a price.
- Additional Consideration #3: **Method of Distribution.** There are only two ways of taking annuity income: 1) annuitization and 2) withdrawal. Annuitization is the normal method of taking the income. Once annuitization begins (the income stream starts), the owner loses control over the cash value of the policy. It can no longer be cashed out and the income stream can't be turned off. The tax treatment of an annuitized income stream is different from an income stream produced by withdrawals. In an annuitized income stream, a percentage of each payout will be considered return of premium and excluded from taxation. The remaining part is considered a gain and taxed

at ordinary rates. Tax treatment of an annuitized income stream will vary depending on the funding sources of the annuity. The best thing is to consult a tax professional with all the details. Now, instead of annuitizing the income stream, it is possible to take out money as withdrawals. This allows the annuity holder to turn on and off the income stream as needed. The policy can also be cashed out as a lump sum payment as needed. To do this, though, purchase an extra rider on the policy.

- Additional Consideration #4: **Death Benefit.** Annuities are generally not purchased for legacy reasons. People's natural tendency, though, is to want to leave loved ones something when they pass on. Be sure to find out what death benefits are on the policy before purchasing it, and any rules attached to that death benefit.
- Additional Consideration #5: **Cost-of-living-adjustment (COLA).** When annuity income stream begins, it can be paid out in a level payment option, or buyers have the option for payouts to slowly increase over time to address the issue of inflation. With this route, payments start lower and then gradually increase by a fixed percentage or cost-of-living index. This should all be spelled out in the annuity contract.
- Additional Consideration #6: **Long Term Care (LTC) Coverage.** Some annuity policies and/or riders may contain provisions for accelerated payment if the annuitant needs long term care. This accelerated rate is usually two times the regular rate for a specific amount of time, or until the cash value is completely depleted. Read the fine print. Find out what is available in the policy.

**Step 4**: When the first three steps are completed and all the information needed is gathered, organize everything in such a way to be able to quickly compare and contrast the various annuities being considered.

Based on my limited research, an annuity could be a good investment vehicle to consider for a person who has built up some sizable assets (in the $300,000 to $500,000 range) and about ten years from retirement. This would be an ideal time to contemplate a deferred fixed annuity. So, for someone 55 to 57 years old with at least $300,000 in retirement savings, it would be a good idea to talk to an annuity expert about options.

This will be my approach with annuities moving forward: because of their complexity and high fee structures, I'm going to place annuities on the back burner to re-visit at a later date. This makes more sense for me, personally, because I'm still twenty to twenty-five years away from retirement. I'm currently building my assets to these kind of annuity investment numbers, anyway. I have more pressing matters where I need to focus more thought energy, time, and money. Perhaps in a few years I'll revisit my research on the subject and then speak to an insurance agent who is an expert in this area.

*Quick Tip: For a FREE list of the Action Steps and Resources for each chapter of the book, simply go to:* http://www.heroicpersonalfinances.com/for-christians-book-action-steps/

# CHAPTER 11
# PROPERTY OWNERSHIP

"But the humble will inherit the land
And will delight themselves in abundant prosperity."
— Psalm 37:11 NASB[cxii]

"Our economic freedom is founded on individual property rights; government should never be permitted to take those away."
— Ernest Istook

According to Wikipedia, this is the definition of wealth:

*In economics, net worth refers to the value of assets owned minus the value of liabilities owed at a point in time.* **Wealth can be categorized into three principal categories: personal property, including homes or automobiles; monetary savings, such as the accumulation of past income; and the capital wealth of income producing assets, including real estate, stocks, bonds, and businesses.** *All these delineations make wealth an especially important part of social stratification. Wealth provides a type of individual safety net of protection against an unforeseen decline in one's living standard in the event of job loss or other emergency and can be transformed into home ownership, business ownership, or even a college education.*

*"Wealth" refers to some accumulation of resources (net asset value), whether abundant or not. "Richness" refers to an abundance of such resources (income or flow). A wealthy individual, community, or nation thus has more accumulated resources (capital) than a poor one. The opposite of wealth is destitution. The opposite of richness is poverty.*[cxiii]

The wealthy own property. Period. It's difficult to build wealth over time while holding all wealth in low-yield bank accounts and renting out someone else's apartment. The statistics are clear that homeowners (mortgage holders) are wealthier, at least on paper, then their renting counterparts.

I realize the above statement is a blanket one. I do believe there is wisdom in renting under certain conditions. I rented for almost ten years as I was dealing with the following circumstances: getting out of debt, going through a difficult divorce, re-marrying and then paying off an even larger amount of debt ($100,000) over a three-year span. Now, my wife and I are home mortgage holders again, working hard at building our family's wealth through mortgage pay down, saving, and investing. We're working together as a couple to build a strong financial foundation for future success.

In an article titled "Private Property Ownership Is the Only Way to Eradicate Poverty" written by Tom DeWeese, Mr. DeWeese explains why the West has prospered while other nations have struggled with poverty. Here are excerpts from his article:

*Why did the United States become so wealthy? Was it the possession of vast natural resources? Africa has more. Was it the existence of greater industry? Japan has more. Was it the existence of a superior education system? The United States now ranks below the top ten nations in education.*

*The reason the United States has led the world in wealth, standard of living, and abundance is that* **the average resident of the United States has had the ability and the opportunity to invest and produce capital.**

*Why could ordinary citizens of the United States produce their own capital to create personal wealth, while most of the rest of the world failed at such an attempt? The answer is actually very simple. The United States created a very easy, immediate, complete system for recording and securing ownership of private property.*

*Peruvian economist Hernando de Soto explains the root of American wealth in his book, The Mystery of Capital. De Soto asks, "Why does Capitalism thrive only in the West, as if enclosed in a bell jar?"*

*Capital, he argues, "is the force that raises the productivity of labor and creates the wealth of nations, It is the lifeblood of the capitalist system, the foundation of progress, and the one thing that the poor countries of the world cannot seem to produce for themselves ..."*

***... While it is common practice in the United States to buy property, hold it for a few years and sell it at a substantial profit or move up to a better home, thereby creating individual wealth, such a***

*system is basically unheard of in most nations of the world.* If one doesn't have or can't prove title, then no bank will make loans on the property. In nations where property cannot be easily and legally registered, the only recourse is to go to friends and relatives, get a smaller loan (thereby reducing one's ability to build a company) and still never have title to the business or the business property financed that way. Though people may live on and pay for property for years, it is hidden in an underground economy not beneficial to the individual or the national economy because ownership cannot be shown.

"In the West, by contrast," de Soto argues, "every parcel of land, every building, every piece of equipment, or store of inventory is represented in a property document that is the visible sign of a vast hidden process that connects all these assets to the rest of the economy." Seventy percent of all small businesses in the United States are started by equity loans on personal homes. Small, independently owned businesses employee the majority of people in the United States.

This then is the hidden secret of why the West became so wealthy and the rest of the world has been mired in poverty. I put this statement in past tense because the United States is now losing wealth as a result of a massive campaign to reduce private property ownership through the policy of Sustainable Development. If not reversed, the United States will find itself in Third World status for exactly the same reasons other nations have landed there — destruction of private property rights.[cxiv]

Anyone living in the United States is surrounded by opportunities that the majority of the world can't even comprehend. For those desiring to be excellent managers of all God has given them should "go to school" on personal finances. It's time to read every financial book available to absorb the knowledge of other experts. It's time to take advantage of the vast opportunities in the areas of capital, in the right way.

On the journey to wealth, a family should make every attempt to at least own their own home versus being a renter, but only under the right circumstances. I am in complete agreement with experts such as Dave Ramsey that broke people have no business buying homes because it will make their situation even worse. If currently living with a bunch of debt while working to pay it off with a weak cash flow, fix those two areas before even considering home ownership.

From this point forward, though, I will assume my readers have worked through or are at least working through the steps to pay off debt and build emergency funds. I also assume they are working through the areas I've touched on in this book so far: investing in one's self, emergency preparedness, tax strategies, taking the match on 401(k)s or 403(b)s, and then putting money to work through strategies such as IBC, peer-to-peer lending, tax liens, or annuities. I will also assume that my readers are homeowners or at the least working toward owning their own home.

In the rest of this chapter, I will focus on acquiring more property, both physical and virtual, for the purposes of investing for long-term wealth building.

## Real Estate
## (Physical Property)

No one has a burning desire to be a slumlord or deal with the hassles of maintaining a property. My guess is that most people have their hands full just maintaining their own personal residence.

Owning rental property has its share of issues—dealing with difficult tenants, the possibility of needing to repair the property at all hours of the day and night and possessing adequate savings to deal with those repairs as well as the inevitable gaps in vacancies between tenants, and much more.

In spite of all the problems with rental properties, though, owning real estate can be an excellent long-term strategy to build wealth. Ask the Trump family—that's how they have made their billions. Dave Ramsey himself freely admits that he invests heavily in rental property. I believe he has stated on his national radio show that he owns more than 1,000 properties in the Nashville area. I'm sure he has contracted an excellent property management company to take care of all his investment real estate!

There are many more "millionaire next door" types who are on the same track as the Trumps and the Ramseys. Real estate is a part of their short-term cash flow strategy as well as long-term investing strategy. When it comes to real estate, there's a saying that goes something like this: "Buy and sell to make CASH. Buy and hold to build WEALTH."

Now when it comes to real estate investing, I do believe that Dave's wisdom is sound—go slow. Never rush to buy real estate just to buy real estate. Don't fall in love with the property. Take time. Look for bargains. Have lots of money in the bank to deal with real estate problems.

When it comes to investing in real estate, one can go about it a few different ways. The safest route possible, like Dave does, is to buy investment property with cash. Since Dave doesn't take on debt of any kind, he pays for his properties outright. They cash flow from day one—very wise. When making the kind of money Dave does through his Ramsey Solutions business, however, it's a whole lot easier to work this kind of real estate investment plan.

Or, the opposite end of the spectrum is to attempt No Money Down deals by using OPM (other people's money). In this way, the property is highly leveraged, and the buyer has a higher rate of return on the investment from the beginning. Unless landing a steal of a deal, though, the property will not cash flow at the beginning. Plus, without a bunch of emergency cash sitting in the bank, it's possible to lose the house at the first sign of a significant problem with a tenant or the property itself.

I do think there is a "middle of the road" approach to take with real estate investing. It takes most of the front-end risk out of mortgaging the investment property and at the same time leverages other people's money through tenants paying off the majority of your mortgage(s) on your properties.

The more "balanced" approach I plan on taking as I move into this phase of my own investment strategy is the following:

1. Build up our personal emergency fund to an even higher level to protect my family from potential problems with rental property investments. I plan on creating a separate real estate investment emergency fund. This will mean increasing my level of financial insurance while I am also increasing my level of financial risk.
2. Increase our personal liability umbrella insurance policy to protect my family from any potential, future legal problems when people will be in and out of our investment property.
3. Restructure our business and legal entities for maximum personal protection and tax savings with investment property in our portfolio.
4. Save up cash over time for a healthy 20 percent down payment on our first property. In this way, we can avoid PMI on the mortgage and maximize cash flow as much as possible. I may also consider

5. Study and learn how to be a wise landlord for our first property. I plan on reading up as much as I can on the mechanics of land lording and property management as well as learning from others who own rental property.
6. Move SLOWLY and start small. I'll be looking for a small, simple property such as a townhouse, duplex, or small home to begin my real estate investment journey.
7. Buy discounted property. This will be the challenging part. In real estate, it's easy to "fall in love" with a particular property and not think through whether this is a wise, long-term purchase. With a discounted property, I'm hoping to maximize our cash flow from day one.
8. Avoid major rehab/renovation costs on the property as much as possible. When you buy property at a discount, there's a good chance you will need to do some updating and repair work. I will do my best to minimize this to small, cosmetic fixes.
9. Find quality tenants to fill our first property. In my research on this particular topic, the majority of rental property owners get into a huge rush when it comes to getting a tenant into the property. A few months later they regret their decision when their tenants are behind in their rent. Then, they are forced to go through a difficult eviction process. I will be better off to move slowly and to even make an extra month's mortgage payment to find quality people to fill our property. Another quick note on quality tenants: never rent to ANYONE you know at any level whether family, friends, acquaintances, friends of friends, or fellow church members. The tenants need to be total and complete strangers so that you can keep everything businesslike in order that the tenants don't attempt to take advantage of you. I've heard too many horror stories about tenants taking advantage of their landlords because of personal relationships. Just don't even attempt it!
10. In my search for quality tenants, I will be sure to have them fill out a thorough application and pay a small processing fee. I will run the background checks and the credit report. I will call past landlords

and get the real scoop on these people to make sure they will be quality tenants. *Quick Tip: A wonderful idea I found in my research on this subject is to ALWAYS introduce one's self as the property manager, not the landlord/owner of the property. This will help in keeping everything more business-like and less personal with the people you are trying to "vet."* I will also attempt to find out if the tenants are "handy" at all with tools and small repairs (see my next point).

11. Once I feel that I have found excellent, potential tenants for our property, I will set forth high expectations for living in the property. Here's a listing of expectations as well incentives that I am considering:

- Monthly walk-through. I will explain to the tenants that as the property manager (wink, wink), I have been directed by the owner to schedule monthly a walk-through to ensure there are no problems with the property. If problems are discovered on the walk-through, they need to be addressed immediately.
- Small repairs. As the property manager (again—wink, wink), I will explain to the tenants that I have a lot on my plate and prefer not to receive the late night calls about small repairs that they can possibly do on their own, assuming they are handy with tools. I will offer the tenants repayment of supplies plus a little extra for time and hassle.
- Lawn maintenance and landscaping. Assuming the property (single family) has a yard and any kind of landscaping, I will place the expectation that they will keep the grass mowed and landscaping neat and tidy in the rental agreement.
- No smoking will be allowed in the home. This one is a no-brainer in today's world. It's difficult to get the smell and stains out of the interior of the home.
- No cats will be allowed. Period. They like to mark their territory with their urine—and once this happens, the stink will never come out of the property.

- I will consider allowing dogs on several conditions including a pet deposit for any kind of damage they may cause.
- Auto payment of rent. I plan on offering a slight discount of $25.00/month for the tenant to set-up their rent payments on auto payment through the online portal of their bank. If I can get the tenants thinking auto payment of rent each month, the better off things will be in the long term.
- I will give the tenants a small monthly discount to go through Financial Peace University if they have never been through it (say $10/month over a twelve-month period to repay the kit purchase). This idea may be a little "radical," but if they can get their finances in order at the beginning of their being our tenants, the better off we're all going to be. To verify class attendance, I would ask the tenants to give me the contact information of their FPU coordinator. President Ronald Reagan had a saying, "Trust, but verify."
- I will offer other "discounts" on rent. If the tenants won't go for auto payment or FPU, I will still offer some type of "discount" for paying early and definitely no later than the 1st of every month. If they are more than five days late, then they will pay a $50 late charge and the new rent will go up by that amount next month.

After starting small and putting two to three years under my belt as a landlord/property manager, I would assess if I believe I have enough experience to go up another level. I could then go a couple of different directions. First, I could sell the smaller property and upgrade to a larger property, such as a duplex or four-plex. Second, I could keep my smaller property and buy another smaller property, such as owning two townhouses or two small homes. Then, after I expanded the first time, I would follow the same pattern: go three years with this new property, see if I can handle it, and then consider expanding up to a small commercial business property or small apartment building. Once achieving this level, I would consider hiring a property management company to help me.

I've heard too many horror stories about real estate investors becoming greedy and trying to expand their financial empire way too fast. Most crash and burn in a big way at some point down the line. I would definitely take a slow, long-term approach to keep me in the real estate game for a while to invest for the future for my family.

## Raw Land

Another possible direction in the area of real estate investing is raw, undeveloped land. Believe it or not, there's actually a thriving market for buying and selling large tracts of land out in the middle of nowhere that don't even have buildings on them!

Mark Podolsky (thelandgeek.com) said buying and selling raw land has been declared by experts as one of the "best passive income models" out there, especially in regard to real estate investing. There are no hassles with toilets, repairing roofs, or renovating kitchens because there are no buildings on the property. Investing in raw land can be done without a huge upfront investment, too. It can cost $100,000 and up to buy a traditional home investment property. But with raw land, under the right circumstances, the investor may spend only a few thousand dollars. The majority of the work on raw land is researching available properties and pitching offers to the current landowners. Some investors preview the property, but the majority of land available for purchase will be hundreds of miles away from the person's home.

Successful land investors have systems they have developed to find and buy land. The first step is looking for land in which the property owners are behind on their taxes. These people may live out of state. They may have inherited the property. In general, they are just not interested in owning the property to begin with. The land is more of a curse than a blessing in their lives. Step two is finding the names and contact information for these distressed property owners. Finding these owners can be a little bit of a challenge. One can purchase a pre-produced list, or hire professionals who do automated "screen scraping" of county websites that have online property tax payment options. These professionals can produce a list of owners, contact addresses, and an estimate of the market value of these properties.

In step three, send them a "low ball" offer letter for their property. The best approach in this letter is to offer a cash purchase, take the tax burden off the seller's hands, and state a specific closing date for purchase.

*Quick Tip: With this in mind, the "meat" of the offer letter may read something like this: "I'm going to buy your property. I'm going to give you cash for your property. I'm going to take this tax burden off your hand. For your forty-acre property, I'll give you $3,000 cash, and we'll close before May 24th. The amount that we agree on is the amount you get in your hand. There will be no fees or additional charges. A notary will show up at the time and place of your choosing with the deed. You sign and notarize, and then the notary will hand you a cashier's check."*

In step four, a small percentage of these owners will accept the offer made. The key to this system is sending out a lot of offer letters. A typical direct mail response is around 3 percent. For every 100 letters mailed, three owners might respond—not a great response, but if just one of those owners sells the property at a steep discount, all that work is worth it.

*Quick Tip: Handwriting the owner's name and address on the envelope may slightly increase the open rate of the letter. Enclose a more professional, typed letter inside that includes the offer. Another trick to increase the possibility of the letter being opened is the "lumpy mail trick." Go down to the toy store and buy a package of those small army men and place one of those guys into each envelope. People will open the letter just to figure out what's in there!*

Once people have responded to a few of the offers, proceed to step five—the due diligence phase. Turn over every rock, making sure to understand how large the land parcel is and if any back taxes are owed on the property. At this point, it may be wise to set foot on the property or hire someone to go and take pictures and videos. Be sure there is legal access to the property—ingress and egress. It must be possible to actually access the property. Don't buy a parcel in some strange location that no one would be able to get to! Also look for something compelling about the property. Maybe there are mountain views or a stream. Perhaps the land is in the path of growth. Look for a good story related to the property so it's easier to sell.

Consider, too, hiring a title company to complete the due diligence. If they are willing to sell a title insurance policy on it, then their due diligence is good. Once research is complete and ready to proceed, finalize the purchase of the property. The costs of doing a land deal will include the purchase price, any back taxes to be paid, notary fee, and recording fee for the county.

After purchasing the property (hopefully at a discount), monetize the property. This can be done a couple of different ways. One way is to flip the property for a quick profit with a cash-only purchase. For example, buy a piece of land for $800, and turn around and sell that property for $1,995—a $1,195 profit! The return on investment is 149 percent! Another way is to sell parcels of land via seller financing. According to The Land Geek, Mark Podolsky, consider running a seller-financing deal like a car note. Buy a piece of property for $1,000. Sell it for $10,000. Have the buyer put a $1,000 down, and then pay $249/month at 8 percent interest. This is true "migraine free" real estate investing according to Mark.

*Quick Tip: Use resources and tools such as pictures of the property, Google Earth, Powerpoint, and any and all tax and appraiser information. Compile this into a PDF. Using Screen Recorder, narrate this PPT slide deck into a video and upload it to YouTube as part of a property-marketing package. List the property for sale on popular land websites such as LandFlip.com, LandHub.com, and LandandFarm.com.*

Here's how to set-up owner financing. Utilize owner financing on a promissory note—a land contract and a purchase-sale agreement. A traditional deed of trust puts a lien on the property that the new buyer technically now owns. The problem with this traditional approach is that if the buyer defaults, an attorney will need to be hired to facilitate the foreclosure process, which could cost $2,000 to $3,000 and take ninety to 100 days.

A land contract protects the seller. The property stays in the seller's name. If the buyer is thirty days late on their payments, the seller sends them a certified letter stating they are in default per the land contract and they have thirty days to bring their payments current. If they don't pay, the seller can turn around and resell the property because the property is still in the seller's name. This is a total win-win!

What are the risks to this type of investing? The first risk is not having enough due diligence education. People get themselves in trouble for buying the wrong parcel of land. The second risk is the unknown. The third risk is overpaying for the property. To maximize raw land investment, strive to only pay around 30 percent on the comps for that land.

To find out more information on Land Investing, check out the following resources:

- Listen to three podcasts on land investing on the Side Hustle Nation Podcast:
    - The Best Passive Income Model: http://www.sidehustlenation.com/the-best-passive-income-model/
    - The Best Passive Income Model: Raw Land Investing Update (Part 1): http://www.sidehustlenation.com/raw-land-investing-update-part-1/
    - The Best Passive Income Model: Raw Land Investing Update (Part 2): http://www.sidehustlenation.com/raw-land-investing-update-part-2/

- The Land Geek (thelandgeek.com). This site is run by a gentleman named Mark Podolsky. Mark offers a lot of free content through his website, podcast, Passive Income Blueprint, and Land Geek Community.
- The Land Academy Podcast with Steve Butala (LandAcademy.com)
- Mark Podolsky's Investor Toolkit: https://thelandgeek.thrivecart.com/ivtwso/#_l_3q
- Josh Brooks' Free PDF Land Investing Guide: www.sidehustlenation.com/land1
- Chris Prichard's Land Investing Action Guide: www.sidehustlenation.com/land2
- LandFlip.com
- LandHub.com
- LandsofAmerica.com
- LandandFarm.com

- LandWatch.com
- LandsofAdventure.com

**Virtual Property**

Since the Internet came online for the masses over the last twenty-five years there is a new avenue available for investing: virtual property. Billions of dollars have been created through virtual property on the worldwide web. This money has been made through domain names, website building, website flipping, website business purchases, advertising, affiliates, and product sales. Just as there are many different ways to make money with physical property, the same is true in the virtual space as well.

In the opinion of many, the best avenue to create long-term income on the Internet is through a private business, not taking on someone else's project. This echoes Chapter 6, "Invest In Yourself." With one big idea that people want more information about and are willing to pay money for, a platform can be created. This platform could consist of a "home base" website. Once that has been created, monetize the big idea through the website in several different ways.

For example, sell information products through the website. These products could consist of books, eBooks, audio books, specialized bundled programs, and even ongoing subscriptions for loyal fans. Sell advertising (with banner advertising) displayed right on the site. Sell advertising through email blasts to subscribers.

*Quick Note: Spamming people with email they have not requested is illegal. The email blasts I refer to above is through your own email list you have created through your website. The people you are emailing have subscribed to your email list.*

Establish relationships with other online personalities and companies and embed affiliate links in website pages and email correspondence. There are many creative, reliable ways to create multiple streams of income. I touched on this back in the "Invest In Yourself" chapter. Create a big idea in a particular niche that interests enough people, monetize that big idea in many ways, and focus a majority of time and energy on that big idea. Some great examples of specific individuals who have excelled in this area include:

- Dave Ramsey (daveramsey.com)
- Michael Hyatt (michaelhyatt.com)
- Tim Ferriss (fourhourworkweek.com)
- Pat Flynn (smartpassiveincome.com)
- Ramit Sethi (iwillteachyoutoberich.com)

Whenever I have one of those "big idea" moments of inspiration, I will head over to godaddy.com and see if one or more domain names are available for that particular big idea. If they are available and inexpensive, then I will buy the domain(s) for at least one year while I develop my ideas to see whether they are viable.

Some readers may not feel like they are "big idea" types of people. They can use other approaches when it comes to virtual property on the Internet. Before taking up any of these ideas, though, make sure to have plenty of liquid cash available to make these virtual property purchases. Treat these virtual purchases as risky investments at the top of the investment pyramid discussed earlier in the book. Assume money will be lost. I would move slowly on these purchases and not bet the farm on any one virtual property.

The first way to buy virtual property on the web is to purchase already established website businesses for sale. In these website sales, either the original website owner/builder is retiring from the business or tired of owning the business because of the time and hassle factor. These folks just want out, plus make a little money on their business as they get out. Many times these website businesses are mature and well tested. They have already been around several years. They could be cash flowing a few thousand dollars a month selling specific products. Websites such as EmpireFlippers.com, Flippa.com, WebsiteBroker.com, Sedo.com, and BuySellWebsite.com all specialize in selling and buying websites and domain names.

Another reason these business websites are sold is that there are plenty of website developers out there that will come up with a business idea, build a website around that idea, and then see if they can get it to cash flow a little bit. They aren't interested in building a particular website into a roaring, fully developed business. They would just like to take a few months to get a website business off the ground, and then sell it for a few thousand dollars to someone interested in taking the business to the next level.

Another approach to take in virtual property is buying and selling the actual domain names themselves, without going through the hassle of trying to actually build any kind of website connected to the domain name. Here's a quick listing of several domain names that have been bought and sold to the highest bidder in recent years:

- Insurance.com $35.6 million in 2010
- VacationRentals.com $35 million in 2007
- PrivateJet.com $30.1 million in 2012
- Internet.com $18 million in 2009
- Insure.com $16 million in 2009
- iCloud.com by Apple for $6 million in March 2011
- GiftCard.com by CardLab for $4 million in October 2012
- Shop.com sold for $3.5 million in November 2003
- Software.com sold for $3.2 million in December 2005
- Pizza.com sold for $2.605 million in April 2008
- Coupons.com sold for $2.2 million in January 2000
- Savings.com sold for $1.9 million in February 2003
- Mortgage.com sold for $1.8 million in March 2000
- Branson.com sold for $1.6 million in June 2006[cxv]

Although buying and selling domain names has lost some of its appeal as the Internet has now become more mainstream, it is still possible to make some money by grabbing a good idea, product, service, or company name that hasn't been registered. If creative and fast enough, luck might be in store and that winning website name could set a person up for life. Of course, this would be considered risky investing (borderline betting), so I would definitely play this conservatively. Don't put your family's life savings down on a particular name that you think is suddenly going to become so valuable to a particular company that they are willing to cough up millions of dollars and simply hand it over. But, for some good bargains on domain names that hold promise—I say go for it!

Whether creating a personal website business from scratch and creating multiple streams of income from that one site, buying someone else's website business to have an extra stream of income, or buying and selling domain names for a profit–there are still plenty of opportunities for people to invest in virtual property for short and long-term gains.

*Quick Tip: For a FREE list of the Action Steps and Resources for each chapter of the book, simply go to:* [http://www.heroicpersonalfinances.com/for-christians-book-action-steps/](http://www.heroicpersonalfinances.com/for-christians-book-action-steps/)

## CHAPTER 12
## STOCK MARKETING INVESTING: PART 2

"Be diligent to know the state of your flocks, and attend to your herds."
– Proverbs 27:23 NKJV[cxvi]

"Investing should be more like watching paint dry or watching grass grow. If you want excitement, take $800 and go to Las Vegas."
– Paul Samuelson

In this chapter, I'd like to circle back to discussing stock market investing. In Chapter 9, Stock Market Investing: Part One, I mentioned that in the early stages of investing, the best approach could be to take a company's 401(k) or 403(b) match and stop there for a while. At the time of my writing these investing chapters of the book, the year is 2016. The stock market has experienced one of the worst beginnings of a new year. In January 2016, the Dow lost 5.5 percent of its value. The Nasdaq fared worse by losing 8 percent of its value in the first month of the year. Analysts fear a rocky road for stock market investing for the rest of this year.

One of the big reasons the stock market can be a risky investing strategy and at the top of the *Financial Fitness* investment pyramid is the fact that the stock market is so speculative and emotion driven. Also, we have so many media reporting on the stock market every minute of every day—one bad news report sends the market into the tank. Something bad happens in the country, such as a terror attack or a major winter storm, and the stock market takes a nose dive. People grow fearful, have a gut reaction, and respond by pulling their money out. Then a few weeks go by and things seem to be going better, and these same people put their money back in. The stock market becomes a roller coaster of ups and downs, reflecting the emotions of a large group of investors. There doesn't seem to be a good, long-term strategy for many of the current investors in the stock market. But, market volatility can be used as an advantage. The best investors do it all the time. The key is to not get caught up in the emotional reactions of everybody else in the market.

Regarding long-term stock market investing, I understand the whole "start investing at an early age," "stay in it for the long haul," "diversify your investments," "throw extra money in the market when it goes way down," and "you profit from dollar cost averaging by investing the same amount every month" mantras. On many levels, all these truths are good advice. But, I am still somewhat persuaded by the advice given in the book *Financial Fitness* that stock market investing is speculative on many levels, unless it is played super safe. What's the point of that? If played *too* safe, money will be lost through inflation and investing fees.

I'd like to lay out my current approach to any further stock market investing past the initial "take the match" from one's employer. Those who have worked hard by investing in themselves, are prepared for emergencies on all levels, have taken care of tax strategies, have already taken the 401(k) or 403(b) match from their employer, have put money to work like banks do, and have invested in property — they have set themselves up to consider finishing out the top of the investment pyramid by completing their stock market investing strategy.

## Let's Return to 401(k)s and 403(b)s

The majority of a company's 401(k) and 403(b) investing options just plain stink. They don't offer many choices in which to invest, and the options they do give are usually not good. Because of this fact, it doesn't make a lot of sense to put more money into these accounts beyond the employer match. After investing in other areas mentioned in previous chapters, the next step should be to take advantage of other stock market investing opportunities.

Bypassing company retirement options to invest in a different stock market investment vehicle, though, will not result in the same <u>immediate</u> tax advantages. According to my research, the majority of companies will not allow people to set up their own pre-tax deductions to a personal IRA plan. It would seem the only way to get to the pretax deduction is to fund a personal IRA plan with post-tax dollars. When tax time rolls around, take the deduction offered on tax forms to get tax money back from the previous year's installments. Then, of course, once reaching retirement and making the decision to start withdrawing money from an IRA, taxes on that money will need to be paid.

If paying with post-tax money anyway on the front end, consider setting up a Roth IRA. With a Roth, it's not possible to claim a tax deduction on yearly taxes, but taxes will have already been paid upfront. When ready to withdraw money from a Roth in retirement, those withdrawals will not be taxed. Everything will be tax-free coming out of the Roth. Based on my research, there are some pros and cons to the Roth. The younger a person is, the more benefit they will potentially receive from utilizing the Roth and paying taxes upfront. If older, a person may be better off going the tax-free route on the front end with a traditional IRA. Taxes will need to be paid upon withdrawal of money during retirement. Remember, I'm not a tax expert, so please consult one before making investment decisions.

*Quick Tip: Let's take a moment and look at the main differences between a Roth IRA and a Traditional IRA. Anyone younger than seventy-and-a-half with earned income can contribute to a traditional IRA. Roth IRAs, however, have income limits for contributions. In 2015, the rules are the following: single tax filers must have modified adjusted gross incomes of less than $116,000 in order to contribute (there is a phase out between $116,001 and $131,000). Married tax filers must have adjusted gross incomes of less than $183,000 (there is a phase out between $183,001 and $193,000). But, it is the same as Traditional IRAs though; the money that is invested must have been made with "earned income." It can't be inheritance money from Uncle Buck!*

*There are tax advantages for both Traditional and Roth IRAs. In a Traditional IRA, pre-tax dollars are invested in the account (or, this money is tax deductible on both state and federal tax forms the year the contribution is made). These funds are allowed to grow tax-free until the person is allowed to withdraw them after age fifty-nine-and-a-half. As soon as monetary withdrawals begin, taxes will need to be paid at ordinary income tax rates. For a Roth IRA, there are no tax breaks for contributions, but earnings and withdrawals are generally tax-free. Taxes are avoided on this money when taking it out in retirement.*

*There are many other rules and restrictions, and these change from year to year. I recommend checking out the following web page for more information: http://www.rothira.com/traditional-ira-vs-roth-ira.*

Another factor to consider when deciding between a Roth or Traditional IRA is what tax bracket the person is currently in and what tax bracket he or she believes they will be in once they decide to retire. If there is a possibility of moving from a higher bracket to a lower bracket, it's best to go with a traditional IRA. The money will grow to a larger amount by being tax-free on the front end. However, if a higher tax bracket is likely at retirement, then the Roth could be the way to go. I found a handy, free app to run financial calculations such as these. The app is available for both Android and iOS users. In the Apple App store, the app is under the title "Ez Calculators." Right now, I find myself going to this app a couple of times a day to run various calculations that range from IRA contributions to paying off the mortgage early to inflation calculators to salary increase calculators. This little freebie app has a lot of useful tools. If avoiding downloading yet another app to the phone, visit their website for the exact same tools at www.fncalculator.com.

Stock market investing—whether in individual stocks or diversifying a portfolio through an IRA—could be considered risky, speculative investing, especially in today's crazy, emotionally-driven stock market culture. In my humble opinion, I would consider putting my money to work in other ways such as IBC's, peer-to-peer lending, infopreneuring (having a private online information business), and real estate investing before maxing out my IRA contributions. Once other investment opportunities are maximized, consider coming back around to stock market investing.

## Index Funds

Say a person returns to investing in the stock market through an IRA. They believe they maxed out their potential in the areas of putting money to work, their own business, and real estate investing, or perhaps they just want to diversify their investment money at another level. If this is the case, then I would recommend diversifying IRA contributions through index funds as I previously mentioned in Chapter 9 – Stock Market Investing: Part One.

Why index funds? Index funds are more desirable than standard mutual funds for many important reasons. Before jumping into those reasons, let me first take a moment to explain what an index fund is. According to Investopedia.com, an index fund is defined as:

" … a type of mutual fund with a portfolio constructed to match or track the components of a market index, such as the Standard & Poor's 500 Index (S&P 500). An index mutual fund is said to provide broad market exposure, low operating expenses and low portfolio turnover."[cxvii]

Index funds are superior to mutual funds for several different reasons. First, they are usually less expensive than traditional mutual funds because they are not actively managed. And second, index funds are diversified to keep pace with the market, typically the S&P 500. Index funds aren't set up to beat the market. The reality is that the majority of fund managers (96%) for actively managed mutual funds can't even match or outpace the market. Jack Bogle, the creator of the first index fund and founder of Vanguard, says this about them, "maximum diversification, minimal cost, and maximum tax efficiency, low turnover [trading], and low turnover cost, and no sales loads." This is the beauty of the index fund.

Here are the next steps in investing in index funds after receiving the employer match discussed back in Chapter 9. Depending on age and tax bracket, consider opening either a Roth IRA or Traditional IRA with a company such as Fidelity, Vanguard, or TD Ameritrade. Once establishing a new IRA, check out all the available index funds. Next, diversify index funds based on risk tolerance. If a more aggressive investor, especially if younger with more time to spare, consider the all-stocks Dave Ramsey approach of:

- 25 percent in Growth and Income Stock Index Funds
- 25 percent in Growth Stock Index Funds
- 25 percent in International Stock Index Funds
- 25 percent in Aggressive Growth Stock Index Funds

If time is scarce and a more conservative approach is enticing, then I would consider the following allocation I mentioned back in Chapter 9:

- 20 percent in Growth and Income Index Funds

- 20 percent in Growth Index Funds
- 10 percent in International Index Funds
- 10 percent in Aggressive Growth Index Funds.
- 40 percent in Bond Index Funds (another recommendation you often hear is to reallocate your bond funds based on your age. For example, if thirty years old, invest in 70 percent stocks and 30 percent bonds.)

*Quick Tip: I'm going to talk more about bond funds in the next section. The more I study investing and the more I invest, the more wisdom I find in moving away from the Dave Ramsey four-part (25/25/25/25), stocks-only investing strategy and making sure that there is a certain percentage of bond funds in the mix. Before setting asset allocations, I highly encourage taking time to read and study investment strategy and not just taking Dave's strategy as gospel truth.*

How should a person decide on which index funds in each of these categories to invest in? Excellent question! Here are a few criteria to look at when considering a specific fund:

- **Fund tracking.** Determine what index a particular fund is tracking. When index funds were first created, they simply indexed the S&P 500. Today, index funds track US Stock Indexes (such as the Wilshire Large Growth and the Russell 2000), International Indexes, and even Bond Indexes. There is a lot of variety in today's sophisticated financial world. Consider a diverse portfolio with a variety of index funds.
- **Expense ratios.** The main reason to go with index funds over mutual funds in the first place is their lower costs. Index funds are not all created equal, and their expense ratios will vary. Look for quality funds at a minimum cost.
- **Tax efficiency.** Many index funds are tax efficient. Depending on the sector a particular fund is indexing, though, there could be some tax inefficiencies. Morningstar tracks information such as this. Strive to make funds as tax efficient as possible.
- **Morningstar rating.** This is a good guide to check once you look at expense ratios. Four and five-star ratings will certainly be

attractive funds to consider, but three and even two-star ratings aren't necessarily a reason to dismiss a particular fund.

If you're going to take part in the stock market, then going with quality, low-cost index funds is a much better approach to track with the markets instead of trying to beat the markets in higher cost mutual funds managed by ineffective managers. In addition to index funds, including a solid percentage mix of bond index funds is a good way to "smooth out" the roller coaster ride of the stock market.

## Bonds and Bond Funds

Most insurance companies (which are considered stable wealth producers) and wealthy individuals have much of their wealth in bonds. Why bonds, though? According to an article titled "Are there any safe investments?" by Ellen Cannon,[cxviii] the wealthy like bonds for two primary reasons. One, they are predictable, and two, the principle always gets repaid.

To my knowledge, Dave Ramsey has never recommended bonds or bond funds in a balanced investment strategy. He always stays consistent with his four-part mutual fund allocation of 25 percent in Growth, 25 percent in Growth and Income, 25 percent in Aggressive Growth, and 25 percent in International. Dave considers this approach to be "conservative." And, from what I recall, he encourages people to stay in this fund allocation even into their retirement years. I've coordinated a lot of FPU classes, and this has always been the standard mantra.

Yet, research in the "real world" of investing reveals this four-part allocation to be aggressive and risky. There is no balance to this approach. Yes, there is diversification among the various stock classes, but all that money is still in stocks. Pick up any investment book out there, and the majority of financial experts believe in balancing out investment strategies with a mix of both stocks and bonds. When nearing retirement age, it may even be wise to have some cash instruments in the investment mix as well.

What are bonds? Before answering that question, I'd like to back up a second and define stocks. Buying stocks, or at least investing in an index or mutual fund, means buying small portions of companies. It means actually owning a tiny little sliver of equity in several companies. If these companies do well financially, then the value of a share of the company will rise. If companies are struggling, then the value of a share in the company will decline.

Bonds are the opposite of stocks. They are debt instruments. Companies, municipalities, state governments, and even the federal government will issue bonds to finance various projects and expansions they want to do. Here is a quick rundown of the main differences between stocks and bonds:

- **Bonds are considered "safer" and more predictable than stocks.** Investing in debt is actually safer than investing in equity. In a corporation structure, debt holders have priority over shareholders. If for some reason a company goes bankrupt, bondholders are paid before the stock owners.
- **Bonds are not as volatile as stocks.** Yes, they can lose value and are influenced by stocks and interest rates, but they are still considered a good investment for slow, steady, predictable returns.
- **Bonds are better than banks.** Better returns are made on bonds than in bank savings accounts.
- **Bonds help smooth out stock market portfolios.** In the major ups and downs of today's stock market, bonds can help smooth out the financial journey, especially if the market is in decline. If the market goes down, the value of bonds will increase. This is especially useful nearing retirement. It would be wise to shift to a progressively higher rate of bonds over stocks closer to retirement age. The "rule of thumb" is to match the percentage of bonds with a person's age. So a forty-year-old should have 40 percent of their retirement account allocated to bond funds. A fifty-year-old should have 50 percent in bonds. A sixty-year-old—60 percent in bonds, and so on.

When investing in individual bonds (as opposed to bond funds) here are some other bond basics to know. First, municipal and state bonds have tax advantages. They are free from any federal taxes and could be free of state taxes depending on which state you live in. Second, bonds are sold at a specified annual interest rate also called the "coupon rate." It is easy to know exactly what the rate of return will be. Third, bonds are bought and sold with a guaranteed return of principal. When buying a short-term, one-year bond for a $100, that $100 is guaranteed to return at the end of the term of the bond. Fourth, there are three types of bond terms: short (0-2 years), intermediate (2-10 years), and long-term (10+ years). Fifth, bonds come with a credit rating. The "safest" bonds are rated A to BBB. Anything rated lower than BBB will be a riskier investment. These lower rated bonds are not considered to be "investment grade." US Treasury bonds are regarded as the safest. Corporate bonds are treated as riskier than federal, state, or municipal bonds, especially those known as "junk bonds." A junk bond is defined as "a high-yield, high-risk security, typically issued by a company seeking to raise capital quickly in order to finance a takeover." Sixth, bonds can be "callable," meaning that at any point in the term of a bond, a government or corporation can "call" or redeem the bond from the bondholder. Usually, a premium is paid to the bondholder as a result.

There are several different types of individual bonds (as opposed to bond funds) to invest in:

- **Municipal and state bonds.** These types of bonds are often known as "Muni's." When a city or state has capital projects that need funding or debt to be refinanced, they will issue bonds for investors to invest in.
- **Federal bonds.** The federal government issues marketable securities when capital projects need funding or debt needs to be refinanced. These securities are collectively known as Treasuries. All debt issued by the US Federal government is considered extremely safe. There are three main categories of government, fixed-income securities that are classified based on length of time before maturity. Bills are debt securities maturing in less than one year (also known as T-bills). Notes are debt securities maturing between one to ten years. Bonds are debt securities maturing after ten years. There are several types of federal bonds to choose from. There are bonds called "TIPS." TIPS are treasury securities that are indexed to inflation to protect investors. They are considered extremely low-risk investments. Somewhat like TIPS, "I Bonds" are interest bearing, federal bonds that have a variable inflation rate

that is adjusted semi-annually. They are only taxed at the federal level, but I Bonds can be tax-free if utilized for higher education. "EE Bonds," also known as Patriot Bonds, are government savings bonds guaranteed to double in value over the initial term of the bond, which is usually twenty years. Most EE bonds will even pay interest beyond the initial maturity date, up to thirty years.

- **Corporate bonds.** When corporations need to raise capital, they will issue bonds. Corporate bonds are considered riskier than government bonds, but that risk is rewarded with higher yields. Corporate bond terms are also typically longer: short-term is less than five years; intermediate is five to twelve years; long-term is longer than twelve years.
- **Zero-coupon bonds.** A zero-coupon bond is "a type of bond that makes no coupon payments but instead is issued at a considerable discount to par value. For example, let's say a zero-coupon bond with a $1,000 par value and ten years to maturity is trading at $600; you'd be paying $600 today for a bond that will be worth $1,000 in 10 years."[cxix]

If bonds are recommended for balancing out investment retirement portfolios, what then is the best way to invest in bonds? The easiest method to start in bond investing is through bond mutual funds as part of a company's 401(k), 403(b), or IRA. Start with diversifying retirement accounts with bonds by investing money into a "one and done" approach such as target-date funds. These types of funds are set-up to automatically diversify and balance portfolios according to age and retirement horizon. Many so-called "experts" don't recommend target-date funds because they believe they are structured too conservatively. But, if just beginning the investing journey, this is as good a way as any to get started. Consider parking retirement funds in an appropriate target date for retirement age, and then take a few months to read and research about investing best practices. With increased knowledge about building a portfolio, consider reallocating retirement money if comfortable doing so. Most brokerage company websites such as Fidelity and Vanguard are loaded with all sorts of helpful information on asset allocation as well as research on the various funds in which to invest. Again, the only thing needed is a little time and patience to sift through quite a bit of investment information. You can also pay for the advice of a financial planner to help set-up a balanced retirement account within 401(k), 403(b), or other IRA accounts.

The majority of individual investors can get plenty of bond diversification through their IRAs. Unless a person is wealthy with large amounts of money laying around in which to invest, I'm not sure there is much value in buying individual bonds. Let's say in a few years, though, cash assets are built up and it's time to consider individual bonds. How is this done? In my research on buying individual bonds outside of bond funds, there are several options for investors. The first option is to buy Federal bonds through the government TreasuryDirect.gov website. Set-up an online account; an option will open up to "purchase and hold Treasury bills, notes, bonds, Floating Rate Notes, Treasury Inflation-Protected Securities (TIPS), and savings bonds, and it's available to you 24 hours a day, 7 days a week."[cxx]

A second option is to buy individual municipal bonds from bond dealers, banks, brokerage firms, and in some cases directly from the municipality. Check out the following websites if interested in pursuing individual muni bonds purchases:

- muniadvocate.com
- municipalbonds.com
- fmsbonds.com
- investinginbonds.com
- finra.org
- emma.msrb.org
- munimarket.com
- fidelity.com
- scottrade.com
- tdameritrade.com
- tradeking.com

There are several options to choose from when it comes to brokers. Be sure to research and pick the one that personally works best.

A third option is to buy bonds on the secondary market. This involves buying from individuals trying to unload bonds earlier than the bond maturity date. Any brokerage firm will sell bonds on the secondary market. Look for secondary market bonds on the websites I mentioned above.

The majority of investment planners encourage investing in bonds. Investing a percentage of money into bonds helps smooth out the rollercoaster ride of the stock market. The easiest and safest way to invest in the bond market is through bond funds offered in your IRA. Look for low cost short-term and intermediate-term bond funds.

Most experts generally discourage long-term bond funds. If desiring to purchase individual federal securities or muni bonds, I would have all my other stock market and bond market investing "ducks in a row." Treat individual bond purchases as riskier investments near the top of the investment pyramid as proposed by LIFE Leadership. Be cautious and conduct plenty of research.

## Robo-Advisor Investing Companies

There are several different types of grocery stores. Many tend to be on the large side like Walmart stores. A few stores such as Aldi stay small on purpose. The main difference between grocery shopping at an Aldi store versus a store such as Walmart is that Walmart attempts to stock as much product as possible. Aldi, though, goes a different direction. They only stock a few, select grocery choices at a lower cost than their larger competitors. The hope is to have a better shopping experience through staying small and inexpensive. A similar approach has been taken by some competitive start-ups in the world of investing.

With the rise of technology over the last several years, there have been new, innovative companies that have entered the marketplace to fill the void of lower cost financial investing. The two companies that have risen to the top of this new automated, "robo-advisor" investing market are Betterment (betterment.com) and Wealthfront (wealthfront.com).

There are two basic premises behind companies such as Betterment and Wealthfront. First, they assess risk tolerance depending on whether the person is a conservative investor or risk-taker. Second, based on risk tolerance, a robo-advisor takes the person's account and puts their money to work in a specific mix of exchange traded funds (ETFs). The principle behind a robo-advisor is to provide a personal investment advisor for the fraction of the cost.

Let me stop here for a moment and explain ETFs. Exchange traded funds are defined as "a marketable security that tracks an index, a commodity, bonds, or a basket of assets like an index fund. Unlike mutual funds, an ETF trades like a common stock on a stock exchange. ETFs experience price changes throughout the day as they are bought and sold. ETFs typically have higher daily liquidity and lower fees than mutual fund shares, making them an attractive alternative for individual investors. Because it trades like a stock, an ETF does not have its net asset value (NAV) calculated once at the end of every day like a mutual fund does."[cxxi]

With Betterment and Wealthfront, there are only a few, select choices for the individual investor to make. These companies have a limited number of ETFs in which they will invest a person's money. Whether grocery shopping or investing, fewer yet quality choices can make the job easier for the individual shopper or investor.

Every investor who invests in a company such as Betterment or Wealthfront has the exact same, limited number of investment choices. So, the only difference between investors will be their personal allocation of their investment money based on risk tolerance.

This entire investment model is based on a concept called Modern Portfolio Theory (MPT). This theory holds to the idea that the individual security selection is not nearly as important as the proper allocation into the appropriate asset classes.

So what are the individual securities that these robo-advisor companies invest in? Betterment invests in 6 Stock ETFs and 7 Bond ETFs. To see a listing of the primary and secondary ETFs, as well as taxable or IRA choices, go to https://www.betterment.com/resources/investment-strategy/etfs/good-investment-selection-science-art/.

Wealthfront invests in 11 asset classes—4 stocks, 5 bonds (including TIPS[cxxii]), real estate, and natural resources. To see a complete listing of these asset classes, as well as a thorough explanation of Wealthfront's investing methodology, go to https://research.wealthfront.com/whitepapers/investment-methodology/.

Which one is better? The answer: it depends on what investment options the person is looking for exactly. Although there are many similarities between the two companies, here are the major differences between the two services that I could find:

- Wealthfront doesn't hold the person's portfolio. They just manage it. Actual holdings are with Apex Clearing Corporation[cxxiii].
- Wealthfront has two funds that Betterment doesn't invest in: real estate and natural resources. If complete diversification is the goal, Wealthfront seems to be the stronger choice.
- Betterment offers US Bonds as part of their asset allocation. Wealthfront does not, possibly due to low returns.
- Wealthfront offers government-issued Treasury Inflation Protected Securities (TIPS).

So, why even consider investing in a robo-advisor such as Betterment or Wealthfront? If new to the world of investing or if the person prefers a more hands-off approach, the primary benefit is a low-cost, low-maintenance, professionally managed investment portfolio. Once risk-tolerance allocations are determined, the account needs only to be funded. Either company will ask a series of questions upon signing up to determine needs and risk tolerance. Based on those answers, they will then set a level of risk. They both also offer a slide bar that allows some control of portfolio allocation.

This has been a simple overview of the new world of robo-advisors along with the two most popular companies in this area—Betterment and Wealthfront. I recommend checking out the following blog post on the website Investor Junkie[cxxiv] for an even more detailed analysis to make an informed decision if considering investing this way: https://investorjunkie.com/36355/betterment-wealthfront-compare/. This post has abundant, excellent lists and charts of the pros and cons, plus similarities and differences between the two companies. Check it out and see if the world of robo-advisors might be a good choice for second level stock market investing.

## Motif Investing

Before diving into the world of stewardship and personal finance, I was (and still am) a musician. I am a trumpet player as well as an orchestra conductor. In my college years, I attended two music schools: The Cleveland Institute of Music[cxxv] and The Peabody Conservatory of Music[cxxvi] (now part of Johns Hopkins University).

As part of my musical training in college, I learned form and analysis of music. The concept of a "motif" is especially popular in analyzing opera music. According to Wikipedia, a musical motif or motive "is a short musical idea, a salient recurring figure, musical fragment or succession of notes that has some special importance in or is characteristic of a composition: 'The motive is the smallest structural unit possessing thematic identity.'"[cxxvii]

Similar to the Betterment and Wealthfront web sites and in connection with the accelerating development in tech in recent years, another company has developed that puts an additional new spin on the world of investing. This website-based investing company is called "Motif."[cxxviii]

In 2010, Hardeep Walia was looking for a way to invest in the "mobile Internet." While his friends told him to just buy Apple (AAPL) stock, Hardeep was looking for a broader diversification of the "mobile ecosystem," such as chip manufacturers, cell phone towers, and operators. There were no specific funds or ETFs available to cover this investing concept. Hardeep struck upon a great idea and a need in the investing marketplace. As a result, motifinvesting.com was born.

In trying to explain what his company is about, CEO Hardeep Walia claims that Motif is like combining the investment experience of Peter Lynch with the diversification of Jack Bogle. The principle idea behind Motif Investing is investing in groups of investments that share similar characteristics. A "motif" or thematic investment package features twenty to thirty stocks or ETFs (exchange traded funds) that follow a specific theme. Some motif examples include "Precious Metals," "3D Printing," and "Black Gold."

There is a lot of flexibility with the Motif Investing platform. Although the company offers more than 150 professionally built portfolios, they also allow investors a lot of flexibility in altering and creating their own motifs. Creating a motif can be done inexpensively for $9.95 per motif. Motif understands that each investor is unique with respect to financial goals, time horizons, risk profiles, investing interests, and personal values. This unusual investing company provides investors with a platform and tools to achieve their unique investing goals.

According to the Motif website, it's possible to "look for motifs using different criteria, such as exploring by industry or looking for themes based on current events. It's also possible to screen motifs by looking at daily change, one-year return, and popularity. The screener allows you the chance to find just what you're looking for in an investment."

Here's a quick rundown on the basic details of utilizing the Motif Investing website:

- A motif is a basket of up to thirty stocks or ETFs weighted to reflect an investment theme, market insight, or trend.
- There is great flexibility in motifs. Choose from professionally built motifs, and customize them if desired. Motifs can be personally designed and bought with one click.
- Costs: Pay just $9.95 total commission per motif trade or $4.95 per single stock trade.
- Account minimums: According to their website, "There is no account minimum. To invest in a motif, you can start investing for as little as $300. You need to deposit $250 to make a trade. If you want to buy on margin, you will need to maintain a minimum balance of $2,000. Please note that margin trading is not applicable to IRAs. Motif Investing is a member of FINRA and SIPC insured."
- Motif's trade in real time, both buying and selling.

Motif investing is an interesting twist on investing in today's marketplace. Again, going back to the investment pyramid as proposed by Brady and Woodward, Motif investing would be considered the top of the pyramid. This would be speculative investing. After some initial research and smaller investing "experiments" in the platform, and working toward becoming an "expert" in Motif, it might be wise to consider investing more money in the platform. Once the hard work is done and the investor feels well educated, there should be less risk—investing through Motif will be based on firsthand knowledge and not speculation.

## Dividend Investing

There are many, well-known companies that sell dividend growth stocks. These dividend companies include Coca-Cola, Johnson & Johnson, Walmart, Proctor & Gamble, General Mills, Aflac, AT&T, Exxon Mobil, and many others. These are companies people do business with every day. They buy their products. They observe their current growth as well as their potential growth in the future. Who wouldn't want to own a piece of these companies?

What exactly is a dividend? A dividend is defined as "a distribution of a portion of a company's earnings, decided by the board of directors, to a class of its shareholders. Dividends can be issued as cash payments, as shares of stock, or other property."[cxxix] In other words, a dividend is a small "extra" part of the company's earnings that is paid out to its shareholders on top of the value of the stocks that is (hopefully) increasing over time.

If one is not familiar with dividends and the companies that issue them, there are a variety of resources available to assist self-educating investors to learn more. I have listed several different websites in the resources section at the end of this chapter. The top five places I would investigate first include the following:

- **Dividend Stocks Rock** (www.dividendstocksrock.com). This website recently turned into a subscription website for serious dividend investors. There is still plenty of free information to be had here, though.
- **The Dividend Guy** (www.thedividendguyblog.com). This website is run by the same guy, Mike, who owns Dividend Stocks Rock. Both sites pretty much run in tandem with one another, although this site doesn't have a subscription side to it. I receive Mike's email newsletter from this blog and it contains many great stock charts that he generates over on his other website.
- **DRiP Investing Resource Center** (www.dripinvesting.org). Go to the Info/Tools/Forms page. This is an excellent resource for Excel Spreadsheets and PDF forms that contain lists of dividend champions. There are many other dividend investing resources on

the other pages as well. If searching for pure dividend information, this is a great source!
- **Dividend.com.** Abundant lists, charts, and other research goodies may be found on this site.
- **S&P 500 Dividend Aristocrats list.** Finding a decent listing of this will require a bit of hunting around Google. I finally stumbled across one at the following website: www.buyupside.com/dividendaristocrats/dividendaristocratsyields sorted.php.

After doing research, create a stock watch list of fifty dividend growth stock companies. When money becomes available to invest, come back to this list, which will assist in making wise investment choices.

There are several considerations to keep in mind when shopping for dividend stocks. First, look for companies that have at least five years of dividend increases. Choose companies that are committed to paying out higher dividend income to their shareholders each year. Second, many investors recommend buying dividend stocks that have at least a yield of 3 percent and higher. There are a few companies that may be considered below the 3 percent level. If a certain company below 3 percent is going to aggressively raise their dividend yield soon, or it's a solid company that will likely do well in the future, consider buying their stock due to potential growth. When considering dividend stocks that are currently paying a yield between 2 and 3 percent, be sure to require strong growth from these companies. If they aren't strong, don't buy them.

Third, when evaluating these companies, look at their ten-year historical dividend rate. This number should be above the rate of inflation. If it's lower than inflation, move on. Fourth, look for the earnings per share (EPS) over the past ten years to be trending upward. EPS is your share of the company profits. Solid companies grow their profitability for their shareholders over time. If profits are decreasing or erratic, move on to a better company. Fifth, look for a price to earnings ratio (P/E) under twenty-five. Price to earnings ratios are calculated by taking the current market price divided by the most recent EPS. The historic average of the stock market P/E ratio is around fourteen. Since dividend growth companies are usually more established companies with slower growth, expect the P/E valuation to be lower than faster-growing companies.

There are two primary benefits of owning dividend growth stocks. First, an ideal retirement situation would be to have enough invested in a diversified portfolio of dividend growth stocks that one could live off of the income generated by the dividends themselves. Stocks would never need to be sold off. The dividends being paid out by the stocks would perpetually pay income for one's entire retirement. How cool is that! Second, dividends are (currently) taxed at favorable rates. In fact, those who are in the lowest two tax brackets will pay zero income tax on dividends. Even people in higher tax brackets will pay lower income tax rates for dividends, depending on the type of account used and the tax consequences for that particular account.

*Quick Tip: When investing in dividend growth stocks, keep a diversified portfolio just like diversifying a 401(k) account. Don't "keep all your eggs in one basket," so to speak. In the world of dividend investing, there are several sectors to diversify portfolios that include the following: healthcare, utilities, financial, basic materials, and consumer goods.*

There are a couple of ways to go about setting up an account to buy dividend stocks. One way is by investing through a Roth IRA. Contributions can be withdrawn at any time without penalty—a positive point of investing through a Roth IRA. There are no age restrictions like other tax-advantaged retirement accounts. Also, there is no required withdrawal age. The only drawback to investing through a Roth IRA is the restriction to a $5,500 (under 50) or $6,500 (over 50) contribution limit. A second way is to open a taxable brokerage account. Invest whatever amount with no contribution limits, but as the name states, these accounts are taxable. Those with a large amount of money to invest can work dividend stock investment strategies through both accounts. Contribute up to the maximum in a Roth IRA and then switch over to a regular taxable brokerage account for any additional money to invest.

*Quick Tip: Be careful not to contribute beyond the maximum allowable amounts for every IRA-type account. If contributing to more than one at a time in a given year, by law contributing cannot exceed the $5,500 (under 50) or $6,500 (over 50) limits,* *combined. For example, Jeffrey, forty-five, has both a traditional IRA and a Roth IRA and can only contribute a total of $5,500 to either one or both in 2016. Consult a tax or investment expert with questions about contribution limits.*

When investing in dividend stocks, be careful not to fall into what is called the "dividend trap." The dividend trap is when people value the dividends that a specific company pays out over the actual value of the company. People can fall into this trap for a variety of reasons. One reason is since dividend stock is for the long term, people are paid to wait around anyway. If just the dividends themselves look good, it will be worth it over time. A second reason is even during times of past market instability, dividends continued to be paid to investors. And a third reason? Dividends may even *increase* during bad markets.

Dividend investors can become caught up in this line of reasoning and forget to take a holistic view of the companies in which they are investing. They become blinded by dividend growth in mediocre companies that have a mediocre future. Investors should desire companies that pay solid dividends over the long term as well as have a promising future and growth track. For example, in the past McDonald's (MCD) has been a well-established business with a decent track record until recent years from 2012 to 2015 when it has faltered for several different reasons. But many investors have chosen to hold on to McDonald's stock primarily because of good dividend payouts. It became a dividend trap.[cxxx] But, comparing that same timeframe from 2012 to 2015, a company such as Disney (DIS) had a positive, steady stock growth. The company seems to have a bright future ahead without any slowing down. A decision to buy Disney stock would avoid the dividend trap. Yes, both dividends would be received as well as long-term stock growth over time. The main point is to thoroughly research the companies that pay dividends before investing in them. Look at the company's long-term business forecast, not just dividend yield.[cxxxi]

This final section on dividend investing has been placed at the end of this Part Two chapter on investing for a reason. Going back to the *Financial Fitness* investment pyramid model I referenced at the beginning of Part Two of this book, dividend stock investing is considered to be speculative. In my opinion, though, I see the wisdom in doing research on dividend stocks, buying intelligently, and diversifying a portfolio of individual dividend stocks within different sectors. This type of investing is a good decision for strong, steady growth over a long period of time.

*Quick Tip: For a FREE list of the Action Steps and Resources for each chapter of the book, simply go to:* [http://www.heroicpersonalfinances.com/for-christians-book-action-steps/](http://www.heroicpersonalfinances.com/for-christians-book-action-steps/)

# CHAPTER 13
# WRAP-UP: PUTTING IT ALL TOGETHER (MY 21-BULLET POINT VERSION OF THE BABY STEPS)

Christian finance classes such as Financial Peace University™ have been such a useful tool for millions of families because of their simplicity, along with the fact that these programs just plain work. If willing to WORK hard (you know, put the effort and energy into actually getting the job done), results will be positive! In FPU, Dave Ramsey provides seven "Baby Steps" to work through in personal finances. While Dave's approach utilizing seven steps seems simple enough, sometimes doing the actual work in each Baby Step is where the challenge in the program lies.

- Can you and your family focus enough to get $1,000 in the bank for your baby emergency fund?
- Are you really committed to cutting up your credit cards and getting out of debt by using the debt snowball method?
- Are you the type of person that is fully committed to the program and able to follow through?

I am currently living the Baby Steps. I have found huge success executing the first four Baby Steps at the time of my writing this book. I will keep using the Baby Steps as a good general guide for my family's personal finances. Based on the information I have shared in this book, though, I would like to synthesize everything down to a modified version of Dave's seven Baby Steps. Here is my personal, 21-Bullet Point Version of Dave's plan along with my own recommendations taken from this book—an "executive summary" to come back to for reminders and inspiration:

- **Pre-Baby Steps/Foundation to success:** This is a combination of all the things I share in Part One of the book. Recognize God as the source of everything. Live out an attitude of gratitude in life, and be generous with God's money on many levels. Establish morning routines that, over time, hardwire one's brain for success.

Learn to manage personal energy at a higher level through diet, exercise, sleep, emotional control, and sexual energy. Take on the wealthy mindset through reading, quality habits, mentors, buying assets, leveraging all tax advantages, and protecting one's self, legally. Establishing these various habits will set people up for success as they work their way through all the Baby Steps.

- **Baby Step 1: $1,000 in the bank.** Yes, do this Baby Step! This is the baby emergency fund to kick the habit of relying on credit cards and other types of long-term debt.
- **Baby Step 2: Debt snowball.** Yes, do this baby step! Get out of debt using this plan as fast as possible. Depending on how much debt one has, getting through this Baby Step could take a while. Have patience and persevere to the end of it!
- **Baby Step 3a: The fully funded emergency fund of 3–6 months worth of expense money in the bank.** Yes, do this Baby Step along with the following modifications I present in the book:

    - Get 3–6 months worth of expense money in the bank. Consider breaking up this amount into a "baby-ish" emergency fund that is immediately accessible in a bank savings account tied directly to a checking account. Keep the rest of the emergency fund in a higher rate of return savings account or money market account that takes a couple of days to actually access the money.
    - Get $3,000 to $5,000 in cash together in smaller bills and store in a fireproof safe at home. This is for an emergency situation when access to bank accounts might be blocked and money is needed to simply survive (situations like Category 5 hurricanes, blizzard of the century, zombie apocalypse, or maybe even the looming US Debt Crisis).
    - Consider small silver coins stored in a safe for extreme situations, such as the ones I just mentioned.
    - Have survival food and water stored (in the house) for extreme situations.
    - Get a decent generator, fuel, and power cords for extreme situations.

- ☐ Consider buying guns and ammo to protect the family.
- **Baby Step 3b: Saving for a home down payment.** For those who don't own a home (or perhaps better stated, don't have a home mortgage), this is the altered Baby Step in which Dave recommends saving at least a 10 percent down payment, getting no longer than a 15-year mortgage, and keeping mortgage payments at 25 percent or less of monthly income. Other than buying a home outright with cash, this is a "safer" way to be right-side-up on a home mortgage and pay it off sooner than later. While I agree with the main plan for the 10 percent down payment, 15-year mortgage, and 25 percent payment, everyone's situation is a little different. While I won't go into all the specific details, my family did a modified version of Dave's plan in August of 2015, mainly because it was becoming increasingly advantageous for us on several different levels to mortgage a home than to continue renting. We rented for almost ten years to get out of a lot of debt on two separate occasions, and it was finally time to pull the trigger on a home purchase. As of today, I feel like we made a wise decision. If Dave looked at our financials, he would have told us to wait a little longer based on his formula, but, again, everybody's circumstances are unique. Everyone can't be forced into a cookie-cutter method.
- **Baby Step 4: Invest 15 percent.** Yes, once the various parts of the first three Baby Steps are completed, step on the gas and move on investing money for the future. This is where I begin to move away from Dave's simplistic "invest 15 percent in mutual funds" approach and move toward the investment pyramid as proposed in the book *Financial Fitness: The Offense, Defense, and Playing Field of Personal Finance* by LIFE Leadership. Using the investment pyramid as a guide, here are my recommendations under an altered Baby Step 4:
    - ☐ **If one's company or non-profit organization offers a match in a 401(k) or 403(b), invest enough money to receive the matching funds, and stop here for now on stock market investing.** If at all possible, try to find

index funds in which to invest in the company's plan. Use Dave's allocation strategy of 25 percent in International, Large Cap, Mid-Cap, and Small Cap. In today's volatile markets, though, I would seriously consider adding bond index funds into the mix to even out the roller coaster ride of the stock market. The majority of investors I have studied recommend a mix of 60 percent stocks and 40 percent bonds. Also, do the ratios based on age that I mentioned back in Chapter 12.

☐ **If currently an employee for someone else, maximize personal productivity. At the same time, increase time flexibility.** Be a great, productive employee, but also allow for personal time and energy to pursue other business and investment strategies in the investment pyramid.

☐ **Next, invest in yourself.** Invest especially in the areas of reading, writing, and public speaking. These will pay huge dividends later on, especially in the current Information Age. Also, figure out ways to create multiple streams of income. Passive income streams are ideal. Create an information product (print book, eBook, or online course) that people will pay decent money for. Create some type of membership website that people will pay a monthly fee to keep coming back to the site. Market and sell a product on a website. If not creative in producing a product, consider buying a website businesses that would create income streams.

☐ **Put your money to work like banks do.** First, based on my own personal experience, I believe it's wise to care a little more about your FICO® score than Dave does. Keeping a decent credit score comes in handy for home mortgages and insurance purchases. Second, consider an IBC (Infinite Banking Concept) policy to have a personal cash flow management strategy by becoming a personal "bank." Third, consider peer-to-peer lending strategies. Fourth, look into tax deeds and tax lien certificates. Finally,

around age 50–55, investigate the potential of an annuity becoming a lifetime stream of income in the golden years.
- **Buy real estate and virtual property.** Wealthy people such as Robert Kiyosaki and Dave Ramsey invest heavily in real estate.[cxxxii] This tells me everything I need to know. Virtual property—domain name buying and selling, website flipping, and website business purchases—could be another stream of income as well.
- **Return to the stock market.** If already at maximum potential of investing in one's self, putting money to work like banks do, and investing in property, then consider returning to the stock market. Examine the possibility of using a mix of additional index funds, bond funds, ETFs, automated strategies, as well as dividend investing.

- **Baby Step 5: College saving.** I'm not completely convinced that Education Savings Accounts (ESAs) are always the best vehicle to use for college savings. The only positive upside I see on these is tax advantages. If a person's children need help financially through college, many of the cash flow suggestions I make in the last investing step, Baby Step 4, will probably be adequate for some money for college. These cash flow suggestions include passive income streams from owned businesses, IBC policy loans, peer-to-peer lending investments, tax liens, and real estate. Moving sooner than later on these suggestions will leave more time for money to be working to eventually help children through college.
- **Baby Step 6: Pay off the house early.** When maximum potential has been reached in passive income streams, IBC policies, and other investment strategies, use all available, extra money in the budget to pay off home mortgages as soon as possible. After paying off a personal home, consider completely paying off any real estate investment property mortgages as well.
- **Baby Step 7: Build wealth and give.** In this final stage, continue working on businesses, passive income streams, and other wealth building, investment strategies. Always give generously in each

Baby Step, but this is the phase in a person's personal finance journey to give at an even higher level than ever before.

*Quick Tip: Interested in receiving a printable checklist of my 21-bullet point version of the Baby Steps? Simply head over to <http://www.heroicpersonalfinances.com/21-bullet-checklist/> to download your copy.*

# OUTRO: CRANK THE FLYWHEEL OF SUCCESS!

In Chapter 5, I referenced one of my favorite business books of all time, *Good to Great* by Jim Collins. In his book, Mr. Collins researched several companies to determine how they made the transitional leap from a good company to a great company. Collins includes such "good-to-great companies" as Abbott, Fannie Mae, Gillette, Kimberly-Clark, Kroger, Nucor, Pitney Bowes, Walgreens, and Wells Fargo.

After investigating what causes these companies to move from good to great, Jim Collins believes he has uncovered the "secret sauce" of great companies. The three main ways companies become great is through Disciplined People, Disciplined Thought, and Disciplined Action. If companies spend time getting these disciplines nailed down, then they have a higher potential to become great.

But, becoming a great company is not a "get these three areas nailed down and move on to the real work" type of process. This is a continuous process of making sure the right people, engaged in the right business thought patterns, are taking the best course of action. Collins refers to this continuous process as the "Flywheel Effect."

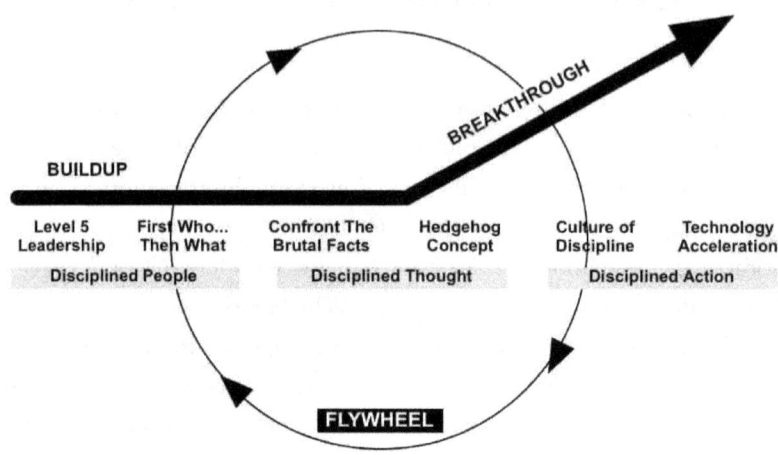

Copyright © 2001
Reprinted by permission of Curtis Brown, Ltd.

According to Wikipedia, a flywheel is "a rotating mechanical device that is used to store rotational energy. Flywheels have an inertia called the moment of inertia and thus resist changes in rotational speed. The amount of energy stored in a flywheel is proportional to the square of its rotational speed. Energy is transferred to a flywheel by the application of a torque to it, thereby increasing its rotational speed, and hence its stored energy. Conversely, a flywheel releases stored energy by applying torque to a mechanical load, thereby decreasing the flywheel's rotational speed."[cxxxiii]

A flywheel is a very interesting, mechanical device. It takes some time and effort to get a larger flywheel spinning. Once moving, though, watch out! It will have gathered so much momentum that it becomes extremely difficult to stop.

The same is true with attempting to start, change, or improve anything. This could be an established Fortune 500 company, a brand new start-up business, a new relationship, or a family's personal finances. Most effort must be applied on the front end, keeping in mind that disciplined people, thought, and action will be needed through the entire process. Assuming everything needed to get things moving in the right direction is in place, movement from small to bigger successes will occur. Once this begins to happen, the flywheel of success kicks in which creates almost unstoppable momentum.

Just like companies that establish the right people, thoughts, and actions to make the transition from a good company to a great company, I would say the same is true for personal life and finances. To transition a household from good over to great, establish strong, consistent, small habits that are constantly reinforced day by day; this will propel a family up to that next level. Be disciplined in all areas of life. Be thinking disciplined thoughts, together. Apply disciplined action at *all* times.

Part One of this book dealt with the concept of being disciplined people with disciplined thoughts. Using this as a guide, become disciplined in both spiritual and personal life. Acknowledge God as the source of everything. Grow in the area of generosity. Establish disciplined morning routines. Eat well. Exercise regularly. Get enough rest. Control emotions and sex drive. Also, become disciplined in thought. Use meditation, affirmations and writing, focus on big ideas, and take on the wealthy mindset.

Part Two of this book dealt mostly with disciplined *action*—establishing a Pareto Principled (80/20) focus in work, creating multiple streams of income, being prepared for the unexpected, plugging up any tax leaks, utilizing wise stock market strategies, and finally, putting money to work through a variety of methods.

A disciplined person who has disciplined thoughts and takes disciplined action opens up the potential to crank the flywheel of success to become an unstoppable force not only in personal finances but also in virtually every area of life. Start sooner than later to create that unstoppable success!

Peter Drucker, the famous American management consultant, educator, and author has said, "What gets measured, gets managed." To make positive, long-lasting changes in personal finances, track progress along the way. A great online tool that has been a huge help to me with financial tracking is Mint.com. At the time of this writing, I have been using Mint for the last three years as our family has dug out of $100,000 worth of debt and gotten back on track with our financial plan. There is another online tool that does a better job tracking investing strategies called PersonalCapital.com.[cxxxiv] Because our family is now focused on the investing side of our financial plan, we have been using the Personal Capital app to help us in this area as well.

Imagine a world filled with this type of a disciplined Christian—one who understands his or her responsibility as a manager of everything God has given them to manage. Imagine believers who comprehend that God cares just as much (and probably more!) about how they manage the other 90 percent of their finances as opposed to just caring about a 10 percent tithe. Imagine disciples who are maximizing their potential in the area of personal finances. If this was happening in the *Christian* community, I believe the world would be a much different place. It would be a more prosperous world where the gospel would be spread around the world at a faster rate. The (universal) church would care for the poor and needy as opposed to reliance on government programs. There would be less divorce and more intact family units. There would be less financial stress and more financial peace. I believe this is completely possible if Christians took serious responsibility of being financial managers of God's wealth.

Will you take up the challenge? Will you maximize your potential not only in your personal finances, but, more importantly, in your walk with the Lord? All these areas of life I have mentioned in this book are interconnected. All touch one another and impact the outcomes in each area.

My prayer is that one day the Lord will be able to say to you as an excellent manager of His wealth, "Well done, good and faithful servant! You have been faithful with a few things; I will put you in charge of many things. Come and share your master's happiness!"

May God bless you richly on this journey of a lifetime.

S.D.G.

# TIME TO TAKE ACTION

I read a lot of books. I gain a lot of knowledge and wisdom from these books. I highlight a lot of sections of these books in my Kindle app and store these highlights as notes in my Evernote app. Many times, I go back and review my notes from these books.

With most books I read, I come away with two or three "nuggets" of wisdom that I attempt to put into action in my life as soon as possible. This book is really just the outcome of putting a bunch of ideas together from a bunch of different books. I gathered ideas and put them into action. The results of action on these ideas have been tremendous. Action is the key to accomplishing anything great in your life. Knowledge alone does little.

I pray you have received several, solid ideas from this book that you can put into action as soon as possible. Before you finish this book, let me ask you to take action in four ways with what you have read:

1. Download your FREE copy of the Action Steps and Resources for all the chapters of this book at heroicpersonalfinances.com/for-christians-book-action-steps/.
2. Print off the checklist version of my **21-Bullet Point Version of the Baby Steps** from Chapter 13. Simply go to heroicpersonalfinances.com/21-bullet-checklist/ to download your copy.
3. With the 21-Bullet Points checklist in hand, go through the list and highlight three items you can take action on right away. For example, maybe you are currently building your emergency fund in Baby Step 3a and never considered emergency preparedness at home. You could take action in three ways by purchasing a safe, placing larger amounts of cash in that safe at home, and preparing emergency food and water supplies.
4. If you found value with this book, would you be willing to share it? **The best way you can share the value of what you learned is by leaving a book review on Amazon.com**. The more reviews I receive, the more exposure the book gets, and the more impact this book can have in other people's lives. **Thank you in advance for leaving a review!**

If you made it this far in the book, I know you will take action in at least these four ways and many others. I pray God's richest blessings on you and your family. Enjoy the journey!

For more information about *Heroic Personal Finances for Christians*, go to HeroicPersonalFinances.com.

# ABOUT THE AUTHOR

Larry Jones is the Generosity Pastor of First Baptist Raytown, Missouri, located in the Kansas City Metro Area. Larry first joined the staff in 1999 as the Associate Minister of Music. After life-changing experiences with Crown Financial Ministries (2000) and Dave Ramsey's original Financial Peace book (2004), he found himself with an extra staff role in the area of stewardship in 2008. This second role came about as a result of living out the principles that are taught by Crown Financial and Financial Peace — creating financial margin with cash reserves, debt free living, wise investing, and generous giving.

As a writer, Larry has been a successful serial blogger for almost a decade. He has also written a couple of smaller eBooks., but *Heroic Personal Finances for Christians* is his first long-form personal finance, self-help book.

Larry's mission is to help as many people as possible move into a state of abundance and generosity in their lives. Life is too short and there's too much for the people of God to accomplish for the Kingdom. Christians need to shed the shackles of debt and poor financial thinking and move to a place of prosperity so that they can help more people.

When Larry isn't writing or performing his Generosity Pastor duties, he is directing a 37-member volunteer worship orchestra at First Baptist Raytown.

Larry currently lives in Lee's Summit, Missouri, with his amazing wife Jennifer, four beautiful daughters, and one handsome son.

Here's how you can connect with Larry:

- LinkedIn: https://www.linkedin.com/in/joneswlarry
- Facebook: https://www.facebook.com/larryjones.biz
- Twitter: @JonesWLarry
- Google+: https://plus.google.com/u/0/104214976165798488810/posts
- Book Website: HeroicPersonalFinances.com

# ENDNOTES

## Introduction

[i] Source: https://www.intouch.org/read/life-principle-6-the-principle-of-sowing-and-reaping

[ii] Source: http://rickwarren.org/devotional/english/the-law-of-the-harvest-you-reap-more-than-you-sow_963

[iii] Source: http://www.daveramsey.com/baby-steps

## Introduction to Part One

[iv] Wikipedia: https://en.wikipedia.org/wiki/One_World_Trade_Center

[v] Who is T. Harv Eker?: https://en.wikipedia.org/wiki/T._Harv_Eker

## Chapter 1: God Is The Source

[vi] Scriptures taken from the Holy Bible, New International Version®, NIV®. Copyright © 1973, 1978, 1984, 2011 by Biblica, Inc.™ Used by permission of Zondervan. All rights reserved worldwide. www.zondervan.com The "NIV" and "New International Version" are trademarks registered in the United States Patent and Trademark Office by Biblica, Inc.™

[vii] Source: Salvation Prayer: http://peacewithgod.net

[viii] Scriptures taken from the Holy Bible, New International Version®, NIV®. Copyright © 1973, 1978, 1984, 2011 by Biblica, Inc.™ Used by permission of Zondervan. All rights reserved worldwide. www.zondervan.com The "NIV" and "New International Version" are trademarks registered in the United States Patent and Trademark Office by Biblica, Inc.™

[ix] Scriptures taken from the Holy Bible, New International Version®, NIV®. Copyright © 1973, 1978, 1984, 2011 by Biblica, Inc.™ Used by permission of Zondervan. All rights reserved worldwide. www.zondervan.com The "NIV" and "New International Version" are trademarks registered in the United States Patent and Trademark Office by Biblica, Inc.™

[x] Scriptures taken from the Holy Bible, New International Version®, NIV®. Copyright © 1973, 1978, 1984, 2011 by Biblica, Inc.™ Used by permission of Zondervan. All rights reserved worldwide. www.zondervan.com The "NIV" and "New International Version" are trademarks registered in the United States Patent and Trademark Office by Biblica, Inc.™

[xi] Source: http://www.businessinsider.com/17-lottery-winners-who-blew-it-all-2013-5?op=1

[xii] Source: (Book) Rich for Life by Dennis Sy

[xiii] Scriptures taken from the Holy Bible, New International Version®, NIV®. Copyright © 1973, 1978, 1984, 2011 by Biblica, Inc.™ Used by permission of Zondervan. All rights reserved worldwide. www.zondervan.com The "NIV" and "New International Version" are trademarks registered in the United States Patent and Trademark Office by Biblica, Inc.™

[xiv] Scripture quotations from THE MESSAGE. Copyright © by Eugene H. Peterson 1993, 1994, 1995, 1996, 2000, 2001, 2002. Used by permission of NavPress. All rights reserved. Represented by Tyndale House Publishers, Inc.

[xv] Scriptures taken from the Holy Bible, New International Version®, NIV®. Copyright © 1973, 1978, 1984, 2011 by Biblica, Inc.™ Used by permission of Zondervan. All rights reserved worldwide. www.zondervan.com The "NIV" and "New International Version" are trademarks registered in the United States Patent and Trademark Office by Biblica, Inc.™

[xvi] Scripture quotations from THE MESSAGE. Copyright © by

Eugene H. Peterson 1993, 1994, 1995, 1996, 2000, 2001, 2002. Used by permission of NavPress. All rights reserved. Represented by Tyndale House Publishers, Inc.

[xvii] The Holy Bible, English Standard Version® (ESV®)

Copyright © 2001 by Crossway,

a publishing ministry of Good News Publishers.

All rights reserved.

ESV Text Edition: 2011

[xviii] Scriptures taken from the Holy Bible, New International Version®, NIV®. Copyright © 1973, 1978, 1984, 2011 by Biblica, Inc.™ Used by permission of Zondervan. All rights reserved worldwide. www.zondervan.com The "NIV" and "New International Version" are trademarks registered in the United States Patent and Trademark Office by Biblica, Inc.™

[xix] https://evernote.com/?var=c

[xx] https://en.wikipedia.org/wiki/Andy_Stanley

**Chapter 2: Living The Generous Life**

[xxi] Scripture quotations are taken from the Holy Bible, New Living Translation, copyright ©1996, 2004, 2007, 2013, 2015 by Tyndale House Foundation. Used by permission of Tyndale House Publishers, Inc., Carol Stream, Illinois 60188. All rights reserved.

[xxii] Tony Robbins story source: "Money, Master The Game: 7 Simple Steps to Financial Freedom" by Tony Robbins, published by Simon & Schuster, pages 644-645 (Kindle version).

[xxiii] Scriptures taken from the Holy Bible, New International Version®, NIV®. Copyright © 1973, 1978, 1984, 2011 by Biblica, Inc.™ Used by

permission of Zondervan. All rights reserved worldwide. www.zondervan.com The "NIV" and "New International Version" are trademarks registered in the United States Patent and Trademark Office by Biblica, Inc.™

[xxiv] Source: http://www.thechangeblog.com/gratitude/

[xxv] Scriptures taken from the Holy Bible, New International Version®, NIV®. Copyright © 1973, 1978, 1984, 2011 by Biblica, Inc.™ Used by permission of Zondervan. All rights reserved worldwide. www.zondervan.com The "NIV" and "New International Version" are trademarks registered in the United States Patent and Trademark Office by Biblica, Inc.™

[xxvi] Check out what Pastor Rick Warren says about the Law of the Harvest: http://rickwarren.org/devotional/english/the-law-of-the-harvest-you-reap-more-than-you-sow_963

[xxvii] Scripture quotations from THE MESSAGE. Copyright © by Eugene H. Peterson 1993, 1994, 1995, 1996, 2000, 2001, 2002. Used by permission of NavPress. All rights reserved. Represented by Tyndale House Publishers, Inc.

[xxviii] Scriptures taken from the Holy Bible, New International Version®, NIV®. Copyright © 1973, 1978, 1984, 2011 by Biblica, Inc.™ Used by permission of Zondervan. All rights reserved worldwide. www.zondervan.com The "NIV" and "New International Version" are trademarks registered in the United States Patent and Trademark Office by Biblica, Inc.™

[xxix] Ibid.

[xxx] Ibid.

[xxxi] Ibid.

[xxxii] Ibid.

[xxxiii] Scriptures taken from the Holy Bible, New International Version®, NIV®. Copyright © 1973, 1978, 1984, 2011 by Biblica, Inc.™ Used by

permission of Zondervan. All rights reserved worldwide. www.zondervan.com The "NIV" and "New International Version" are trademarks registered in the United States Patent and Trademark Office by Biblica, Inc.™

[xxxiv] "Scripture quotations are from the ESV® Bible (The Holy Bible, English Standard Version®), copyright © 2001 by Crossway, a publishing ministry of Good News Publishers. Used by permission. All rights reserved."

[xxxv] Scriptures taken from the Holy Bible, New International Version®, NIV®. Copyright © 1973, 1978, 1984, 2011 by Biblica, Inc.™ Used by permission of Zondervan. All rights reserved worldwide. www.zondervan.com The "NIV" and "New International Version" are trademarks registered in the United States Patent and Trademark Office by Biblica, Inc.™

[xxxvi] "Scripture quotations are from the ESV® Bible (The Holy Bible, English Standard Version®), copyright © 2001 by Crossway, a publishing ministry of Good News Publishers. Used by permission. All rights reserved."

[xxxvii] Ibid.

[xxxviii] Ibid.

[xxxix] Ibid.

[xl] Amazon book link for Happy Money by Lania Buenostar: http://www.amazon.com/Happy-Increase-Simple-2-Step-Formula-ebook/dp/B008EED35I/ref=sr_1_fkmr0_1?ie=UTF8&qid=1461492315&sr=8-1-fkmr0&keywords=Happy+Money+by+Lania+Buenostar

[xli] Book: *Happy Money (Increase the Flow of Money with a Simple 2-Step Formula)* by Lania Buenostar. Copyright 2012 by Lania Buenostar.

## Chapter 3: Morning Routines And Habit Formation

[xlii] Scriptures taken from the Holy Bible, New International Version®, NIV®. Copyright © 1973, 1978, 1984, 2011 by Biblica, Inc.™ Used by permission of Zondervan. All rights reserved worldwide. www.zondervan.com The "NIV" and "New International Version" are trademarks registered in the United States Patent and Trademark Office by Biblica, Inc.™

[xliii] Scott Adams story source: http://www.businessinsider.com/the-creator-of-dilberts-morning-routine-2015-3#ixzz3kmuwqAW9

[xliv] http://www.stress.org/holmes-rahe-stress-inventory/

[xlv] Link to my first Christian personal finance blog: http://www.richchristianpoorchristian.com

[xlvi] Podcast Link: http://fourhourworkweek.com/2015/04/20/triple-h/

[xlvii] Podcast Link: http://fourhourworkweek.com/2015/09/18/5-morning-rituals/

[xlviii] Scriptures taken from the Holy Bible, New International Version®, NIV®. Copyright © 1973, 1978, 1984, 2011 by Biblica, Inc.™ Used by permission of Zondervan. All rights reserved worldwide. www.zondervan.com The "NIV" and "New International Version" are trademarks registered in the United States Patent and Trademark Office by Biblica, Inc.™

[xlix] Ibid.

[l] Ibid.

[li] Scriptures taken from the Holy Bible, New International Version®, NIV®. Copyright © 1973, 1978, 1984, 2011 by Biblica, Inc.™ Used by permission of Zondervan. All rights reserved worldwide. www.zondervan.com The "NIV" and "New International Version" are

trademarks registered in the United States Patent and Trademark Office by Biblica, Inc.™

[lii] Article written by Ray Williams, "Do Self-Affirmations Work? A Revisit." https://www.psychologytoday.com/blog/wired-success/201305/do-self-affirmations-work-revisit

## Chapter 4: Energy Management

[liii] Scriptures taken from the Holy Bible, New International Version®, NIV®. Copyright © 1973, 1978, 1984, 2011 by Biblica, Inc.™ Used by permission of Zondervan. All rights reserved worldwide. www.zondervan.com The "NIV" and "New International Version" are trademarks registered in the United States Patent and Trademark Office by Biblica, Inc.™

[liv] Source: *The 4-Hour Body: An Uncommon Guide To Rapid Fat-Loss, Incredible Sex, And Becoming Superhuman* by Timothy Ferriss

[lv] Who is Paul Michael Levesque?: https://en.wikipedia.org/wiki/Triple_H

[lvi] Who is Joyce Meyer? https://en.wikipedia.org/wiki/Joyce_Meyer

[lvii] Scriptures taken from the Holy Bible, New International Version®, NIV®. Copyright © 1973, 1978, 1984, 2011 by Biblica, Inc.™ Used by permission of Zondervan. All rights reserved worldwide. www.zondervan.com The "NIV" and "New International Version" are trademarks registered in the United States Patent and Trademark Office by Biblica, Inc.™

[lviii] Who is Paulo Coelho? https://en.wikipedia.org/wiki/Paulo_Coelho

[lix] Scripture quotations are taken from the Holy Bible, New Living Translation, copyright ©1996, 2004, 2007, 2013, 2015 by Tyndale House Foundation. Used by permission of Tyndale House Publishers, Inc., Carol Stream, Illinois 60188. All rights reserved.

[lx] Source: *Think and Grow Rich* by Napoleon Hill

## Chapter 5: Take On The Wealthy Mindset

[lxi] Scriptures taken from the Holy Bible, New International Version®,

NIV®. Copyright © 1973, 1978, 1984, 2011 by Biblica, Inc.™ Used by permission of Zondervan. All rights reserved worldwide. www.zondervan.com The "NIV" and "New International Version" are trademarks registered in the United States Patent and Trademark Office by Biblica, Inc.™

[lxii] Who is Sara Blakely? https://en.wikipedia.org/wiki/Sara_Blakely

[lxiii] Source Note: These 20 items were actually contained in a Dave Ramsey blog post: https://www.daveramsey.com/blog/20-things-the-rich-do-every-day

[lxiv] Who is Zig Ziglar? https://en.wikipedia.org/wiki/Zig_Ziglar

[lxv] Scriptures taken from the Holy Bible, New International Version®, NIV®. Copyright © 1973, 1978, 1984, 2011 by Biblica, Inc.™ Used by permission of Zondervan. All rights reserved worldwide. www.zondervan.com The "NIV" and "New International Version" are trademarks registered in the United States Patent and Trademark Office by Biblica, Inc.™

[lxvi] Scripture quotations from THE MESSAGE. Copyright © by Eugene H. Peterson 1993, 1994, 1995, 1996, 2000, 2001, 2002. Used by permission of NavPress. All rights reserved. Represented by Tyndale House Publishers, Inc.

[lxvii] Check out Michael Hyatt's wealth of information on Virtual Assistants on his blog: http://michaelhyatt.com/tag/virtual-assistant

[lxviii] Source: http://abovethelaw.com/2012/07/infographic-of-the-day-american-litigiousness-statistics-that-will-make-you-angry/

---

**Part Two: Introduction (An Explanation And Framework)**

[lxix] Source: A special thank you to Life Leadership (lifeleadership.com) for the use of the You, Inc. Investment Hierarchy pyramid as found in *Financial Fitness: The Offense, Defense, and Playing Field of Personal Finance* by LIFE Leadership. Used by permission.

[lxx] Source: http://national.deseretnews.com/article/16282/one-man-interviewed-1200-wealthy-people-and-heres-the-free-activity-he-found-they-all-do.html

## Chapter 6: Invest In Yourself

[lxxi] Scriptures taken from the Holy Bible, New International Version®, NIV®. Copyright © 1973, 1978, 1984, 2011 by Biblica, Inc.™ Used by permission of Zondervan. All rights reserved worldwide. www.zondervan.com The "NIV" and "New International Version" are trademarks registered in the United States Patent and Trademark Office by Biblica, Inc.™

[lxxii] Source: http://www.brainyquote.com/quotes/quotes/r/renzopiano575230.html

[lxxiii] http://www.crown.org

[lxxiv] https://en.wikipedia.org/wiki/Diminishing_returns

[lxxv] Source: Wikipedia. https://en.wikipedia.org/wiki/Pareto_principle

[lxxvi] Source: The Urban Dictionary. http://www.urbandictionary.com/define.php?term=Passion

[lxxvii] Source: http://rickwarren.org/devotional/english/god-is-waiting-for-you-to-plant-a-seed

[lxxviii] Scriptures taken from the Holy Bible, New International Version®, NIV®. Copyright © 1973, 1978, 1984, 2011 by Biblica, Inc.™ Used by permission of Zondervan. All rights reserved worldwide. www.zondervan.com The "NIV" and "New International Version" are trademarks registered in the United States Patent and Trademark Office by Biblica, Inc.™

[lxxix] Ibid.

[lxxx] Ibid.

[lxxxi] Ibid.

[lxxxii] Scripture taken from the NEW AMERICAN STANDARD BIBLE(R), Copyright (C) 1960,1962,1963,1968,1971,1972,1973,1975,1977,1995 by The Lockman Foundation. Used by permission.

[lxxxiii] Ibid.

[lxxxiv] www.michaelhyatt.com

[lxxxv] www.fourhourworkweek.com

[lxxxvi] http://www.meetup.com

[lxxxvii] https://www.toastmasters.org

[lxxxviii] http://freedomtospeak.toastmastersclubs.org

## Chapter 7: Emergency Preparedness

[lxxxix] Scriptures taken from the Holy Bible, New International Version®, NIV®. Copyright © 1973, 1978, 1984, 2011 by Biblica, Inc.™ Used by permission of Zondervan. All rights reserved worldwide. www.zondervan.com The "NIV" and "New International Version" are trademarks registered in the United States Patent and Trademark Office by Biblica, Inc.™

[xc] Quote source: http://www.brainyquote.com/quotes/quotes/r/robertbade138358.html

[xci] For more information on Ron Popeil: http://www.biography.com/people/ron-popeil-177863

[xcii] Definition: Fiat money is currency that a government has declared to be legal tender, but is not backed by a physical commodity. The value of fiat money is derived from the relationship between supply and demand rather than the value of the material that the money is made of. Historically, most currencies were based on physical commodities such as gold or silver, but fiat money is based solely on faith. Fiat is the Latin word for "it shall be." Read more: Fiat Money Definition | Investopedia http://www.investopedia.com/terms/f/fiatmoney.asp#ixzz4CaNJSWNx

[xciii] http://www.emergencymgmt.com

[xciv] Website source link: http://www.newjerusalem.com/PureWater.htm

## Chapter 8: (Interlude) Tax Strategies

[xcv] Scriptures taken from the Holy Bible, New International Version®, NIV®. Copyright © 1973, 1978, 1984, 2011 by Biblica, Inc.™ Used by permission of Zondervan. All rights reserved worldwide. www.zondervan.com The "NIV" and "New International Version" are trademarks registered in the United States Patent and Trademark Office by Biblica, Inc.™

[xcvi] Source: Book - Multiple Streams of Income: How to Generate a

Lifetime of Unlimited Wealth by Robert G. Allen. Kindle locations: 226, 653.

[xcvii] Source: Book - How to Pay Zero Taxes 2015: Your Guide to Every Tax Break the IRS Allows by Jeff Schnepper Kindle location: 856.

[xcviii] Source: http://www.gobankingrates.com/personal-finance/49-special-tax-deductions-dont/

## Chapter 9: Stock Market Investing: Part 1

[xcix] Scriptures taken from the Holy Bible, New International Version®, NIV®. Copyright © 1973, 1978, 1984, 2011 by Biblica, Inc.™ Used by permission of Zondervan. All rights reserved worldwide. www.zondervan.com The "NIV" and "New International Version" are trademarks registered in the United States Patent and Trademark Office by Biblica, Inc.™

[c] Source: https://propelsteps.wordpress.com/2014/05/10/story-stock-monkey-market-funny-explanation/

[ci] Source: http://www.fool.com/retirement/general/2016/01/11/criticizing-financial-guru-dave-ramsey-for-this-ad.aspx

## Chapter 10: Put Your Money To Work Like Banks, Insurance Companies, And The Wealthy

[cii] Scriptures taken from the Holy Bible, New International Version®, NIV®. Copyright © 1973, 1978, 1984, 2011 by Biblica, Inc.™ Used by permission of Zondervan. All rights reserved worldwide. www.zondervan.com The "NIV" and "New International Version" are trademarks registered in the United States Patent and Trademark Office by Biblica, Inc.™

[ciii] Source article by K. Mike Merrill: http://bigthink.com/capitally/re-thinking-the-game-of-monopoly

[civ] Source: Bill Gates article: http://www.businessinsider.com/this-man-made-bill-gates-so-wealthy-2014-9

[cv] Source: http://consultingbyrpm.com/drop/ibc.pdf

[cvi] Source: https://fundresearch.fidelity.com/mutual-funds/summary/315792655

[cvii] Source: https://www.amazon.com/How-Profit-Peer-Peer-Lending-ebook/dp/B00APBK6T4

[cviii] Web link: Investopedia.com

[cix] Source: http://www.investopedia.com/terms/t/taxliencertificate.asp?layout=infini&v=5A&adtest=5A

[cx] Source: http://www.investopedia.com/terms/t/tax-deed.asp?o=40186&l=dir&qsrc=999&qo=investopediaSiteSearch&ap=investopedia.com&layout=infini&v=5A&orig=1&adtest=5A

[cxi] Source: *How to NOT Get Ripped Off when Buying an Annuity* by Alessandra Derniat

## Chapter 11: Property Ownership

[cxii] Scripture taken from the NEW AMERICAN STANDARD BIBLE(R), Copyright (C) 1960,1962,1963,1968,1971,1972,1973,1975,1977,1995 by The Lockman Foundation. Used by permission.

[cxiii] Source: Wikipedia: https://en.wikipedia.org/wiki/Wealth

[cxiv] Source: http://americanpolicy.org/2012/11/19/private-property-ownership-is-the-only-way-to-eradicate-poverty/

[cxv] Source article: MILLION-DOLLAR URLS: The Most Expensive Domain Names Of All Time from the Business Insider, http://www.businessinsider.com/most-expensive-domain-names-2014-7?op=1}:

## Chapter 12: Stock Markey Investing: Part 2

[cxvi] Scripture taken from the New King James Version®. Copyright © 1982 by Thomas Nelson. Used by permission. All rights reserved.

[cxvii] Source: Investopedia: http://www.investopedia.com/terms/i/indexfund.asp?o=40186&l=dir&qsrc=999&qo=investopediaSiteSearch

[cxviii] Online Article: http://www.getrichslowly.org/blog/2013/04/14/are-there-any-safe-investments/

[cxix] Source: Investopedia

[cxx] Source: TreasuryDirect.gov. http://www.treasurydirect.gov/indiv/myaccount/myaccount_treasurydirect.htm

[cxxi] Source: Investopedia, http://www.investopedia.com/terms/e/etf.asp

[cxxii] http://www.investopedia.com/terms/t/tips.asp

[cxxiii] https://www.apexclearing.com

[cxxiv] Website: https://investorjunkie.com

[cxxv] https://www.cim.edu

[cxxvi] http://www.peabody.jhu.edu/conservatory/

[cxxvii] Source: Wikipedia. https://en.wikipedia.org/wiki/Motif_(music)

[cxxviii] https://www.motifinvesting.com

[cxxix] Source: www.investopedia.com/terms/d/dividend.asp

[cxxx] Note: After McDonald's announced the all day breakfast menu at the end of 2015, their stock price has begun to climb once again. Perhaps MCD stock isn't a dividend trap? Only time will tell!

[cxxxi] Source of comparing MCD and DIS stock valuations is www.dividendstocksrock.com

## Chapter 13: Wrap-up: Putting It All Together

[cxxxii] Check out this article regarding the wealthy and real estate: http://www.worldpropertyjournal.com/north-america-residential-news/millionaires-see-real-estate-as-top-investment-in-2014-morgan-stanley-reits-collectibles-spcase-shiller-property-market-7979.php

**Outro: Crank The Flywheel of Success**

[cxxxiii] Source: Wikipedia. https://en.wikipedia.org/wiki/Flywheel

[cxxxiv] Online Article: a comparison between Mint and Personal Capital can be found at https://investorjunkie.com/44628/personal-capital-vs-mint/

www.ingramcontent.com/pod-product-compliance
Lightning Source LLC
Chambersburg PA
CBHW071452040426
42444CB00008B/1302